ARMY

Process Vs Practice

(Straight Trees are Cut First)

Attention Authors

ARMY
Process Vs Practice

(Straight Trees are Cut First)

Brigadier AN Suryanarayanan

Foreword by

General S Padmanabhan
PVSM, AVSM, VSM (Retd)
Former Chief of the Army Staff

Manas Publications
New Delhi-110002 (INDIA)

Manas Publications
(Publishers, Distributors, Importers & Exporters)
4402/5A, Main Ansari Road,
(Opp. HDFC Bank), Darya Ganj,
New Delhi - 110 002 (INDIA)
Ph.: 23260783, 23265523:, 23842660 (R)
Fax: 011-23272766
E-mail: manaspublications@vsnl.com

2009

ISBN 978-81-7049-350-1
Rs. **695/-**

Typeset at
Manas Publications

Printed in India at
Shakti Printing Press, Delhi
and Published by Mrs Suman Lata for
Manas Publications, 4402/5A, Main Ansari Road,
Opp. HDFC Bank, Darya Ganj,
New Delhi - 110 002 (INDIA)

CONTENTS

ACKNOWLEDGEMENTS

My first debt of gratitude goes to my 'Defenders': Colonel (later, Brig and Dr) V Ramanan, my friend-philosopher-guide in those 'terrible' years; Lt Col HS Bedi, my indefatigable Defending Officer (who, unfortunately today cannot even acknowledge my debt, as he is suffering from loss of memory) and late Col NS Bains, (Retired), B.A. (Hons), LL.B., (Punjab University, Lahore) and Advocate, Delhi High Court, my very able Counsel, whose brilliance and legal acumen would match those of 'Sydney Carton' of *'A Tale of Two Cities'*!

I am thankful to General S Padmanabhan, PVSM, AVSM, VSM, ADC, former Chief of Army Staff, who not only exhorted me to write this narrative so that posterity may benefit but also consented to write the Foreword.

I owe my gratitude to my younger daughter, Vinita who was a child then; and now, despite being committed as a social worker and first time mother of an infant girl, found time to goad me repeatedly to write out my experiences of that dark period of five years and read through the first draft; also to Nagesh, my son-in-law, who patiently went through my drafts and offered suggestions.

How can I forget my course-mate and friend, Lt Gen Raj Kadyan, PVSM, AVSM, VSM who was instrumental for the past year, in persuading me to pen this narrative?

Thanks are also due to Manas Publications, who, despite my being author of a book for the first time, accepted to publish this book and have done so in good time.

I dedicate this book to Kay and Anu, who are not with me today but their memory continues to sustain me.

Brigadier A N Suryanarayanan

FOREWORD

It gives me great pleasure to have been asked to write the Foreword for Brigadier A.N. Suryanarayanan's book "Army: Process Vs Practice". Surya is my former instructor, fellow student at the Staff College, Wellington and my long time friend.

In this book, Surya describes the legal web in which he got entangled and his resolute struggle for justice over a period of four years. At the end of it, Surya emerged relatively unscathed, his honour restored and his military career repositioned on the growth path. He tells his story in detail–factually and without rancour or animus towards anyone.

There may be many more 'Suryas' in our million plus Army who may need encouragement to stay on in their fight for justice. Reading Surya's book will certainly steady them on their course. Others too, soldiers and civilians alike, will benefit from this book as it contains useful information on military law and how it is administered in our country.

The military legal system, despite many drawbacks it suffers from, is an essentially fair and humane system, which ensures that accused persons receive justice sooner rather than later. Like civilian courts, military courts too depend heavily on the testimony of witnesses and the contents of documents. If witnesses lie to courts marital despite being under oath and documents are forged or falsified, the accused will receive less than justice. The onus of ensuring that justice is actually done lies squarely on authorities who deal with courts marital, the courts themselves, counsels appearing in trials and, above all, the accused persons.

Surya's book implicitly advises wrongly accused persons to fight for justice, howsoever long and tortuous the road may be, to the desired end - the clearing of one's name.

S. Padmanabhan

PRELUDE

THE GIST OF THE CASE

"A person should not be too honest.
Straight trees are cut first; and
Honest people are victimized first."
Chanakya (350 BC-275 BC)

However good any system may be, it just takes some unscrupulous persons to manipulate it for vicarious pleasure or revenge, or to satisfy their ego. That it can happen in the Indian armed forces too is a painful warning. This is the core of this story.

This narration begins on a day 25 years ago. It is the saga of a lone man's crusade against the misuse, by some, of the Indian Army's system of justice and how he fought single handed against such misuse by his immediate superior and others. That *superior* had a previous grudge and was looking for an opportunity '*to catch*' (his words in 1981); the year was 1983 when '*catching*' began and would only end in February 1988, a good 5 years, 4 Summaries of Evidence and 4 Courts Martial later in 3 stations; but some consequences of it had to be fought till retirement.

It all began in 1982, when the Indian Army carried out its biggest Exercise till then, codenamed Dig Vijay. Preparation started in Aug 1982; move by both rail and road and concentration were to be completed by mid Dec 1982. *Though not authorized,* two camouflage nets each of the correct pattern and size had to be carried for every vehicle, gun, fieldwork and personnel. Ordnance was unable to provide the full quantity of 'scrim garnish' to be knitted into them... definitely not the unauthorized quantity for two nets... and issued Non Availability Certificate on 21 Nov 1982, whereby Local Purchase, an option, became a must.

When approached, the Brigade Commander volunteered to speak to the authority in Corps and get the necessary sanction for Local Purchase. Transaction was entered into and the nets were duly prepared. But my Regiment's first celebration of Honour Title for 1971 Operations which had just been awarded and my own selection for the prestigious 10-month Higher Command Course possibly lulled me into a false sense of security and total trust in people. I went in for splitting of the single transaction into 6 so as to make each fall within the powers of the authority *ibid* and left everything to my implicit trust in the efficient and experienced Quarter Master, after signing the papers in Dec 82/Jan 1983 and AFTER using up the item in Dec 1982, in the nets prepared for the Exercise!

During the preparatory stage for the Exercise, my Regiment got appreciation for organizing a demonstration for the entire Corps on total camouflage, thus proving we had indeed purchased and used the necessary material, whereas earlier, my Battery Commanders had clamoured repeatedly for the item!

Certain unpleasant exchanges had taken place between my immediate superior and me two years earlier (1981) at Army HQ, whereby he was looking for an opportunity '*to catch me*'. Some other events took place by which my own immediate subordinate, the Number Two, became unhappy and a willing tool in helping my boss, so as to '*fix*' me. Events were so stage-managed that being on leave and confined to bed with severe back ache, I had neither advance information nor the resources to counter the treachery by some who ganged up against me at the last moment, for whatever reason. The 'coup' was staged just after I handed over to my successor. It was too late for me to do anything.

I lost my wife after two weeks and both my minor daughters had to be separated from me (*and* from each other, to enable their looking after); but I fought with my back to the wall like a cornered cat; and, *after 4 Summaries of Evidence* (including 1 of my Quarter Master), *4 General Courts Martial and moves to three different stations over 5 years,* I came out unscathed! But I had to struggle for it, day and night for 5 years, and some of the rippling consequences shadowed me all the way to retirement.

In these pages you will read the details of all my suffering for those 5 years, where I hope to bring out the inept and ham-handed handling of disciplinary cases of even such senior officers of the rank of Lt Col by some incompetent A Branch and Judge Advocate Branch staff!

I have tried my best to make reading this book simpler by keeping, as far as possible, military jargon and abbreviations (except universal ones) out. To give you, the reader, a clearer perspective and background, I have also added a few pages about my Regiment, some brief explanations of army terms and a sequence of how a disciplinary case is progressed. To ensure that the identities of those concerned are protected, I have created alternate characters to go with the actual events. These are described in the Chapter on Dramatis Personae and they do NOT bear any resemblance to any person, living or dead. (You may hazard a guess but are bound to be wrong!) Summaries of some lengthy addresses and a few provisions of the Army Act and Army Rules (as they existed from 1983 to 1987) are covered in Annexures. I hope this way the narrative is easy to understand and follow, not only for those fortunate officers and jawans who did not have to undergo a similar frightful experience, but also for the 'civilians' unconnected with the Army, who may read this.

There are lessons I learnt from this entire saga; I have summarized the major ones in the very end. These may benefit posterity. I hope it is never too late for any other soldier-victim being treated thus to realize in time, what to do under such trying circumstances. I'd like to reiterate that

I am NOT bringing out the laundry of the Army into the open by this book but only highlighting how even a tried and tested system can be misused to settle a personal score. Lastly, my sole aim is that the system should not hound a man and "*hang him, because his name is Bhutto*"! If that is achieved, I would be happy.

"When a good man is hurt, all who would be called good, must suffer with him"

Euripides (484-406 BC)

CHAPTER 1

HOW IS THE INDIAN ARMY ORGANIZED?

Information in this Chapter is only for the purpose of understanding. A totally non-army reader will benefit by knowing at least an outline of organization of the Indian Army as it existed in the Eighties, and probably does today. It would also help if the reader understands *some* terms peculiar to the army used in this book; *some* staff functions; the local purchase procedures; and how disciplinary cases are progressed.

For a quick grasp, a chart showing the bare outline of organisation as explained below is placed at Annexure 1.

Outline of the Organization of the Indian Army (IA)

The Army HQ, with a General as Chief of Army Staff (COAS), functions under the overall control of the Ministry of Defence at New Delhi, like the Navy and Air Force HQs.

Chief of Army Staff is assisted by a Vice Chief of Army Staff (VCOAS) and a number of Principal Staff Officers (PSOs), all Lieutenant General: some of them being: Military Secretary (MS), Adjutant General (AG), Quarter Master General (QMG), Master General of Ordnance (MGO), Deputy

Chief(s) of Army Staff (DCOAS) etc, each heading a Branch at Army HQ. Chief of Army Staff Secretariat has an independent Complaint Advisory Board, introduced by General K Sundarji, which examines every petition and complaint addressed to the Chief of Army Staff, independent of Adjutant General's/Judge Advocate General's Branches and discusses direct with the Chief of Army Staff.

For purposes of this book, we should also know in further outline, the AG's Branch. AG has two Lieutenant Generals: Director General Organization and Personnel; and Director General Discipline, Ceremonials and Welfare. The latter has Judge Advocate General (JAG), a Major General under him as well as two 'Additional Directors General': one for Discipline and Vigilance; and the other for Ceremonials and Welfare.

MS Branch mainly deals with postings, promotions, appointments and career planning.

Armoured Corps, Artillery, Engineers, Signals, and Infantry are considered "*Arms*" and are headed by a Lieutenant General, generally called Director General (DG) or an equivalent designation, functioning under a Deputy Chief of Army Staff. Similarly *Services*' like Army Services Corps (ASC), Army Ordnance Corps (AOC), Electrical and Mechanical Engineers (EME), Army Medical Corps (AMC) etc also have Lieutenant General as Head. All are part of the Army HQ.

Indian Army today has six territorial commands (Northern, Central, Southern, Eastern, Western (and a recent addition, Southwestern) and an Army Training Command (ARTRAC), each under a Lieutenant General as General Officer Commanding in Chief (GOC in C).

Each command (barring the ARTRAC) consists of one or more Corps, whose head is a General Officer Commanding (GOC), Lieutenant General in rank.

Each Corps has two or more Divisions (Armoured, Mechanized, Mountain, Artillery, or Infantry) depending upon the terrain, perceived enemy threat etc, commanded by a Major General, called General Officer Commanding (GOC). There may also be some brigades, directly under a Corps, and *not as part of any Division;* these are called Independent (Indep) Brigades and may again be Armoured, Mechanized, Mountain, Artillery or Infantry, each commanded by a Brigadier.

Each Division, in turn, has three or more brigades of one particular type and also one Artillery Brigade, each commanded by a Brigadier.

Brigades generally have three or more *'units'*, that is, Regiments/Battalions with a Commanding Officer of Colonel's rank; (Lieutenant Colonel till 1984/85), assisted by a 2 IC and two staff officers: Adjutant and Quarter Master.

A unit has three/four or more sub units: squadrons (sqns)/batteries (btys)/companies (coys) under Majors. Second in Command (2 IC) normally deals with: Security; Accounts; Regt Institutes like Officers Mess; and Training etc. Adjutant deals with Adjutant General Branch (Discipline, Welfare, Pay, Promotions, Leave, Guards etc) and most of General Staff Branch subjects less Training (such as Operations, Intelligence, etc); and Quarter Master, with Q Branch matters (like, Rations, Fuel, Ordnance Stores, Clothing, Barracks etc). Each company/battery/squadron may have three or more platoons/troops with three sections/ detachments in each.

A Section/Detachment is the very basic sub unit.

On an average, a Division may have about 10-12,000 all ranks; a Brigade about 3,000-3,500 and a Regiment/Battalion about 500-700.

Some Appointments and Designations

It is good to know about some appointments and designations from a Corps downwards to a Unit, for ease in understanding some procedures, pertaining to Discipline and Local Purchase: the topics in this narrative.

In Corps HQ, there is a Chief of Staff, a Major General under whom the General Staff (GS), A Staff, JA staff, Q Staff, and Heads of Arms and Services function:

- A Branch or the Adjutant General's Branch deals with discipline and has a Brigadier looking after it, assisted by a Colonel, known as Colonel A.
- Judge Advocate General's Branch in a Corps HQ normally has 2 JAG Branch officers: Deputy Judge Advocate General (DJAG), a Brigadier and a Deputy Assistant Judge Advocate General (DAJAG), a Major; there may also be an AJAG (Assistant Judge Advocate General), a Lt Col and additional DAJAG.
- Ordnance Branch under a Brigadier, Deputy Director of Ordnance Services (DDOS) deals with ordnance stores/supplies; and thus Local Purchase of such items.
- There are many more branches, such as Artillery, Engineers, Signals, Electrical & Mechanical Engineers, Medical and so on; but we are not concerned with most of them for this narrative.

A Divisional HQ too has General Staff Branch etc; we are not concerned with Adjutant' General Branch in a Divisional HQ, as all actions in this narrative are in Independent Brigades (Armoured/ Artillery) and Artillery Regiment; but the general principles, sequence etc remain the same everywhere.

In a Brigade, Commander is assisted by a Deputy Commander (Colonel) and three staff officers (SO): General Staff, A & Q. Till 1984, A & Q were under one SO, known as Deputy Assistant Adjutant and Quartermaster General (DAA& QMG). The functions were separated in 1984 into Adjutant General Branch under a Deputy Assistant Adjutant General (DAAG) and Q Branch under a Deputy Assistant Quarter Master General (DAQMG). *You will come across many of these terms in this narrative.*

As stated above, at a unit level, 'A' matters (like Discipline, Welfare, Pay, Leave, Promotions, Guards etc) are dealt with by Adjutant; and Q matters (like Rations, Fuel, Ordnance Stores, Clothing, Barracks etc) by Quarter Master. 2 IC is NOT a Staff Officer; but is kept in picture by a copy of all important outbound UNCLASSIFIED and RESTRICTED mail of each Branch in the Circulation File, which as the name implies, is *circulated daily* to Commanding Officer, 2 IC, Adjutant and Quarter Master, who get to see mail signed by the others. Mail classified as CONFIDENTIAL, SECRET and TOPSECRET are carried by Adjt/QM personally to the Commanding Officer/2 IC for information/directions.

CHAPTER 2 GETTING TO KNOW MY REGIMENT

For purposes of this book, I was the Commanding Officer of what I'd like to call "Medium Regiment' (*my Regt or* simply, *Regt*) which was raised on 18 Jan 1966 at Maude Lines, Delhi Cantonment. In the 1971 War as part of I Corps, it had brought laurels to add to its history during the Battle of Basantar River and had successively served in places such as Alwar and Nasirabad before being moved to Akhnur (J & K) in Oct 1977 for three years.

Under a normal planned relief programme, it was to move to Delhi in Oct 1980. CO of the relieving unit at Delhi was planning to use political influence of a VVIP on Monday, 20 Oct 1980; their Military Special train was to leave Delhi Cantonment that very night! 16 to 18 Oct were Dasehra holidays and 19 was a Sunday. Regt got wind of it on 15 Oct and informed me. Being in Delhi, I met a very senior Railway official to find out as to what could be done. He said, as the next 4 days were to be holidays, he was anyway issuing just then, a signal regarding placing the train for the outgoing Regt on 20 Oct and he was not doing me a favour! And, he did, just before closing hours on 15

Oct! I thanked him profusely, but he waved me away with a smile!

Arrival close to Delhi

After being relieved by the incoming Regt, my Regt arrived on 2 Nov 1980, at Dundahera Camp, (just outside Delhi Cantonment, short of Gurgaon), sandwiched between the Indian Potassium and Maruti factories, (the latter to come into production two years later). I took over as its Commanding Officer on 20 Nov 1980. I had earlier served in it from Feb 1976 to Aug 1978, at Nasirabad and Akhnur. My predecessors had toiled hard and set Standing Operating Procedures (SOP) and drills, whereby it had a fine reputation, by the time I assumed command as the 7th CO.

Problems Galore

The area occupied by the Regt was huge and one had to travel almost 800 M from the National Highway-8 (leading to Jaipur), before reaching the main office. There was no perimeter fence, nor a compound wall. The *Layout Chart*, at *Annexure 2* will aid you in understanding certain important events later in this narration. Land was available for making accommodation for all ranks; but successive defence budgets never catered for it, as the location was merely treated as a Staging Camp for refuelling etc for formations moving North, in the event of an external emergency, as we would have moved out too!

While we were then a part of an Independent Artillery Brigade at Delhi Cantonment, directly under a HQ Corps, we were also under HQ Delhi Area for local administration. But the CO at this location was Station Commander, Gurgaon under Ambala Sub Area, in turn under Punjab, Haryana and Himachal Pradesh Area, then at Simla! We had only temporary accommodation for single Junior Commissioned Officer(s) (JCOs) and Other Ranks; but none for officers, including single ones. While my station HQ had to allot married accommodation already hired, for officers of IAF, a few of my own officers had to stay in Delhi Cantonment,

16 KM away! Officers Mess and single officers' temporary accommodation were, however, within the IAF Ammunition Dump, 5½ KM away in Gurgaon. Once IAF established its own Station in May 1982, we had to find a place for both. Some officers preferred staying in Gurgaon, just 7 KM away, rather than Delhi, 16 and more KM away. So, I consulted the defence and audit authorities and hired flats/ houses for single officers, some married ones and the Mess in Gurgaon. So my officers and men were distributed from Gurgaon (Sector 14) via Delhi Cantonment, right up to Naraina/Janakpuri in one direction to Karol Bagh in another, in a stretch extending almost 30 KM! Some men had married accommodation in Delhi Cantonment, while some stayed in Gurgaon in CILQ (Compensation In Lieu of Quarters) accommodation.

Physical Training (PT) used to be at about 6.30/7 AM and Night Training on some days was upto 9/10 PM! Regt was also supposed to be 'mobilization-ready' in less than 4 hours! Rations, clothing and other necessities had to be collected from Supply Depot at Delhi Cantonment (17 KM away) and Ordnance Depot at Shakurbasti, 47 KM away, all by road! Regulations existed that living accommodation should be within 8 KM of the Regt, but practical difficulties denied it; so how do officers and men commute? Or even communicate? These were not the days of competitive cellular companies, or even competitive landline: monopoly of Delhi Telephones ruled the roost! *This was the daily routine! You can well imagine the daily stress and strain for the officers and men; and tension for the CO*!

I had been an extremely strict Commanding Officer at work; but was very friendly when off-parade; just as I had seen and learnt from my second Commanding officer in 1963-65! I always went out of the way to ensure that all facilities were provided to all ranks of my unit, before asking them to produce results that I wanted, for which I brooked no delay. It was working without a problem, as I watched! As a welfare measure, while at the same time, to extract results, I decided to run two 3-ton lorries, modified with hard bottom benches for men and officers to commute between Delhi and Gurgaon, after consultation with audit authorities; and made Standing Operating Procedure for their use, besides arranging for their parking overnight, till my Regt itself was asked to establish a Detachment to look after the 'Rear'-interests of Brigade HQ and other units moving to Meerut in Aug-Sep 1981! Major Crass (you will be introduced to him soon in the chapter on *Dramatis Personae*) had sometimes misused the vehicle late at night for totally private work and when asked not to repeat it, began simmering with jealousy and anger, though he had been passed over for a Lieutenant Colonel finally, by the time I wrote his ACR for the second time.

The reader must be wondering why bore him with all this information? Well, I am sure you can better appreciate the constraints under which I had to work, as *'the buck stopped at my desk, as the Commanding officer'*! All just because I was as ambitious as my contemporaries to rise higher! The tension and stress increased manifold, when two or three accidents involving my men and vehicles took place on the highway. In the Army, if there is an accident, it is never treated as just an incident but as totally avoidable, *purely due to the army driver's fault*; a Court of Inquiry would only find ways to 'fix' the driver and the 'co-driver' sitting beside him, as if the latter could apply the brakes or lower the gear or whatever! 2 IC/concerned Battery Commander and sometimes even I, invariably visited the accident spot; and if convinced that it was not my driver's fault, I used to support his case for justice. This was never liked by my Commander. You will get to know him too in the Chapter on *Dramatis Personae*!

Our Move to Meerut dropped

There had been talk about the Independent Artillery Brigade being moved out of Delhi, to bring in an Infantry Brigade from Meerut, for operational reasons. This became a fact under serious consideration, within a few months of arrival of my Regt close to Delhi. We too came to know. My men raised the point in a Sainik Sammelan, as, in anticipation of the move to Delhi, they had moved their families for their children's education, which is permitted 6 months ahead, according to regulations. A few officers too had done so. Now if there is to be another move so soon, what happens to their family lives and children's studies? Accommodation at Meerut would be allotted only as per norms: as an incoming unit, just 4 for officers and a few for the men; the rest have to wait in queues for upto 2 years and more! Whereas in Delhi, with their field seniority, almost all including the men, had accommodation soon, even if spread out as described by me earlier! They had just finished 3 full years in Akhnur, without proper facilities for even temporary accommodation and schooling. The entire Regt had been under tents; though some families had moved into self-constructed mud-brick and tent/bamboo roof homes, with the permission of General Officer Commanding, Major General (later Lieutenant General and Governor of J & K) SK Sinha. Luckily for us, he had moved as AG to Delhi, and successively became General Officer Commanding, (our) Corps and General Officer Commanding in Chief Western Command later! He was fully aware of our problems.

Besides taking up the matter through proper channel, I had, as the CO, included the difficulties as a Morale Point in the Quarterly Security Intelligence Report (QSIR) on 28 Mar 1981! There was an enquiry through army's intelligence channels to the Brigade HQ and the new Commander who had arrived shortly thereafter, took offence, by indirectly referring to it in his first visit to my Regt, asking me, as to why I did not wish to move directly under his eyes at Meerut, when his HQ, Workshop, Signal Company and 3 other Regts were to do so! I explained the details to him; but because of his 'previous prejudice' against me (you will be reading about it later!) he was biding his time, when the matter came up through normal channel for his recommendation, to say a firm NO!

In the meantime, Gunners Day Cocktails were held on 17 Jan 1981 at Station Artillery Mess at Parade Road, Delhi Cantonment. General OP Malhotra was not only the Chief of Army Staff but was Senior Colonel Commandant of Artillery too! Thus he was both the Chief Guest and the Chief Host! Readers may be aware that Gunners Day used to be 15 Jan every year, but because of the Army Day Reception at Army House which VVIP attend, this one used to be held on 16th or 17th. (*To celebrate the raising of the first Indian Artillery unit, i.e., 'A' Field Brigade at Bangalore on 15 Jan 1935, that date was initially chosen as the Gunners Day; but was changed to 28 Sep, after research found that the oldest Indian Battery has been continuously existent from 28 Sep!*)

During the cocktails, Chief of Army Staff used to go around and meet as many officers and families as possible, to feel the pulse; besides he was our *'mai-baap'* (a 'parent'). When he came to our Bar, I happened to be away and my officers and families had buttonholed him with all their apprehensions about the impending move. He just smiled and said, he will look into it; by then Commander and I rushed there. After a short while, ADC to General Officer Commanding in Chief, Western Command came to me and said that the former would see me at 8 AM, the next morning at the Inspection Bungalow. When I asked him the reason, he said he knew nothing! I got the jitters, as knowing Lieutenant General KV Krishna Rao's views on the Gunners, if this news about my officers and families raising the move with Chief of Army Staff had reached him, I was bound to be admonished! All my 'spirits' (*pun intended*) evaporated! Lieutenant General Sinha, who was there, spoke nicely to my officers and families and promised to do his best for cancellation of the move. Only then did I heave a sigh of relief!

The next morning I was there on time, along with my Officiating Subedar Major, Munshi Ram, at 7.45 AM, pacing nervously, like an expectant first-time father! ADC came out and asked me to wait. In the meantime, General Officer

Commanding Delhi Area who also arrived to meet the Army Commander wanted to know why I was waiting; I told him that I had been summoned! In a few minutes, Army Commander came out and summoned me first; I went with the Subedar Major trailing, whom I introduced! General Rao said in his typical drawl: *"I called to compliment your Regt, for the excellent Guard you have provided me, during my stay. I did not expect such a standard from an Artillery Regiment. Well done!"* I did not lose time in telling him: *"Sir, your words carry more significance for us today, as it is our Raising Day; I shall convey them to my men in the Sainik Sammelan"*. I could see from the corner of my eyes that the ADC was smiling! Gen Rao shook hands with both of us and off we rushed to Gurgaon, with me fully relieved of all tension built up since last night! I learnt from a Major General at Army HQ in July 1981 that the same Gen Krishna Rao, who became Chief of Army Staff on 1 June 1981, had written a strong comment on my QSIR (mentioned earlier) that *'this CO needs to be taught a lesson on morale'* or some such words; luckily nothing happened to me then, *probably because worse was in store two years later*!

The dreaded move day came and went but no orders for us and another Regt at Anand Parbat. The others moved out, yielding place to an Infantry Brigade with 3 Battalions. Brigadier Scraggly, who had come as Brigade Commander only a few months earlier, left his family behind in separated family accommodation at Pratap Chowk. He also ordered his pet-Regt to establish a detachment to look after the interests of Meerut Regts (and *'of his family'?)* But, he was still keen to move my Regt (while leaving the 5th, his pet) back. Once I came to know of it, I mentioned it during a formal first visit by the new General Officer Commanding Corps to my office on 9 Oct 1981, when there was a one to one operational discussion. I still remember his words: *"Who is the CO ..."*? I was confused and told him, *"Sir that is me"*. *"Well, then, the CO's wishes shall prevail"* he said and put a final stop to the subject. His staff conveyed it to Scraggly in writing as *'Notes of Visit by General Officer*

Commanding... Corps to ... Medium Regiment' and this obviously annoyed him even more! (When he was Director,. Military Operations, I had met the General a few times to get the award of an Honour Title for my Regt for its role in 1971 Operations, although I had *not* served with the Regt then but elsewhere; that *esprit de corps* had impressed him, as he told me himself on 9 Oct 1981 during his first visit! I was pleasantly surprised that such a senior General would remember a Major, whom he had met in 1978-79. He was to *'bail me'* out twice more, but NOT at the most needed juncture; read on!)

CHAPTER 3

DRAMATIS PERSONAE

It is difficult to speak or write with becoming moderation or propriety, on topics to which we are biased by prejudice, interest, or even principle.
– Joseph Lancaster

Why should you know who is who? **"The further backward you look, the further forward you can see."**
– Winston Churchill.
That is why!

Every person about whose actions over the few years of my command I write here had something in common with the others against me, so that even if individually he could not harm me, they all found common ground and bonded together at the most critical time to try and achieve it. In order to know the genesis of ill-will against me by this *band of brothers*, it would help if you know their mindset and some of their actions.

Brigadier 'Scraggly'

Scraggly was already a Brigadier in 1978-80, commanding a Brigade close to Dehradun. As he owned a house in

Defence Colony at Delhi, he used to frequently visit Army HQ and my office. I was then a Major in the Military Secretary's Branch at Army HQ; my immediate superior and he were good friends, but the latter would always refer his requests to me for scrutiny! Scraggly would like all high calibre officers to be posted to him; especially every gunner-Major returning from a foreign staff college course; there usually was only one; or at best two per year! Since he was a friend of my superior, initially I had posted two bright Majors as minor unit commanders. (*After two decades, one of them rose to be an Army Commander and the other, the Adjutant General: both my juniors and friends*!). He still wasn't happy. When his demands became excessive, I had to convey through my superior, with facts and figures, that the same were not feasible! In less than a year, my superior moved out and I was promoted to stay back in his appointment, *with the offer of the carrot of command of my own Regt*, which was what any Lieutenant Colonel would have loved. It was still July-Aug 1979. I continued, as it well suited me, as I would not be disturbed for 5 years from Delhi! That was the first mistake by me, as you will learn after reading this book.

Once in early 1980, I was in the midst of drafting an important Note from the Director General Artillery to Chief of Army Staff, on the promotion prospects of senior gunner officers vis-à-vis general cadre officers. I had bolted my cabin, as I did not want to be disturbed in my trend of thought. In any case, visiting hours were 3 to 5 p.m., by when I would have been free to attend to visitors. To my bad luck, Brig Scraggly wanted to visit me just then, at about 12 noon. He probably knocked on my door; tried to peep etc, besides shouting my name from outside. I was engrossed in my work and neither heard nor responded. So he went to Coordinating Office, 3 rooms away, to another staff officer, again a good friend of his. The latter called me on the PABX telephone. I did not respond once or twice, though its tone resembles a fire alarm! The third or the fourth time, I picked up! When I found it was the Lt Col from Coordination, I politely told him that I was unable to attend to him till about 2/2.30 p.m. He said Brigadier Scraggly wished to see me for just 5 minutes; I said I did not want my drafting to be interrupted and put it down. It was about 1 p.m. and lunch time; but the Brigadier wouldn't give up; he had a bright idea: he went to my Head Clerk's office, alongside mine and through the recess for the common telephone called out to me and said he wanted just 5 minutes. I told him very politely the nature of the job I was committed in and that I would not be able to meet him till it was done, possibly by 3 p.m., the visiting time! That raised his hackle and he asked me: *"Do you mean to tell me that you have no time for me?"* I replied in exasperation at being disturbed: *"Sir. If that is what you feel, you are putting words into my mouth!"* He walked off from the clerks' office in a huff mumbling: *"Will see you some day"*! *How prophetic he proved to be*! When I carried the final Note to Director General Artillery for him to take it personally to the Chief of Army Staff for a discussion, I told him the sequence; he asked me not to worry but enquired anxiously if I had had my lunch! I said no, but that I would shortly!

Brig Scraggly did not visit my office for the next one year; but, his staff used to write Demi Official letters, quoting his name! I did what was possible.

One day in late June 1981 in the Regt, I was called urgently to the telephone, to ring back the Director General Artillery who had just called for me. I did, with a premonition that he may not have good news for me, as I was all along aware of Brig Scraggly's request to be posted to Delhi. I was hoping against hope that it wasn't the news! Imagine my shock, when THAT was the news! When I mentioned to him that for having waited for over a year for command of my own Regt and having earned more *'enemies'* in my appointment at his office, he could have been more judicious. He understood my angst and gave another shock: *"Don't worry. I have spoken to him in detail and no harm will come to you"* (thus confirming that he had spoken about 'that incident')! I couldn't restrain myself and said *"Sir. When you retire, I may still be commanding, with this gentleman as my boss"*. He assuaged my feelings by calling me to meet him some time, which I could not do. I wish I had done so, soonest and also sought a change of command.

The 'troubles' started for me thence. In our first meeting in a welcome cocktail at the outgoing Commander's home in the last week of July 1981, all other COs and the Deputy Commander were sidling up to him. But the outgoing Commander, a perfect gentleman, called me for introducing. Without bothering about the time, the place or the people around, Brig Scraggly asked in a loud voice: *"Will you now have time for me?"* I replied as politely as I could, with tongue in cheek: *"Yes sir. 200%, as you are to be the Commander of the Brigade, where my Regt will be serving for the next few years"*. He looked as smug as a Cheshire cat that had just lapped up all the milk! The outgoing Commander knew there was something wrong and moved away; but I did tell him the next day. Though we had had differences of opinion a few times, including his order for 'jacking up all the vehicles of my Regt', (you will read about it when I talk of Colonel Rabbi, the Deputy Commander), he had always respected my professional competence! He wished me luck and asked me to be careful!

Brig Scraggly appeared to follow the words of Dr A Maslow: *"If the only tool you have is a hammer, it is tempting to treat everything as if it were a nail"*! He started visiting Delhi often, citing an official visit to both Regts, usually on Friday or Monday, so that Sat/Sun were available to him with his family; but he will visit my Regt only on a Monday, so that my officers (who knew of our earlier spat) and men had to work over the weekend to present a good impression. He was happy with the other CO at Delhi for many reasons, which I don't wish to go into. While being reasonable with 3 other COs and overly fond of the 4th, he was always on the look out to *'catch me'*, as he himself said more than once in the presence of my subordinates. All for satisfying his

EGO, at a feeling of having been rebuffed once at Army HQ, which he brought out at my Farewell Lunch, two years later! But I had also been 'unbending' (may be *'wrongly'*, as I think back in hindsight) because throughout our stay in the same Brigade for two years, I never called on him even once socially; while I had definitely visited his 'separated' family to check for any problems once in a while!

The first attempt to *'catch'* me was during an Annual Inspection soon after his taking over. The Regt was ready for a 2-mile run and he arrived with his Staff Officer. On seeing me, in normal uniform and not the specified one for a run, he asked, if I wasn't running with the men. I replied that I had been practising with them to motivate but today as the CO, I wished to be at the finish line with him to see if my efforts have borne fruit. Over 92% achieved 'Excellent' grade; 6% 'Good' and the rest 'Satisfactory'. He would not believe it; so asked for the Parade State and the Ration Strength for the day to check, if I had left behind the usual 'Services' personnel or tradesmen like washermen, cooks etc to show abnormal results. Besides the Quarter Guard and Main Gate, only 2 persons each, BUT NOT from these categories, had been left behind in each sub unit as sentries! Then he felt the distance may have been measured less to show spectacular results. *Just see, how a crooked mind works even at that level*! I took the challenge and said that if his surveyors found it less, I would seek premature retirement; but what about the reparation for the insult to my Regt *and me*, if it was found to be more? He said we would speak about it later, once the distance was measured.

Later that day, in one of the battery cook houses, he asked the senior JCO (the same Subedar Munshi Ram), if they had *'surplus'* rations; he replied 'No'. He went around every nook and corner and found in the pantry, placards showing 'Saved Rations' and a few containers with bin cards showing some small quantities! He asked the Subedar as to why he had lied. He replied: *"Sahib, aap ney to, surplus poocha thha. Yeh to saved hai"* (Sir, you had asked about surplus; but these are saved); he then explained how sometimes small quantities of dry rations get saved for a number of reasons, but those are taken on charge in a note book by a committee of men detailed for the purpose, under his supervision and given back to the langar or to the married jawans in station, on festive occasions, after a decision by the men in a Roll Call or Langar Committee meeting. He also offered to stop it, if the Commander so ordered, but said it was a welfare measure and there was no extra expense to the State! Scraggly turned to me and said with a malicious wink: "*... I wanted to catch you; but you escaped this once*!" I replied puffing up my chest: "*Sir, **as long as I am commanding this fine Regt, you can't catch me***!" (Later I got it stopped, foreseeing problems with Scraggly!) How prophetic I was *for once*, got proved on 29 June 1983, just AFTER I handed over!

Instances during the inspection were many; but I have only highlighted some! When the Inspection was over, he left but the staff stayed back; got the distance measured out by a team from the other Delhi-Regt and found it was longer by about 15 metres! I insisted on their giving it to me in writing and kept it in file! I did raise it in his Conference subsequently; he then said a word of praise for my Regt (but not for me); but that was never recorded in the Minutes and I too left it. I had never pointed out many such statements not recorded in Minutes, including *a crucial one regarding Local Purchase of scrim garnish and his volunteering to speak to his batch-mate, Deputy Director of Ordnance Services at Corps HQ*. How I wish I had!

Like the Gunners Day on 17 Jan 1981 (previous Chapter), the next one on 16 Jan 1982 was again at the same venue at Delhi, but arranged by our Brigade ex-Meerut! That morning, Scraggly, finding that flowers had not been arranged due to an oversight on the part of his staff, sent for me from my office (17 KM away) and asked me to get flowers immediately, within Rs 500, for the huge covered accommodation under canvas (*'shamiana'*) for 800-strong crowd! Luckily for me, en route to my Regt everyday, I used to see two floriculture farms. That day, I went there with my wife, to purchase. The owner's son was sweet and said that I could take as much as I liked; we went crazy and picked up half his produce of the day! When we asked for a bill, he took offence and said he is *not to be insulted by offer of money from military officers*! (We became friends after that. Every time I went to his farm short of Gurgaon or his kiosk in Janpath during my stay/visit to Delhi till 1995, he would let us/me pick up whatever and howsoever much I/we liked). When I returned within an hour, with a jonga-load of high quality flowers and said all of it was *my Regt's gift for the Day*, Scraggly wouldn't believe it. He had failed in another attempt at *"catching me"*!

On another occasion, after a sudden visit to my Regt, while driving back, he picked up 50 (or was it 100?) eggs from the unit bania, got it loaded into his car and left without payment! As I had seen his car stop near the wet canteen (see Layout Chart), during the long drive out, I sent the Subedar Major to find out. He brought back this information! I called the bania, got a bill made for the eggs and sent it with a polite handwritten note to Scraggly through a courier. He expressed surprise that he had not paid? The cheque did come and was given to the bania. May be I was injudicious; but how else to convey to him that *I did not want him to get the impression that I or my officers did such things*. We bought our Payment Rations from another Regt just to avoid any adverse comment from any quarter. All this would be of no use, when I was mired in a trumped up case in a year's time, thanks to him.

He used to get *atta*, (wheat flour) on payment from my Regt, after getting it sieved three times. Readers would remember his family remained in Delhi, while he was at Meerut. On one occasion, he did not pay and Quarter Master brought it to my notice. I asked him to tell the staff and get the money; so, another black mark against my name!

One more occasion when he tried to *'catch'* me was when the Summary Court Martial proceedings (only one in my entire command of 32 months) of a driver whom I had dismissed with civil imprisonment, had been returned by Judge Advocate at Corps for commutation by the Commander, with *'advice to be rendered to me'*. Luckily for me, General Officer Commanding Corps who had come to Delhi a few days prior to this, sent for me and spoke to me at length on the case. I explained to him the reasons, which in any case were part of the proceedings too. He told me to relax and not to get perturbed if Scraggly tried to 'bully' me on this, as he would handle it with him as well as the JA. I felt relieved. This had bothered Scraggly no end, as he lost an opportunity for 'counselling' me and thus including it in my ACR later!

This gentleman was an expert in getting anonymous and pseudonymous letters written to himself through his cronies against any subordinate whom he did not like and more so, when the latter was away on leave/duty, thus putting the affected officer under stress! He knew more ways to put his subordinates under tension than there were days in a year. (*He used to say, keep your command under stress for your own success; but I never believed in it, though I was an extremely strict CO*). It had happened not just once, but at least during three periods of my absence as a CO. The first one was sometime in Dec 1981 and he acted as if he was gracious enough not to take notice of it, by just forwarding it to me; still I replied to him with solid proof, to show the allegations to be false. Next, when I went on part of annual leave in June 1982, he got a pseudonymous letter written and sent me a photocopy seeking an explanation. I wrote back a strong rebuttal, while also drawing attention to Army Order 69/73, wherein very clear directions of Ministry of Home Affairs were reproduced that *no action will be taken on anonymous and pseudonymous complaints*. It, however, allowed the superior to forward the complaint to the named person, if they were frequent. Two letters in 2 years is by no means frequent; but an originator of such letters can easily make the occurrences frequent! *The third and the most important that was to affect the course of my life and career was to be conceived yet,* as he was biding his time for the most opportune time!

Despite my sincerity, when my character was doubted through a second anonymous letter, I felt offended and was seriously considering a decision during Aug 1982, to seek premature retirement to rid myself of this tension! But my wife and her brother, a Bengal Sapper Major insisted that I should be stronger and must fight it out. How I wish I had listened to my inner voice and left in Aug 1982, even if I had been considered *weak* by my wife! Since I had strongly rebutted the first two during my command, he bided his time *'to catch'* me and (having apparently discussed its contents with Major Crass before getting it written) sent the third and last one on 27 June 1983, just the night before my handing over command! Readers may recollect my words above, wherein I had told him during his very first Annual Inspection of my unit: *'... as long as I am CO of this fine Regt you can't catch me'*! More about it later!

On the direct orders of Army HQ, I had been attached to MS Branch during Sep-Oct 1982 to prepare a Report as part of a team, when Major Crass was also on leave; so Major Tanjore Doll, the next junior officiated. To ensure I stayed stressed and tense (as per his policy), he ordered my Regt in writing that while attached, CO shall be responsible for every thing and will attend to work daily in the Regt! This exposure would have been good for my career; so I worked hard by going first to the Regt for 2 hours in the early morning; then going in the opposite direction to Army HQ (another 30 KM, though in Govt jeep) for the day's work, leading to 17-18 hours of work a day; on some days, I had made two trips a day to the Regt! This same gentleman, having sanctioned my annual leave in 1983 asked me to adjust the date of commencement of my leave with an expected visit by Corps Commander (about that too, you will read in detail in the General Court Martial (GCM) proceedings, later in this narrative).

When my ACR had to be written by him for 1982-83, he had nothing adverse against my command function, except *a few unfortunate accidents, where too, my regiment or my personnel had not been blamed, even in a single one*. Knowing I was laid with a severe back ache but still upset that I did not go to my Regt ammunition dump on 13 June to meet him (details later), he called me to Brigade HQ on 15 June 1983 to sign my ACR. When it was shown to me, I found a remark: *'Security and administration need improvement'*. I signed the report without a word and then demanded a copy to represent, as no occasion had arisen for any weakness in either of these two heads and never in my 22 years service. He asked me to wait in some other office; discussed with Col Rabbi; called me again and asked me to bring another ACR form with signature of the medical officer (the next day). He knew that my representation would go through the Corps and Army Commanders, who knew my competence for many years. That day one of my young officers was getting married at Delhi; but I could not attend the wedding; I went for the Reception in the evening; and then late at night got the medical officer to sign my new ACR form! (*That was the first time I went out of my home after 10 May 1983 - my 15th and last wedding anniversary!*) Next day, I went again to Meerut and this time he rewrote the whole ACR, removing those words, but adding: *'There were a number of vehicle accidents under his command'*. I signed it but told him I shall be appealing, if my next promotion was denied because of these words, as none of my vehicles or drivers had been blamed in any of the accidents. I ensured he tore up the previous form in my presence; which was a mistake by me, as I had lost the proof of his weak backbone! (*These dates and events are important for the reader to link up certain attempts at false evidence by a few at the General Courts Martial*).

I feel the instance I am about to narrate takes the cake. During late June 1982, he had to move his family also from Delhi to Meerut, when I was away on part of annual leave;

for this, he had a few vehicles attached, including some from mine. A day or so before I was due to return to Delhi in end-June 1982 (though on leave still) he had transported both his buffaloes in one of my unit vehicles from Delhi to Meerut. Military Police Traffic Check Post, at Meerut found the two *'unauthorized passengers'* and seized my 3-ton lorry. The co-driver of the vehicle told the Military Police that the animals belonged to Scraggly; but he did not believe it. The co-driver immediately called up Scraggly from there itself. As per the version given to me years later by my jawan, Scraggly immediately rushed from his home in his private car to the Traffic Check Post, looking dishevelled; took charge of the buffaloes and asked my jawan, if I had reached back and was aware of this. Unfortunately for me, my return had been postponed by 4-5 days, due to the sudden illness of my mother (who subsequently passed away on 6 July 1982, after my return). Scraggly also warned the driver, the co-driver and the Traffic Check Post, not to breathe a word about it to me at any time! The irony of it all was: one of the points in the first anonymous letter in Dec 1981 *ibid* had been that I had a cow at my bungalow and was selling the surplus milk, though no misuse of any Govt person or resources was involved! *(I wish Lalu Yadav had been in Govt of India then!)*

He had the nerve to say in my Farewell Lunch at the Brigade Officers Mess in Meerut on 29 June 1983 that he had *'had difference of opinion with me when I was in MS Branch'*; but that he never carried the 'burden'! I replied that ' *...but from the day the Director General Artillery told me over the telephone about your appointment prior to your arrival, Sir, I knew I had to be extra careful and have been, hopefully, right to this day"*. But, well before we went to the Mess for lunch, he had sent an officer courier to Corps HQ with my Handing and Taking Over Certificate requesting them not to allow me to proceed on the prestigious Higher Command Course. I heard about it after the lunch and just before leaving Meerut. (Again, you will read about this later in detail). I knew I had to step forward and answer the bell and I did not flinch.

Later, during the very last GCM (Revision), I brought it out of the mouth of my successor that months later, during his own Dining Out in my Regt Mess, Scraggly had called my Quarter Master who was later to be my co-accused and told him that he was *'sorry, he could do nothing to save* ***him*** *from the inquiry and its after-effects'* thus proving his target was me and me alone!

Colonel 'Rabbi'

This person about 4 years my senior, was waiting to pick up his promotion to a Lieutenant Colonel and command of a Regt in Feb 1976 in the Regt, when I reported there as a battery commander and in line to replace him. He had no special qualifications, which are stepping stones to pick up the very first rank in selection grade, as a Lt Col. An advantage for me was that the then Commanding Officer had served in the same Brigade in 1971 Operations, as a battery commander, when I was Brigade Major; so his welcoming letter to me calling me a *'known devil'* must have irked this person, who had by then been with the Regt for over 5 years! He used to feel somewhat 'inferior' as his 'employability' was minimal for lack of qualifications, whereas I had qualified in Long Gunnery Officers Course and Defence Services Staff College Course and had been Instructor Class C and B (Captain and Major), as also Brigade Major of Artillery (during 1971 War) and Mountain Brigades (all prestigious appointments) before my arrival there (with 13 years service)! To show his authority as the No 2, he would utilize my services to do any work allotted to him by the CO, saying: *".... The Commanding Officer has particularly chosen you to do this job..."* The gullible person that I had been (at least till 1983); I fell for it every time!

A major instance was within 3 weeks of my joining, when CO who had been tasked in May 1975 itself, to run a quiz on Administration, on Monday, 8 Mar 1976 had asked him to prepare the basics and discuss. Rabbi had done nothing for months and probably wanted to embarrass me; so told me at the last minute at about 1 p.m. on Friday, 5 Mar with his usual words: *"...CO has particularly ... etc"* and asked me to get all preparations done by Sunday and *tell* ***him***. I could not be browbeaten for knowledge of Administration. Not only did I get the quiz with answers and relevant authorities cited, ready in 24 hours, but I also organized the quiz hall with furniture and power amplifier equipment; red and green bulbs for the syndicates as well as the quiz master etc! On Sunday morning, he was NA; so I called up the CO, who was forgetful by nature. He had a shock, realizing he had forgotten his commitment totally and so thought I was only reminding him and asked where Major Rabbi was. I told him what had happened so far. He went with me to the venue and was suitably impressed; but Major Rabbi was unhappy the next day, as he had directed me to tell ***him*** and not the CO, whereby obviously he could have taken the credit.

Rabbi had returned as Deputy Commander to the same Independent Artillery Brigade in July 1981, where I had joined as CO of my Regt in Nov 1980! As the outgoing unit had not bothered to keep their vehicle fleet in tiptop condition that any CO would proudly like to have, I took pains to gradually downgrade/discard vehicles as per policy and with my liaison in Army HQ still current, started getting new vehicles allotted. On one occasion, in early July 1981, my Regt got a letter to detail "*CO's jonga* for a Brigadier from Army Medical Corps visiting Delhi on duty" the next day at 8 a.m.

In any unit, a Commanding Officer's jeep is treated as a sacred cow and never *detailed by order*, for any duty outside; however, if a request is made for any reason, it would be provided willingly. In this case, a new jonga, having just arrived as the first one in my upgradation efforts, was in Workshop, undergoing modifications; so I told Quarter Master to call up Captain *Bandicoot*, (as he was known amongst young officers of my Regt!) who had signed the letter and tell him that as the CO's new jonga was undergoing certain modifications, the next best vehicle will be sent. That upstart Captain iterated that there was no change to the orders. There being NO other better vehicle, the best available jeep out of the remainder fleet went; but the visiting Brigadier was probably not too happy. This information reached Bandicoot and he conveyed something to Rabbi, who, without enquiring, went to the Commander and said that CO...Medium Regt has *'refused to send HIS jonga'* for the visiting Brigadier, who had felt insulted! Though the Commander was an excellent gentleman, he must have been upset at a *'Lt Col refusing orders issued by his HQ'* and so asked Rabbi to direct me to report to his office forthwith. It was around 11.30 a.m. and I left my unit in a jeep for the Brigade HQ in Delhi, 16 KM away. When I was on the move, ALL transport in my Regt had been ordered to be 'jacked up'; meaning NO vehicle could move; *even collection of rations, water, fuel etc will be by men on their shoulders*! But, what was their fault?

I went into the Commander's office and could see him all red. He refused to listen to any explanation and told me to get all jeeps of my Regt lined up outside his office soonest for him to see; he said I could leave. I still did not know of the jack-up orders, which Rabbi, who had been stumped with the jeeps-line-up-order, now whispered to him in his ears! I could see confusion on Commander's face; but he had to support his No 2, so he gave it out now, making exception for all jeeps to come over and me to use my vehicle to go back, which would also return for the line up! I thanked him for the courtesy and said, let my jeep be the first to line up and I would walk, just as everyone in my command would be doing from then, till the order was revoked! I felt pained at this behaviour from Rabbi, an old colleague from the same Regt; but kept quiet and walked out. I marched home (a KM away) in working uniform, with the stick orderly bringing my brief case, marching behind me!

In about an hour, the Commander called me on telephone and said, the jeeps could go back and the jack-up order was also cancelled! I took the opportunity to clarify a few things to him then:

- That all the jeeps including the non-running/ repairable ones (barring the new one in Workshop) would have lined up and he would have seen what type of fleet I had taken over!

- If he felt that I may have acted thus since he was under posting as Sub Area Commander to Madras soon and thus I might not be earning another ACR from him, I requested him to wait till his departure and 'experience' the loyalty of others vs. mine!
- I told him also that his order was not just an insult to me, but to my fine Regt and that the whole station would have known about it by now! I requested him to think as to what would have happened to his reputation, had I refused this *'illegal order of a collective punishment'* to my Regt: it would have spread like wild fire, by the evening and I did not want it that way. (*This Commander had seen my competence in Exercise Shikar during Jan-Feb 1981 and had given me a very good ACR on 31 May 1981; that had helped my selection for a* Higher Command Course *subsequently!* We had *become* socially also close. *He also had the opportunity to experience my loyalty, when he shifted his pets and entire baggage to my Regt—this fact would come up in the trial— and his car to my home, to be looked after, as he was planning to proceed on retirement from Madras soon and would pick it all up! To think that he had: a Deputy Commander, 4 other COs and many staff officers and he had to choose me and my Regt!)*

I must tell you this also: Rabbi, being in Meerut had retained temporary married accommodation at Delhi on Non Availability basis: a small one, opposite mine! I realized after a while that he was keeping a watch on my movements as also those of the unit vehicles such as the Despatch Rider, my jonga/jeep (and my wife) every day! Obviously he was carrying tales to the Commander, as his loyalties no more remained with my Regt but with his new boss, as already experienced by me in the 'jack-up case'! You will also later read about his coming to my home on 26 June 1983, a Sunday! Luckily for him, he never got found out and was (very obviously with such fine qualities) approved for a Brigadier too! While *marking time* for it, he happened to invite one of his previous commanders for a meal and me too, as I had also known that Brigadier for many years. Despite being a strict *Radhasoami* as well as a *Sathya Sai Baba* devotee, Rabbi was having beer (and meat?) that evening: one more indicator to me of his traits as a person! There were more instances; but I am sure you have caught on to my suggestion!

Major 'Crass'

This man was junior to me by a year; very crass and fond of creating and maintaining cliques and spreading scuttlebutts about every one else! The only remarkable point I had found in him was that he would take pains to supervise the practice of Regt teams for major games and put them through the pace for a sure win, many times taking part himself; despite this, unfortunately *he did not have the sportsman-spirit*!

He had been posted to this fine Regt, to report in June 1976; but when his reporting date was still 6 weeks away (I was a battery commander; and Rabbi then a Maj, was 2 IC with us), he made a journey from Central India by car along with his wife, to visit our Regt in Nasirabad (Rajasthan) in Apr-May 1976 to 'check out' things, as a future 2 IC. It was kind and good of them that they dropped in at my place too. It was lunch time and so, we requested them to join. They realized in a couple of minutes two bits of information: one, that my wife and his wife had been classmates in Nursery classes in Dehradun and second, that I had just spent about 2 months and won't be moving out for at least two years till I earn reports in my criterion appointment (as 2 IC) after Rabbi left. I don't know how but my wife had very uncanny intuitive feeling about people and always used to warn me! (*How I miss her*!) In this case too, she told me within a few minutes of their departure and I remember the exact words after 32 years: "*...beware of this man; keep him* *far away and don't trust him easily*!" But the gullible person that I was, I couldn't differentiate between cheese and chalk; Crass and I became very close. From time to time, my wife used to warn me but I never paid heed.

His dream of becoming 2 IC of the Regt soured further, when another Major senior to him got posted in Sep 1977! I got moved to MS Branch soon, first on attachment then retained on posting in Aug 1978. I saw then that he had been graded 'Below Average' with 3 points on a 9-point scale in ALL 4 character qualities by his Reviewing Officer (though on a staff posting) in 2 consecutive ACR; this was bound to come in his way for promotion to a Lt Col and so warned him during one of my trips to the Regt, to work harder. I promised him then that I would soon ensure that he not only becomes 2 IC but if I did become CO of this Regt, he would be my 2 IC, even if he were to be finally passed over for promotion to a Lieutenant Colonel; and I would recommend to my successor too that he be the 2 IC! I did not have to work hard for it, as our CO got moved alongside me to MS Branch and soon that senior Major got passed over and moved to NCC, after applying. Thus with a new CO, he became the 2 IC! When I joined as CO in Nov 1980, the fact that I was willing to carry on with a 'superseded Major' as my 2 IC was very much acceptable to MS Branch, who were finding it difficult to find suitable employment for such Majors who would continue in uniform for 14 to 16 years more! *Probably I was destined to fall into trouble created by him many years later and that is why I promised him and ensured it also*! He continued with my successor also (as 2 IC) who being 2½ years his junior, had a tough time in shedding him, while keeping him in good humour! He had to take my help after 2 more years to get him out of the Regt!

Readers will recall from *'Problems Galore'* above that I had kept a 3-ton vehicle as an Officers Bus in Delhi Cantonment for their daily commute. Once the number of married officers in Delhi reduced when I hired accommodation in Gurgaon in June 1982, I replaced it with a 1-ton truck. This man started misusing it late at night, once even after midnight, when on leave, for picking up his wife from her job! When I came to know of it the next day (and Major Tanjore Doll was officiating as CO), I put a stop to it and told him that *'Uneasy lies the head that wears the crown'* and that as a CO, I alone was answerable; I could not also close my eyes and say that I wasn't aware! He refused to understand. This probably was the start point of more serious differences to follow!

After returning from Exercise Dig Vijay in Rajasthan to Regt's location at Gurgaon by road on 13 Mar 1983, I had made him convoy Commander for the road column. I personally briefed the whole column outside the *Mandir* as was our tradition, in his presence and hearing that the NO vehicle will move beyond Rohtak at night, even though the distance was not much, as the drivers would need rest, after having driven for 300 KM by then. I had sent Major Tanjore Doll (later my successor) with a team to go ahead, reconnoitre and find a suitable halt around Rohtak for the night, which was done. But Major Crass chose to disregard my orders and moved a dozen or so vehicles independently, to Gurgaon in one go! En route there was a fatal accident. I agree that accident by its very nomenclature is just that: an accident; but I was more upset at two things: *blatant violation of my personal directions to the whole Regt* **and** *the totally avoidable loss of a life.* I might have still not lost my cool, had he radioed me for permission to move administrative vehicles at night or sent the First Report of Death or waited for my arrival which I had said, around noon the next day. I heard of the accidents on calling the Regt by telephone. But Major Crass was not there! He had not only gone home, but had allowed all officers to break off too, which was inexcusable till the men had put all stores and equipment in and reported all correct and that report had come to me from him over the radio! Even more upsetting was the fact that repeated log messages were waiting for me to call up Scraggly, obviously about the accidents, what else? What choice did I have: *did I order a move back in one go at night* OR *did Major Crass disobey my orders*: either way, it would be counted as my 'command failure', for no fault of mine; Scraggly was licking his lips probably! As I did not want to precipitate matters, I sent my jeep to his home to come and see me at home, which I had never done before for official work. He sent it back saying he would follow! He did but leisurely on his scooter after an hour, unkempt and without his head cover. Before I could ask anything he said, when there was no point in waiting at Rohtak as the distance to Gurgaon could have been covered the same night, why should the vehicles have waited? I lost my cool for the first time in 7 years with him and said, the least he should have done was not only radioed the message to me for my okay but also waited in the Regt for my return as ordered. What would be my explanation to the Commander? He shouted: *"Tell him, I did it"*. I asked him to go away. (Later, my wife, who never interfered in my work but had heard this, gave a look of *deja vu*)! I gave him a bit of my mind the next day, 15 Mar 1983 in my office in the presence of the Adjutant. I warned him that if this behaviour repeated even once, I would not keep my promise of his retention as 2 IC, but will also not hesitate to take action as the situation demanded. He apologized immediately and said that he had some personal problems which had upset him, etc. I fell for it, as always and said he could have told me and I could have allowed him to go home direct from Rajasthan; someone else could have been the Convoy Commander! I never realized that he was a *'wolf in sheep's clothing'* and so continued trusting him. I forgot that if you climb on to a scorpion, you should expect to get stung!

On 9 Apr 1983, during the visit of Commander Corps Artillery Brigade to my Regt, Major Crass had collected all the Junior Commissioned Officers outside their Mess after our Tea and abused them, when I was busy briefing the visiting senior officer in my office and then seeing him off. The rank of Junior Commissioned Officers is peculiar only to the Indian and Pak Armies and whatever the provocation, they are always addressed as *"Sahib"* with respect. While seeing off the Brigadier, I found the Subedar Major with a long face. When I asked him, he gave the details but by then Major Crass had pushed off on casual leave; of course sanctioned by me. All Junior Commissioned Officers collected outside my office within a few minutes, wanting individual interviews, saying that they could not work under him! It wasn't mutiny but only genuine expression of a grievance. I promised to talk to them again when Major Crass returned on 14 Apr 1983 and sort out matters. On 14th, when they were with the Subedar Major, waiting outside my office, Crass started talking to them but I told him to go away, as they were waiting to see me, the Commanding Officer, at my bidding. I heard them out and called Crass to my office and made him apologize for the abuse. He demurred but had no choice and so did.

The next instance was at the Officers Mess on 22 Apr 1983. My Adjutant had just got selected for Defence Services Staff College Course at Wellington and insisted on hosting an evening at the Officers Mess by inviting all officers and their wives. During the pre-dinner cocktails, when snacks were being served, Major Crass compelled the waiter to serve him first, even before the ladies. I watched it, so called him aside and ticked him off, saying that I was still the CO and the courtesy shall remain for my wife first, then the ladies and then me; others would be later, just as he would have learnt in the Academy and hopefully been practising for 20 years! He said sorry again, but I could see he was smarting, as news of rejection of his representation against final supersession had come just the day before. (I had drafted that appeal for him after telling him that nothing much may come out of it; *so when the bad news came, he thought that I had spoken to someone in Military Secretary's Branch not for redress but for rejection. He had said so, to many after I went on Course!)* In the same party, after a while, he tried to get pally with my wife by telling her that when she stayed back after my departure for Higher Command Course in July, she could ask him for any help. I do not know what came over her; she said: *"Over my dead body! I will never request you for anything". That proved to be a prophecy, as I had to get a 3-ton as a hearse for carrying her body for cremation on 20 July 1983, just 3 months later.*

During May 1983, instructions were received from Military Secretary's Branch as to the percentage of officers who could be graded at each level, as Outstanding, Above Average, High Average, Average etc on the 9 point rating scale. 1 June 1983 was the first time this would be implemented when Annual Confidential Report (ACR) on officers above 10 years service would be written. I had informal discussions with Major Crass (and one more Major, who had also been passed over), that it may be more appropriate to award better grading to the aspiring ones, than them. They agreed. On 7 June 1983, I requested all of them to come home (as I was confined to bed due to very severe back ache), to read and sign their ACR, one by one. He started arguing with me loudly, despite his earlier acceptance of the suggestion. Thereafter he started spreading canards about me, which I did not know then but much later, when it was too late. Anyway, his antagonistic feelings were fuelled further by Scraggly, who was still waiting to *'catch'*.

An 'Operational Immediate' signal from HQ Western Command was received on 10 June 1983 for 'CO ... Regiment' to be available for a secret discussion at unit location on 13 and 14 June. The same was sent to me through a Despatch Rider, by the Head Clerk, as I had briefed both him and Major Crass in advance about it, I having been informed verbally earlier, direct by General Officer Commanding Corps. After my perusal at home, when this signal went back to the unit; and Crass, as Officiating CO saw it the next day, he wrote on it: *"Please ensure that I see the mail, before it is seen by **the Officer** who is on leave. No by-passing..."* In the meantime, Scraggly had told Crass that as I would be in the unit on 13th, he would visit my Ammunition Dump but I was not informed! On 12th itself I called up the Adjutant to inform both Scraggly and Crass that I wouldn't be able to attend the secret meeting the next day, due to unbearable back ache as I was unable to even get up from the hard floor, where I was lying for many weeks, as seen by some officers, who had come for ACR on 7 June! That absence was misunderstood by Scraggly as defiance, as otherwise I had been keen to visit the Regt on 13th for the other 'secret' board of officers! So, the chain of events started.

Another signal from Corps HQ was received on 11th to confirm action on the first. On it, Crass had written: *"CO ... or Lt Col xxx?"* I saw it when I went to the unit on 18 June (for the first time after 4 May), called and told him he should not have such doubts and definitely not write stupid comments on mail. Later he had written on it, *"Yes, I still* ***has*** (sic) *doubt"*, which I saw during the GCM and brought it out through the then Adjutant, while proving his rancour, animosity and the conspiracy!

While on leave, I could not even go out of station after the first 5 days and was mostly bed ridden with severe undiagnosed back ache; it had all but disabled me and caused me a worry not only about fitness for the prestigious 10-month course starting on 4 July but also about my very retention in the Army! In the meantime, much against my directions and established military convention, the Quarter Master too was sent away on leave by Crass, such that he would not be there when I left for the Course, to help in proper handing over. Taking advantage of my absence, he and Scraggly met at my unit Ammunition dump on 13 June 1983 to decide on *"when and how to catch"* me!

Just around that time two events had happened, which I was unaware of:-

- The Junior Commissioned Officer Quarter Master, *Subedar Never-loyal,* had attempted to misappropriate some dry rations and had been caught. Matter was reported to Crass and his offence was pardoned (without my knowledge) as a rain check for future use! He thus became a willing tool in the conspiracy by disingenuous and anachronistic cooking up of all data. I came to know of it 4 years later. (But he was so badly caught out during the trials that the Court had to warn him many times).

- A thick envelope from Corps HQ Ordnance Branch marked for Quarter Master by name had been received, which contained a Demi Official letter and some documents, presumably of Local Purchase (of garnish), from a Major at Corps HQ Ordnance, asking the former to be careful in typing financial documents. (*Crass* and *Cassius*, the officiating Quarter Master had obviously opened and read the letter between 4 and 12 June 1983 and briefed *Scraggly* in the Ammunition Dump on 13 June, by when *Never-loyal*, the store-holder had also been taken into the plot, as above!) Quarter Master, who passed by Delhi on 17 June collected the envelope and based on its contents, had *allegedly* got the documents amended in the office of Cassius! *(It is interesting to note that no one knows where those documents were, even after 4 General Courts Martial!)* Whatever 'doubts' on Local Purchase those two had, were clarified to their satisfaction, as reported by Crass himself to me over the telephone, in the presence of the Adjutant. (*However, neither the fact of this envelope nor any amendments in dates of my signatures affixed up to 4 May 1983 was mentioned to me by anyone till I rejoined on 28 June 1983, by when Quarter Master had gone to his village for the 'Shradh' ceremony (obsequies) of his mother*).

As discussed during their tête-à-tête, Scraggly and Crass got an anonymous letter written and sent to the former, which he received on 22 June, but did not take action for 5 days. How this came to light is interesting: during cross examination of my successor during the GCM, he stated that on 25 June 1983, after the Promotion Conference, when Crass had raised the point about Local Purchase and I had said where was the problem, as Crass himself had reported to me on telephone that he was fully satisfied with the explanations by the Quarter Master on 17 June (which they foolishly kept insisting as 16 June), he (Crass) had replied that *'Anyone could write an anonymous letter!'*. Lo and behold, that letter was already there in Brigade HQ since 22 June 1983 and he was aware of it, being its author! And, on 27 June 1983, less than 12 hours before I rejoined from leave and unknown to me, a special courier as previously decided between them, was sent by Scraggly at Meerut to Crass, Officiating as CO at Gurgaon, for comments the same night! This was totally against specific orders to the contrary laid down by Ministry of Home Affairs (Govt of India) and reproduced in Army Order 69/73! An officer was sent back by Crass with his comments at 10 p.m. that very night! I was in station attending a Bara Khana in the Regt and due to rejoin from leave in about 10 hours! (*That same Scraggly had ordered me to attend to work in the Regt every day, after full day's work at Army HQ in 1982; to adjust my leave dates for an expected visit of General Officer Commanding, in end-Apr 1983; and for a meeting on 13 June 1983 to meet a special board of officers: **all when I was on leave!***)

On 29 June 1983, when Handing and Taking Over was completed and my successor and I were ready to go to Meerut to report to Scraggly, we kept waiting for Crass who had also been warned by Rabbi the previous night, to go with us, as he had officiated as CO for 2 months of my just concluded leave. When he was delayed, I sent my driver to his home and he brought back a scribble *'NFW'* (not feeling well!) on a piece of paper! It was too late for me to do anything then, as, having handed over, I was no more the CO. I got a funny feeling and a premonition of worse things to follow but consoled myself. My *'bad times'* started right there.

This man claiming to be my younger brother in public for many years and being in station did not attend my wife's funeral on 20 July 1983. This was, to use the Bard's words: "*the most unkindest cut of all!*" I got this out of my successor in the GCM to prove his extreme ill will: all for an ACR, when he had already been finally passed over and his appeal too rejected, over which I had no control!

Incidentally, *it was Crass who had earlier known the Quarter Master (later, my co-accused) and had recommended his name to me for posting when there was a vacancy. We approached Army HQ and waited for over 8 months for him to be posted*!

Lieutenant Colonel 'Shifty Eyes'

This person, 6 months my senior, had been extremely career conscious but fell victim to a heart-problem, after his approval to a Lt Col; so he was posted to a soft appointment, as a Major (Instructor) in Deolali. I was already a Lieutenant Colonel then, in MS Branch dealing with promotions and career planning of Artillery Officers. We had been reasonably friendly for many years. Whenever a vacancy used to arise of a Lt Col either directly or in a cascade, he would call me up or travel to Delhi to meet me (at home) with a request to get him the acting rank of a Lt Col, even in broken periods. In any case, that was the policy too, provided the Director General Artillery, under whom I was working, agreed. I used to help him out invariably, as he was the senior most Major.

He arrived as CO of another Regt in Delhi (which too had been planned by me while at army HQ). I had already been a CO for about 6 months and had a good rapport with the (outgoing) Commander, as explained by me earlier. Immediately after his arrival as CO and to his chagrin, my Regt won two continuous competitions whereas his came second; and the Commander teased him on the second occasion! Shortly afterwards, there was a change and to his good luck now, Scraggly came and he had earlier served under him! But I had had some problems, as narrated by me above! The stage had been set by now. His Regt, just like mine, was not moved to Meerut, whereas 3 others had been. Scraggly started leaning on him for all his '*needs*'!

In Feb 1983, when I got selected for undergoing a 10-month Higher Command Course, (*to train outstanding Commanding Officers for assuming higher ranks and responsibilities*) at Mhow from July 1983, Scraggly was shocked that his pet (this CO) had not made it. In a conference, he even asked me the possible reason in his presence, *hinting that my earlier tenure in MS Branch had probably helped me*! I had to explain the entire tough screening procedure and the need for 2 to 3 'above average' ACR covering 20 months; and that I had earned two (for over 19 months) and would earn one more before moving, while the other person had got only one, of less than a year.

During Exercise Dig Vijay, there was a report in Feb 1983 about an alleged molestation case of a young boy by a soldier; Scraggly was trying to blame my Regt and thus prevent me from proceeding on prestigious Higher Command Course. I could make out his plan! So, I got a *'khoji'* (a local person, who can follow human trail easily in the deserts) and he led us to a Junior Commissioned Officer from Shifty-eyes' Regt (Scraggly's pet)! As the culprit owned up, Scraggly had no go other than to punish that person; but did nothing to Shifty Eyes, his pet, for *'command failure'*. But he felt very humbled by one more *encounter* with me and still bided his time to *'catch me'*!

So when a Presiding Officer was required for a Court of Inquiry, who suited the role better than this Lt Col, who had become jealous after Scraggly's open question about my selection for the Course, which was to open up major avenues for my promotions! One more occasion where I had been a poor judge of human beings.

Some More Disloyal Persons

There were a few more whose loyalty vanished soon after my handing over, as turpentine over oil paint! Meet them now.

My Successor–CO, Lt Col (later Colonel) 'Tanjore Doll'

He was not known to me earlier, but was 'imported' by me from another Regt, on the request of the then CO. For this he remained mostly grateful but only till my troubles started! He was a good worker but had too many family commitments; also he would lean towards anyone who has an upper hand at a given moment. I had helped him out at very high risk to myself with a vehicle and manpower all the way to his village 300 KM away, when his daughter had got married. When Major Crass got finally superseded and no one in the Regt wanted an *outsider* to take over from me, I used all my influence at MS Branch and with the Director General Artillery to get this person to relieve me. He was like my shadow during field manoeuvres and conferences and I introduced him as my successor everywhere right from Feb 1983. When I was on annual leave in May-June 1983, he was also sent on leave so as not to embarrass him by his being subordinate to Crass, just before his own elevation above him in 2 months. When he rejoined, I briefed him in detail about everything. However, he started behaving odd from the moment I voluntarily included in the Handing and Taking Over Notes the point about Local Purchase and after the Court of Inquiry commenced!

He told me much later in 1985 in confidence that he was apprehensive of Crass, *'who could cause so much damage to a super-smart person like you, what could I do when he continues as my 2 IC even today, all thanks to you!"* He requested me to get Crass posted out, using my influence which existed even then in the MS Branch. It took me time but I got it done. Only after that there was some positive change in this person, as I could experience from his general demeanour during the next Summary of Evidence and General Courts Martial. One thing, however, I must grant him: *of his own he never did me any harm and had been polite and courteous throughout*. Knowing all the facts about the whole Local Purchase transaction, he demurred in giving the whole truth: this is what I hold against him. Also, in the so called 'alleged recovery of garnish from the imaginary junk store' (about which you will read later), he should have taken a stand.

Officiating Quarter Master, 'Captain Cassius'

'Yond Cassius has a lean and hungry look... such men are dangerous.'

William Shakespeare (Julius Caesar Act 1, scene 2)

A chain-smoking Captain with a sickly appearance and *'lean and hungry look'*, he was under the thumb of Crass at previous location. He wanted to be posted on staff at Delhi, and Crass wrote me a personal letter in 1980 urgently requesting for it. He had no qualifications. However, I worked out a choice of six stations within 6 to 8 hours of Delhi, to one of which I could consider his move. I sent a signal accordingly direct to the Regt: probably a rare occurrence in the Indian Army. He chose and I issued the posting. En route, he called me up and I invited him home for lunch. 2½ years later, he rejoined my Regt when it was on exercise in Mar 1983 and soon went on leave. In May, he was appointed by Crass to officiate as Quarter Master (QM) during his leave, against the norms of service, when I was away too! Crass took him in his net and used him as a pawn to shoot his arrows at me, at all the Summaries of Evidence and General Courts Martial (GCMs). His lies were laid bare by my Counsel and Defending Officer in the GCMs. One more wrong judgement by me of a human being!

Junior Commissioned Officer Quarter Master, Subedar 'Never-loyal'

"I choose to be among the faithful,
No longer to be betrayed for,
There's something to be said,
About being true to the one you respect!"

By Insync: 2008

A gunner-Naik and a good layer in my Battery in 1976, he got successively promoted to reach a Subedar in 1982, under me. As per recommendations of the Promotion Board, he was appointed Junior Commissioned Officer Quarter Master in Nov 1982. He suddenly turned hostile towards the Quarter Master (and in turn to me) in his depositions by stating he had brought only 19,500 metres of LP Garnish and not 87000 metres as contracted. For this he produced an unsigned, undated and un-numbered Nominal Issue Voucher (NIV) with 4 signatures of sub-unit representatives, two of whom as Defence Witnesses said on oath that neither of them had signed that voucher; nor received the item mentioned therein! It had not been chronologically entered in the relevant register too! I came to know the reason years later, as mentioned earlier. He became a convenient tool in Crass' scheme of revenge against me for perceived 'insults', and made to state on oath that he had brought only 19,500 M!

No one is infallible and surely I do not claim to be; but I was definitely blameless in this case! You have read the quote from Joseph Lancaster at the beginning of this Chapter. I hope I have not fallen prey to that tendency in writing about these persons who had played havoc with my career and life! But you had to know about the major dramatis personae, before I proceed to the next Chapter.

CHAPTER 4

SOME MILITARY TERMS

"What's in a name? That which we call a rose
By any other name would smell as sweet."
William Shakespeare (Romeo and Juliet, II, ii, 1-2)

The Bard may be right; but armies the world over want the correct nomenclature for every thing! Therefore, to follow the trend of events over a period of five years, a broad understanding of some *'military officialese'* is a must. If you want to buy, say a mosquito net, you would ask for it in a shop saying: "Show me a mosquito net, please!" But in the army, which has over many millions of items in each of the many ordnance depots, an indent has to be prepared showing the Catalogue No and Part No (known as cat/part No) and the exact nomenclature. The indent would show something like:

H5-1080-00000134: Net Mosquito Olive Green, nylon, with lining: quantity one.

So, here are some terms, put simply. *These are not official definitions, though!*

Arrest: A person accused of an offence may be placed under arrest by his Commanding Officer to ensure that he neither escapes a trial nor harms himself or commits suicide etc. Arrests are of two types: *Open and Close*. In both cases, the accused is not allowed to appear outside his quarters except in uniform and is not permitted to visit places of entertainment.

- In the case of Close Arrest, a person of equal rank as the accused, duly armed stands guard over him and is normally called an Escort. In Court Martial cases, the accused is placed under close arrest from the time the Charge Sheet is given to him by the CO and till he is arraigned on it in the Court. Later the Convening Authority usually permits Open Arrest (or even, a *release from arrest without prejudice to re-arrest*) till the verdict. Type of arrest after the conviction, if any, depends on the punishment awarded.
- An Open Arrest is exactly like the Close Arrest, except that there is no escort.

Bania: A civilian contractor, who may also be a retired army JCO/jawan; runs a Wet Canteen and provides immediate needs like grocery, confectionery, Indian sweets, hot beverages, cool drinks etc on payment. In many cases he moves with the unit even to forward areas.

Bara Khana: This is a 'feast' on special occasions 'offered' by the men to officers and Junior Commissioned Officers, when everyone drinks and dines together. It enables a CO to know the pulse of the men, by direct contact. It is also usual to welcome and send off a CO and the Subedar Major of a unit with a Bara Khana. Families may be invited on one or two special occasions like Raising Day or Pongal or Onam etc; but those are usually without drinks.

Camouflage Net: This is a net made of jute, knitted into small squares, through which strips of Hessian cloth/coarse jute of varying width, lengths and shades, called Scrim Garnish are inserted to produce an irregular pattern, used for obvious purposes.

Casualty: Indicates someone injured or killed and also a decrease of military personnel or equipment that may be captured or missing in a military engagement. When used 'loosely', it also refers to a Casualty Return, a document published in the armed forces to record an occurrence in personal documentation of any person.

Confirming Authority: This is the officer by rank and designation, who may confirm the Finding (Guilty or Not Guilty) as well as the Sentence of a Court Martial. A Convening Authority may in some cases be the Confirming Authority also. In my case, the Confirming Authority was the Chief of Army Staff, as I was a substantive Lieutenant Colonel, while the Convening Authority was Commander, Independent Artillery Brigade/General Officer Commanding, Corps.

Convening Authority: This denotes an officer by rank and designation who may, under a special warrant signed by the Chief of Army Staff, convene a Court Martial of a particular type. Normally a GCM for an officer may be convened by Commander of an Independent Brigade, or General Officer Commanding of a Division or a Corps.

Court of Inquiry: (C of I, in short). This is an assembly of a suitable No of officers (and Junior/Non Commissioned Officers, as required) and consists of a Presiding Officer with one or more members and is detailed by the orders of a CO or higher Commander(s), in Part I Orders to assemble on date, place and timings fixed by the Presiding Officer to inquire into circumstances under which an event may have happened or may have led to an offence or an attempted one. Cases which involve an officer's character and military reputation are invariably presided over by an officer senior in rank to the affected officer and members are normally at least of equivalent rank. Under Army Rule 180, the affected officer is permitted to sit through the entire proceedings and cross examine witnesses if he so likes. NO counsel is permitted to be present. The proceedings are then seen and further action where necessary, such as recording a Summary of Evidence is progressed. A Court of Inquiry is, however, not a must, except in accidents, financial irregularity, death etc. (*Army Rule pertaining to this term is said to have been changed in 2003*).

Court Martial: This is a military court composed of officers of certain ranks, as laid down in the regulations such as Army Act, 1950; Army Rules, 1954; and Defence Services Regulations (Regulations for the Army) 1962 etc. These are of 4 types: a General Court Martial which alone can try an officer and will always have an officer of the Judge Advocate Branch present as an Advisor but not for voting etc. The other types are: Summary General Court Martial (SGCM), normally during war/operations; District Court Martial (DCM) and Summary Court Martial (SCM). The last named is peculiar to the Indian Army to try plain sepoys, where the CO alone constitutes the Court!

Exercise: Besides physical training, armed forces refer to field manoeuvres as Exercises. These may be with or without firing of weapons involved.

Handing/Taking Over (HTO): Whenever any person holding documents or stores is posted out or proceeds out of a unit for a period exceeding 14 days, proper Handing Over is done as per Ledger Balances, checked against ground holdings. 7 days for store-holders, extendable to 10; and for others, 4 days are permitted as per Defence Services Regulations (Regulations for the Army). Even when not done so due to exigencies/death of incumbent, the person who is functioning will be deemed to have so done.

Hearing of Charge:

- If after a study of the Court of Inquiry proceedings, the convening authority of Court of Inquiry is convinced that further evidence is required to be recorded, he 'takes cognizance of the offence', prepares a Tentative Charge Sheet which explains the alleged offence and carries out what is known as "Hearing of Charge".

- This is mandatory for Junior Commissioned Officers/ Other Ranks; but an officer will have to demand it in writing.

  (The above provisions are stated to have been modified in 1993).

- It is during this procedure that for the first time, the details of the Charge (or offence) is read out to the affected person and he is asked to plead his case, without the presence of a counsel or defending officer; he may produce witnesses in defence. Nothing may be taken down in writing.

- At the end, the "CO" may either dismiss the Charge or proceed with it, when he asks for evidence to be reduced to writing (*'Summary of Evidence'*). The 'accused', so termed hereafter, has to be physically present during the entire recording and may produce witnesses in his defence, a list of which he has to submit to the "CO"; he is permitted to cross examine the prosecution witnesses; (my recommendation: it is best avoided, in order not to let your proposed line of defence out!) He may also make a written statement towards the very end of the recording; see also Annexure 5.

Judge Advocate (JA): He is an officer of JAG Branch, who is posted in Corps and higher HQ for providing legal advice in complicated cases, when so requested by commanders holding warrants for convening Courts Martial. In addition, a JA is a must in every GCM and in some DCM for specified offences, though he is neither a Judge nor an Advocate. A JA is the one who provides a Report on Application for Trial (RAT); is present at a trial; including a Revision, when he provides legal advice; and also provides a Report on Trial (RT), although *not all for the same Court Martial*.

Langar and Langar Committee: The cookhouse of the men is called a Langar. Usually in the sub unit (Battery/

Company/Squadron), a Part One order is issued, which appoints members of a Committee to look after quality, quantity, variety etc besides the issue of rations from the sub unit stores to the langar and its use by it. The Committee also accounts for dry rations that are saved and takes them on charge; and after a consideration by all the men and under supervision of the Senior JCO, it issues it back to the langar for *'Bara Khana'* or to married men in station on festive occasions.

Local Purchase: Sometimes, despite best inventory control at the ordnance depots, stock of some stores gets exhausted. In such cases, provision exists in the Army whereby a Non Availability Certificate (NAC) is obtained from the depot concerned for specified quantity; commanders at various levels may resort to a laid down procedure for purchasing these from the open market by obtaining three quotations, comparing them and ordering from the lowest bidder, checking for quality and quantity as per sealed specimens received. Ceiling Monetary Limits are laid down for the maximum amount that an officer of a specified rank and designation may order for. *(In the instant case, as you will be reading elsewhere, I had resorted to locally purchase a total of 87,000 metres of an item called Scrim Garnish in 6 different transactions for three different shades, for a total of Rs 61,526/20P, within the powers of the Deputy Director of Ordnance Services at Corps HQ - whose powers were Rs 10,000 per transaction - for the biggest Exercise of the Indian Army for 3 months from Dec 1982 to Mar 1983)*

Non Availability (NA) and NA Certificate (NAC): Despite best inventory control at the ordnance depots, stock of some stores gets exhausted, when it is declared as Not Available. In such cases, provision exists in the Army whereby a Non Availability Certificate (NAC) is issued by the dependent depot to demanding units, for the quantity demanded.

Report on Application for Trial (RAT): This is a confidential report prepared by a JA at Corps/Command

HQ, to whom a warrant holder sends all relevant documents, such as a brief of the case; Court of Inquiry proceedings, if held; Summary of Evidence and the Application for Convening a CM. It is only seen and kept in custody by the officer seeking such a report. A Deputy Assistant Judge Advocate General at Corps HQ does not deal with RAT. The DJAG/AJAG at Corps/Command HQ is expected to detail any available officer to write the same.

Report on Trial (RT): This is a report prepared by a JA officer other than the one(s) who prepared the RAT and/or sat as JA during the trial, to see if the trial had any flaws that need rectification before confirmation; or if a Revision is required. This is submitted to the Convening Authority of a Court Martial.

Revision: This is a procedure by which any rectification of proceedings is done after the Court has given its Finding and awarded the Sentence and has adjourned *sine die*, but before confirmation. For this, a full Report like a RT is prepared and reasons, if any, for the necessity to reconvene are given out. However, as per Paragraph 198 of *'The Notes on Indian Military and Air Force Law', "Revision should be sparingly used, as a rule,* ***only with a view to correction of minor errors in the Finding and Sentence;*** *instead of Revision, partial confirmation may be resorted to. The reason for directing Revision should be clearly given, with an indication of the Course(s) Open to the Court and appropriate to the circumstances, but* ***without dictation of any particular course****"*. Revision can take place only once.

Sainik Sammelan: Loosely called *"Durbar"* (legacy from British days), this is a monthly event in every unit and sub unit for its commander to directly interact with the bulk of his command; explain personally points that he may have and what to expect for the next month etc. Jawans are at liberty to raise directly to the unit/sub unit commander, any point affecting them as a whole or even individually, without fear of a tick-off!

Scrim Garnish: These are mere strips of Hessian cloth of two specified widths (50 MM and 75 MM) and varying shades and lengths, which are inserted in a camouflage net to produce an irregular pattern

Summary of Evidence: After 'Hearing of Charge', a Commanding Officer who feels that the Charge ought to be proceeded with may want to get the evidence reduced to writing, so that his decision to proceed with or drop the charge altogether is more reasoned. In such a case, an officer is detailed to record the evidence of Prosecution Witnesses, in the presence of the accused, who may cross examine them, should he so desire. (*I have learnt from my bitter experience of the three Summaries of Evidence which were recorded on the same charge under three different COs, that cross examination of Prosecution Witnesses at Summary of Evidence is best avoided, in order not to give out one's line of defence; as I had almost given out the conspiracy angle in detail, which, later in the GCM, the Prosecution tried its best by coaching of witnesses to disprove*).

Warrant Holder: Officers commanding Independent Brigades, Division and Corps are vested with different types of Warrant authorizing them to convene particular types of Court Martial. They are called Warrant Holders.

Now that you know the outline of organisation, duties of some staff; a brief gist of the Case and the nature of persons whom I was working with; and these terms, it will be appropriate for you to go through the sequence of how a disciplinary case is progressed, after which you will read the details of the progress of just one case over 5 years in various Chapters! I have also summarized the lessons I had learnt from this entire saga!

CHAPTER 5

SEQUENCE OF ACTION AFTER AN OFFENCE IS ALLEGED

You need to understand the sequence of events that take place before convening of a Court Martial; during its currency; and subsequently, till the Finding and Sentence are confirmed/not confirmed/accused get acquitted.

The general sequence in very brief terms is:

A preliminary investigation

Court of inquiry, where required

Its careful examination by the "CO"

'Taking cognizance' of the offence

Preparation of Tentative Charge Sheet

Attachment to another unit for disciplinary proceedings, if necessary by Army HQ

Appointment of a "CO" at the new unit for discipline

'Hearing of Charge'

Recording of Summary of Evidence

Its study by the CO

Application for Trial

Report on the above, called RAT (Report on Application for Trial) by a JA

Composition of the Court

Issue of final Charge Sheet and

Commencement of trial

Routine during the trial

Adjournments

Finding

Sentence

Pre-confirmation petition, if any, by the accused

Revision, if any

Confirmation, Non Confirmation/Acquittal.

The sequence of events after an offence is alleged or comes to notice till a CM is convened:

- A preliminary investigation may be carried out under the orders of the CO, to find out if indeed an offence has been committed and if so by whom, when and where?
- If required, though not obligatory, a Court of Inquiry is set up, again under the orders of the CO with composition depending on the type of alleged offence; this would be a unit Court of Inquiry.
- Where persons from more than one unit are alleged to be involved or in cases where the CO himself may be allegedly involved, the next higher authority orders the Court of Inquiry, when it is known as a Staff Court of Inquiry.
- Where the character and military reputation of an officer is likely to be affected, provisions of Army Rule 180 are invoked and he is permitted to sit through the whole proceedings and also allowed to

cross examine the prosecution witnesses; but he is not allowed to produce witnesses; he may, however, make a statement with evidence.

- If after a study of the proceedings, the convening authority of Court of Inquiry is convinced that further evidence is required to be recorded, he 'takes cognizance of the offence'; prepares a Tentative Charge Sheet which explains the alleged offence and carries out what is known as "Hearing of Charge". This is mandatory for Junior Commissioned Officers/OR; but an officer will have to demand it in writing. In the case of a "CO" or higher officer becoming the subject of a disciplinary case, an artificial "CO" is created, to whose unit the accused then gets 'attached'. For officers, the attachment has to be ordered by the Discipline and Vigilance Directorate (DV Dte) at AG's Branch, Army HQ. (*I learn that this provision has been amended a few years back: firstly Hearing of Charge mandatory for all, including officers and also that it could be dispensed with, if there had been a Court of Inquiry*!)
- It is during this procedure that for the first time, the details of the Charge (or offence) are read out to the affected person and he is asked to plead his case, without the presence of a counsel or defending officer; he may produce witnesses in defence. The "CO", at the end of 'Hearing of Charge', may either dismiss the Charge; or proceed with the charge, when he asks for evidence to be reduced to writing (which is called a Summary of Evidence). The accused, so termed hereafter, has to be physically present during the entire recording and may produce witnesses in his defence, a list of which he has to submit to the "CO"; he is permitted to cross examine the prosecution witnesses. He may also make a statement towards the very end of the recording.

- Again, after a perusal of the Summary of Evidence proceedings, the CO may dismiss the charge; or ask for additional evidence to be recorded or seek a pre-trial advice from the JA at Corps HQ, wherein he also makes an application for a trial by Court Martial.
- JA writes out a RAT, or Report on Application for Trial wherein he examines the legal angle of the charge and the evidence. This is sent to the convening authority and is kept confidential. Simultaneously, where a trial is recommended by the JA, the application goes to the General Officer Commanding Corps through his A Staff.
- Depending on the rank of the accused, composition of the court is ordered to meet on a date and time.
- The accused is informed a minimum of 96 hours in advance (just 24 hours, on active service) along with composition of the Court and a copy of the final Charge Sheet. He is also asked if he is planning to engage a Defence Counsel, in which case, the prosecution too will engage a civilian counsel, besides a legally qualified officer as the Prosecutor. *Many times, the prosecution engages a civilian counsel and lets the accused know only 4 days in advance. How does an accused arrange a civilian counsel practising military law cases in High Court or Supreme Court to turn up at 4 days notice?*
- The accused is asked to give name(s) of any serving officer(s) as Defending Officer. If not given, the Convening Authority arranges one, *where possible*!
- If an offence is alleged to have been committed by two or more persons, a Joint Trial is ordered. There is a provision to seek separate trial; but it is better to undergo a joint one, so that none of the other accused springs a surprise against you!

Sequence after GCM is Convened

The Court assembles on the given date and time, before which the following events take place:

- The accused is 'marched up' to his "CO" under an armed escort (who is generally expected to be of the same rank); CO reads out the Final Charge Sheet and directs the accused to remove his belt and hand it over, in proof of being placed under arrest. He is then 'marched out'! Under both types of arrest ("*Open*" as well as "*Close*"), the accused cannot appear outside his quarters (or the quarter guard, if in custody therein) except in uniform. Belt is an essential part of uniform; its absence 'announces' the fact of arrest!
- If under Close Arrest, the escort remains throughout.
- During the entire Court proceedings, the accused stays under one or the other form of arrest. But, once the arraignment on the Charge is over at the Court, the Convening Authority may (and usually does) direct that the accused be taken off Close Arrest, without prejudice to re-arrest but continue under Open Arrest.
- Before the Court proceedings every morning, the accused is examined medically by an authorized medical officer. If the unit to which the accused is attached has one, it is normally done therein (so that he doesn't become a 'show piece' to spectators, as being 'under arrest'). But the Convening Authority may lay down a different place just to humiliate, as had happened in my case!
- The Court is normally expected to sit for not more than 6 hours **and** only between the hours of 6 a.m. and 6 p.m. ; except that when 'exigencies of service' or the 'interests of justice and discipline' demand, it may continue to sit for longer hours and/or beyond 6 p.m., but will record the reasons in the proceedings.

- The Court assembles and accused is/are brought before it with escort(s); then escort leaves.
- The convening order is read out and members take their seats as per seniority.
- The accused is asked if he has objection to any member serving; if any is raised, that member goes out and waits while JA gives his advice; the Court is closed to consider the same; reopens and decision is announced. If not accepted, the member returns. A few waiting members are present and may be called in to replace any 'objected member' being relieved; but will again be subject to 'objection'. The procedure continues till all members are covered. Once the required number is available, the waiting members are discharged to go.
- The members, the Interpreter if any, the Shorthand Writer and the JA attending the trial are sworn in or affirmed, according to their religion(s): Hindus and Muslims affirm, while Sikhs and Christians swear in the name of God.
- The proceedings are dictated by the JA attending the trial and typed out the same day. The accused is permitted to see them after being typed but cannot make a copy! *(That is why I kept writing out every word that was dictated by the JA and compared it later with the typed pages (noting down even page numbers, as these would be required later for any petitions) and point out any mistakes. Time was always at a premium, with preparation for the next day to be done; so I had to go without sleep for many nights. Even the inchoate proceedings of the first two trials were not given for a reference later, till we raised objections).* However, a considerate court may give a copy for perusal before preparation of Closing Address by the Defence counsel.

- The Charge Sheet is read out, signed by the JA and attached to the proceedings. Accused is asked to plead Guilty or NOT Guilty to the Charge. Silence is taken as plea of NOT guilty. Objection may also be raised to the Charge and plea to jurisdiction of the Court.
- Once those pleas are disposed of, the trial on the Charge commences. Prosecution Witnesses are called in sequence for Examination-in chief by the Prosecution Counsel; Defence may cross examine each; Prosecution may then do Re-examination and Defence may do further cross examination. Both Defence and Prosecution may suggest questions to be asked by the Court; the Court may also ask questions to clarify any point they need to; but ONLY the Presiding Officer (and JA) may do so. Other members may only ask through him.
- The Court may also call for any witnesses to clarify any points; the Prosecutor arranges their presence through the Convening Authority.
- Whenever a difference arises on a legal point between the Prosecution and the Defence, the JA summarizes the relevant provisions of the regulations, reads them out, records in the proceedings and advises the Court to close and then consider it for a decision. When ready, the Court is re-opened and proceedings re-start.
- The Defence gives out its final Closing Address first, followed by the Prosecution and finally a summing up by the JA. The closed Court then deliberates and arrives at the Finding (of Guilty or Not Guilty) and the Sentence, both by majority of votes. They are announced in Open Court. The character, past record of convictions/punishments, if any and plea in mitigation of sentence are heard before the Sentence is announced.

- The proceedings are transmitted to the Convening Authority, who forwards them to the Confirming Authority through the intermediate stages, the JA at each of which may examine and give their views; this is known as RT (Report on Trial).
- The accused may send a Pre Confirmation Petition to the final authority through the intermediate stages.
- Revision may be ordered by any intermediate authority, independent of the examination of any such Petition.
- Proceedings after Revision are sent through the same stages.
- A post confirmation petition and/or a mercy petition is also allowed.

CHAPTER 6

EVENTS LEADING TO THE FIRST GENERAL COURT MARTIAL

"Base Fortune, now I see that in thy wheel
There is a point, to which when men aspire,
They tumble headlong down. That point I touched,
And, seeing there was no place to mount up higher,
Why should I grieve at my declining fall?"
Christopher Marlowe

I was commanding a fine Regiment; most drills were set by my predecessors and things were going beautifully for the Regiment as well as me. Bad luck was waiting for me in the form of a Brigadier, who had previous score to settle with me in our official work and was posted as my immediate superior. He just could not bear to see me doing well, because another Lt Col known to him for many years was not as lucky as me!

Exercise Dig Vijay

Indian Army's largest exercise till then, named Exercise Dig Vijay was to be held in the deserts of Rajasthan, during Feb and Mar 1983. Move and Concentration was to take place before mid Dec 1982. Advance information had been received in all units by Aug 1982 and leave had to be adjusted as such that maximum personnel with guns, vehicles and equipment took part. I requested the Brigade and Corps Commanders to permit my Regt to leave after celebrations on 13-15 Dec (for the first time) of my Battle Honour Day on 16 Dec 1982 and they agreed.

Beg, Borrow, Buy or Steal: 2 nets must for everyone and every thing!

Units were ordered to *carry two camouflage nets each* for all guns, vehicles, equipment etc, in place of just *one, as authorized*. Each net had to be knitted in laid down patterns with strips of Scrim Garnish of different shades and width! Nets were required also for cook-houses, Order Group's seating, all fieldworks, Visitors Vehicle Park, etc.

Bugbear of TWO camouflage nets started! *Indian Army, thy name is improvisation; so, beg, borrow, buy or steal*! Higher HQ just passed the buck down: *'I don't know, how you do it; but these are the orders'* was repeated ad nauseam in every conference at Brigade and higher levels! What does a poor unit commander do, except arrange the nets! I was one such CO; why should I have hesitated, when I too was ambitious and everything was going well for my advancement in the Army? I had two choices: *"Disobey and explain or obey and complain"*. I chose to *obey* but forgot to complain!

We had excellent local liaison with Ordnance Depot Shakurbasti and got the maximum nets and garnish possible but they put their hands up after Nov 1982, as all units had approached them and their stocks were exhausted! So they issued Non Availability Certificate, for 3 shades of Garnish Scrim, 75 mm on 21 Nov 1982: MB Green 62,000 M; Light Green 17,000 M; and Dark Brown 11,000 M; (a total of 90,000 M).

I raised the shortage of camouflage material in a conference at the Brigade HQ. Scraggly ordered us to go in for Local Purchase (LP) for which he would speak to the

Deputy Director of Ordnance Services (DDOS) at Corps HQ, who was his batch-mate. Initially, 100 vehicles and 18 guns needing big size camouflage nets were to take part and the requirement was colossal! The number was later reduced to about 80 including 9 vehicles loaned/attached to other units. The requirement was still huge; we also had to loan 68 knitted nets to Brigade HQ and some garnish to our dependent Workshop!

The requirement for total 235 nets to be knitted worked out to 2,01,160 M; but holding with the Regt as on *25 Nov 1982* was 1,22,400 M in all shades (*including 99,000 M of Undyed Garnish, which was not of much use*); the shortfall even then was 78,750 M. The basis of working as laid down by Army HQ was: 2,360 M per 16x11 M net; 1180 M for 10.7x6 M net; and 590 M for 8x5.5 M net. **The last receipt** of these three shades at the Regt from Ordnance was **10 Nov 1981** (Dark Brown) and **30 Dec 1981** (the other two shades). (During the trial, I brought these out of the Q office Ledger-Clerk, PW-3).

Accordingly, my Regt went ahead with the Local Purchase procedures. 87,000 M of Scrim Garnish (against a Non Availability Certificate of 90,000) was contracted for a total of Rs 61,526/20P; it was received on 13 Dec 1982 during the very first Battle Honour Day celebrations (for the 1971 Operations), which had just been announced. It was distributed to all batteries and some quantity to the dependent workshop (on goodwill). 68 knitted nets (with over 40,000 M of garnish in them) were loaned to the Brigade HQ on 24/25 Feb 1983 in the exercise area but we got back un-knitted nets and only 15,000 M garnish in July 1983, well after my departure for the Course. There was no time for getting into minor details like worrying about vouchers and signatures etc. within the unit, as immediately following the celebrations, we had to get the Rail Column moving, followed by the Road Column. These dates were later slightly delayed.

Nothing was Secret or Hidden about the Local Purchase

"The biggest guru-mantra is: Never share your secrets with anybody. It will destroy you."
Chanakya

"To him that you tell your secret,
you resign your liberty."
(Anonymous)

I believed in the above and never had any secrets with anyone except my wife, to whom anyway I had lost my *liberty* in 1966, when I had proposed 2 years before our wedding!

The fact of Local Purchase (LP) of garnish was openly announced, not only in many of the Battery Commanders' Conferences in my office and the Brigade Commander's Conference of all Commanding Officers but also in my Unit Sainik Sammelan (also called *Durbar*). THUS, THERE WAS NO SECRECY AT ANY STAGE. Thanks to this LP, my *Regt's camouflage and concealment was so good that on one occasion, General Officer Commanding Corps and General Officer Commanding Armoured Division flying low in a helicopter over concentration areas could not locate mine*! So, during the preparatory period for the Exercise, my unit was ordered to lay on a demonstration on camouflage and concealment for all the Corps units. An appreciation was also received and logged in the Exercise Dig Vijay Message Log Book; but all papers of the Exercise had to be destroyed in the end, as ordered; thus one major piece of evidence to help me was lost, though I got it out of the mouth of Tanjore Doll, who was a Prosecution Witness.

My only fault was that I had agreed to the Quarter Master's well-meaning suggestion of breaking up the single local purchase transaction into 6, so as to make each within the powers of the Deputy Director of Ordnance Services at Corps HQ, who had been approached by the Commander already, (instead of Command/Army HQ, from where sanction might have taken even a year)! No dealer would wait that long for payment. The necessary papers were signed by me, well before I joined the Concentration Area in Jan 1983 but **after** the item had been used up in knitting the nets. Thereafter once my name appeared as the only Gunner Officer of my batch, in early Feb 1983, in the list of officers selected to attend the prestigious Higher Command Course at Mhow from 4th July 1983, I was probably in euphoria to worry about mundane things! However, after the sanctions were received, I signed the Contingent Bills etc IN MY OFFICE on 4th May 1983, (before my leave commenced on 5th).

It was decided in a Battery Commanders' Conference that the Quarter Master would stay back in the permanent location as Officer in Charge Rear, i.e., to ensure normal and routine tasks, besides catering to all our logistic needs in exercise area and dispatching personnel returning from leave to the exercise area etc. As I had taken a few days leave at the year-end and also had to further stay back due a fissure in ano, our combined stay 'in the Rear' was also made a matter of *'acting in concert'*!

Mischief by Major Crass Starts

We returned from the Exercise in mid Mar 1983 and routine re-started. But a few events took place as explained by me in the Chapter on *Dramatis Personae* by which Crass developed animosity, rancour and ill-will towards me; he found a willing and ready partner in Scraggly and they hatched a plot as close to the date of my departure for the Higher Command Course as possible, so as to stop me from proceeding on that course.

I had to complete my annual leave as instructed by the College of Combat, Mhow before I reported for the Higher Command Course. Accordingly, I applied for leave from 29 April to 27 June 1983, such that the authorized 4 days were available for me to hand over to my successor, before leaving on 1 July AN for Mhow. *That was another mistake by me*. Knowing the mindset of Scraggly and Crass, I should have finished my leave by end-May and been present for at least a month in command, to nip any attempt at any mischief at all. I had totally lost the initiative by my leave dates!

I shall digress a bit and cover some essential information for you to follow the thread in trial, later. Even these leave dates were doubted in the trial! Scraggly had directed me both verbally and in writing: *'Please adjust the date of commencement of leave, subject to visit by GOC ...Corps to your unit'*! Obviously, leave could not extend beyond 27 June (as above). On 4 May 1983, I found out from AMS at Corps that Corps Commander was not visiting in the near future. I asked Major Bandicoot, DAA&QMG to check with Scraggly if I could proceed on leave. He called back and confirmed. All this: while I was attending work in Regt every day, but had not bothered to check if any Routine Order was published with my original dates of leave and Crass' assumption of the officiating appointment in my place. It was also routine for me to function in the Regt while on leave and other temporary duty, if in Delhi. Readers would recall instances ordered by Scraggly! Accordingly, I commenced my leave on 5 May and went on a trip to Jaipur and Ranthambore Sanctuary with the family. There I got a very severe back sprain within 72 hours; got evacuated in stages to Delhi. Not only was our outing shortened...(*alas, that was also to be the last holiday as a whole family for me, as I lost my wife within 2 months and elder daughter 11 years later*)... but I could not even get up easily and unassisted from the floor where I had made my bed. In that agony, I never bothered to get my leave dates amended, which was later used against me in the trial to show that I had signed the LP documents while on leave and thus had intent to defraud and *'mens rea'* (criminal intent)! Quarter Master had *allegedly* got the dates etc amended in the documents in Cassius' office on 17 June 1983, backdating them to May, about which I was not aware till 28 June, after handing over! *Even the original documents were never produced in trial by the prosecution, but only office copies amended by clerks who stated on oath that they had amended dates etc, AFTER my original signatures of May*!

Crass, officiating in my place but without my knowledge, when I was in station, sent away the Quarter Master also on annual leave from 15 May 1983 for 2 months in such a way that he would rejoin 2 weeks AFTER I had left for the Course on 1 July! This was against all norms of leave planning. Quarter Master's son's marriage had been fixed for 23 May 1983 in Dehradun, for which he would have needed leave; it could have been split and balance taken later in the year! Even after his mother's obsequies he could have been ordered back well before my departure. All Indian army units have an arrangement by which an officer would *'voluntarily rejoin'* when *'advised'* by a private letter/ message from CO/2IC through a courier! If there were doubts in anyone's mind (other than what was sown by Crass himself, in my absence), he, as officiating CO could have advised the Quarter Master to rejoin from leave voluntarily, to clarify. Not only did he not do this, but on the only occasion when the Quarter Master visited the Regt on 17 June 1983 to collect personal mail, Crass allowed him to go, after my specific instructions that he must clarify all his doubts and ONLY THEN allow the Quarter Master to leave. *Crass himself did tell me over the telephone that the Quarter Master had satisfied him and if any points at all remained, he could always clarify after rejoining*! This fact was brought out by me in the GCM both from Prosecution as well as Defence Witnesses, who stated that Crass even saw off Quarter Master in a jeep that day!

Crass again raised the point about LP, after a Promotion Conference in the Regiment on 25 June 1983. I told him that he had himself confirmed to me just the previous week that the Quarter Master had satisfied him with all the answers and that anything left can be clarified on his return; but as Officiating CO, it was within his powers to take any action that he deemed fit; why fire it from my shoulder? (However,

Quarter Master had said in their presence about going to his village in Garhwal for the *'shradh'* i.e., obsequies for his mother). He did not take any action; instead said: *"Anyone can write an anonymous letter"*. On my asking him as to who could, he said: *"As the whole Regt knows, anyone can"*. He later briefed all witnesses in the GCM to say: *'CO said Quarter Master will be in his village and not in Dehradun'*, as if I had conspired with the Quarter Master for his son's wedding and his mother's death! In the meantime, because of doubts expressed by Crass and Cassius and probably with the good intention not to come in the way of my most important career course, Quarter Master sent a letter to the Regt with copies to me, Tanjore Doll and Cassius:

"I, SL...Major...hereby certify that:-

(a) Lt Col.../Cassius are not responsible for any discrepancy in QM stores ...Medium Regt.

(b) They are not responsible for any financial, local purchase/ accounting of local purchase items done any time in the past.

I fully take the responsibility of all the discrepancy, if any, and I am answerable for any sort of deficiency/discrepancy/financial transaction."

(He had also given his address in Uttarkashi till 2 July 1983; and Dehradun after that).

My copy of the above letter was not given to me by Crass till 28 June, when Rabbi came for investigation; till then I had not been aware of this letter!

Pseudonymous Letter received by Commander

"I am no sot, to suffer such abuse
As doth bereave my heart of his delight;
Nor will I frame myself to such as use,
With calm consent, to suffer such despite;
No quiet sleep shall once possess mine eye
Till Wit have wrought his will on Injury."

– Edward de Vere ('Revenge of Wrong', 1576 AD)

As narrated earlier, a pseudonymous letter alleging wrong doing by the Quarter Master and me in the LP transaction arrived in the Brigade HQ on 22 June 1983. Note the convenient timing: I was on leave, with a severe back ache; Quarter Master was away and would not return till I left for the Course; I had to rejoin in 5 days, hand over command and proceed on the most prestigious Course for a Lt Col, for 10 months; *'catching'* me could not be done in the past 2 years! (*As I write this in 2008, I hear news on TV channels as to how 'the most outstanding Commanding Officers alone are chosen for this course and how 15 Colonels have refused to sign the 5-year bond that is required before proceeding on this course'! My mind raced back 25 years!*)

Scraggly waited till the last possible moment, as had been agreed upon between him and Crass; and sent it on 27 June 1983 evening to the latter, by name by a special courier, *with directions to reply by hand of an officer-courier, the same night*! (It could have been done on 22 June itself by *'recalling'* me over the telephone, as neither any permission from Army Commander nor extra expenditure to the State was involved.) The reply was sent at 10 p.m., while I was to rejoin in less than 10 hours. (The same Crass did not agree, despite my advice for a courier on 18 and 25 June, with 'advice' to Quarter Master to rejoin voluntarily!) Scraggly had probably planned the whole thing expecting me to apologize but I was strong and unbending, as I felt I was guiltless to do so. I had no evil intentions before, during or after contracting the above Local Purchase of Scrim Garnish. The proof of the pudding was in the eating; and every one had tasted the success of my Regiment's camouflage, including Scraggly. So I was confident, no harm would befall me for a minor procedural lapse of splitting the transaction and using before obtaining sanction, as there was real, emergent and colossal need for it; and it had arisen due to the *unauthorized* orders for TWO nets each! But that was not to be!

Conspiracy Kicks Off and Enquiry Commences

"The irrationality of a thing is not an argument against its existence; rather a condition of it"
Nietzsche

Scraggly had been waiting since 1981 for me to take just one wrong step, which my procedural mistake and Crass' animosity gave him. Once commenced, even he could not re-trace his steps; however, once in late-1983, he had mentioned to a common friend, a Brigadier at Army HQ that if I apologized, he would get the case closed. I replied to that Brigadier that I was convinced I had done NO wrong and so will not grovel before this vindictive and petty man; let the inquiry keep going and it would lead nowhere. I had added that probably Scraggly was gleeful in his thought that I was not endowed with the anatomical wherewithal of my gender, which indeed I had! But I was wrong in underestimating the *'snake-in–the-grass'* Major Crass, who was well entrenched in the Regiment. Even Tanjore Doll, my successor, though senior in rank to him, but having *'sir-*red' him for the previous 4 years was scared, as he later told me in 1984 that he was apprehensive of Crass (mentioned earlier). Crass had nothing to lose, as he had been finally passed over and by then had done 7 continuous years in the Regiment. After I left, even the Subedar Major fell into his trap with the fear of not getting Honorary Lt's rank and so gave false evidence on a small point in a Summary of Evidence; but nemesis caught up with him and he died soon thereafter, without earning his honorary rank.

Only those who were serving outside the Regiment or those who continued to serve in the Regt after Major Crass was posted out, came forward to speak the truth, in my favour. Any discerning reader of the proceedings of the GCM will find his venomous animosity easily. I wonder why the JA and the members of the GCM could not see through this.

On 26 June 1983, a *Sunday*, Col Rabbi called on me in my friend's flat, where I had just shifted my family for the duration of my Course. He said being an ex-colleague from my Regt, he just wanted to check all well before I left for the course etc and indirectly asked me *if there was any problem in the Regt,* which I wished to tell him about. I had assumed even then that Crass was only acting immature and why take a unit matter to higher HQ, just when I was to leave. I said all well. *Now in hindsight I realize that obviously he was in picture both about the pseudonymous letter and the hobnobbing between Scraggly and Crass; and because of mine being his old Regiment, he felt a prick in his conscience and had got rid of it by this quick visit*! But he stated under oath during my second GCM on 12 Aug 1985 that *he had NO knowledge of the letter till Crass' reply addressed to* ***him*** *was received on 27 June 1983*! The cat was out of the bag; he had obviously known BEFORE he came to my home on 26 June; why else should he have asked about any problems? That became crystal clear in 24 hours!

On 27 June 1983, when I reached the Regt at about 7.30 p.m., for the Bara Khana with the men, Crass showed me the pseudonymous letter, in the presence of all battery commanders/officiating ones, who had been called 30 minutes earlier. Immediately I called the Officiating Subedar Major, Subedar BR Sharma and told him that I had to decline his invitation for the meal, unless the author of the letter came up and explained without any fear of reprisal, any wrong doing by anyone including me and the Quarter Master. On his suggestion, all the officers, JCOs and store-holders, besides the poor jawan with a similar sounding name as the author of the letter were collected in my office. While only Crass, Cassius and Never-loyal made a grimace and Tanjore Doll sat expressionless, the rest shouted in unison that they were with me and nothing had gone wrong, as I had even announced the fact of Local Purchase in Durbar and conferences and had also told them that any difficulty in making two nets each, could be directly reported to me! It was pleasing to hear it but I knew that it was momentary; I could also make out in clear detail the three major mischief makers and the 'plight' of a new Lt Col whose rank will be confirmed only after I was away from the scene and he was wishing it would happen soon! I told Crass that as the letter was addressed to him in secrecy asking him to reply immediately, he could reply whatever he liked and I would deal with it the next day. *This was another mistake by me.*

I rejoined at about 8 a.m. on 28 June 1983 as scheduled and after a Mandir Parade and special Sainik Sammelan, started handing over formally to Tanjore Doll at about 10 a.m. That was a mere formality, as I had been briefing him for a few days since 16 June, (at my home from my *bed*, as he lived close by); so it was over in less than an hour.

Just then, Rabbi landed up with two Majors in tow; he walked up to my office alone and in Tanjore Doll's presence, told me that he had been asked by Scraggly to carry out an *informal investigation* regarding stock holding of Garnish Scrim in my Regt! As I well knew the stock position BEFORE my leave (as explained above), I felt he was not going to achieve anything by this 'informal investigation', but was once again proved wrong; as I had not studied Scraggly, Crass, Cassius and Never-loyal correctly. I however called a Muster Parade at 11 a.m. and told the Regt that anyone with any knowledge of wrong doing in the whole transaction could go direct to Rabbi and report without fear and his name will be kept secret by Rabbi. NO ONE WENT TO RABBI, TILL approx 8.45 p.m. when he and party left; I left for home at 9 p.m. *I did NOT sit with Rabbi any time during the investigation, to ensure a fair one*; this too was brought out in the trial.

Midway during his 'informal investigation' of the Case, Rabbi came to my office at about 6.30 p.m. and told me in the presence of Tanjore Doll: *"Crass says even now, if you apologize, he will sort things out and there may be no further inquiry"*. I replied: *'I have done nothing wrong and in any case, why should I apologize to **him**? Don't you realize that if he can sort it out now after my apology, there was NO case ab initio'*!

What I forgot were the words of George Napper: "*When you are up to your rear end in alligators, it is hard to remember that your purpose is draining the swamp*". And it was sad to remember; I had brought in the alligators in the first place and bred them!

By the time I left at 9 p.m., two major events had taken place, of which I was **not** informed of the first one, till 30 June 1983, by when the Court of Inquiry had started:-

(1) Out of the blue, Cassius asked Never Loyal at about 3 p.m. the same afternoon (*as later stated by him during the trial) to check if any unused garnish was lying anywhere in the unit*! *Where and how did he get the idea that any such garnish was lying at all*? He had been doing Quarter Master's job for over 6 weeks by then and Never-loyal from 16 Nov 1982 and if any was available, it ought to have been within their knowledge as they both, *having been physically performing the job for 7 and more continuous days as per norms, were ultimately responsible for all the stores in the Regt*! Never-loyal who confirmed he had done a proper handing and taking over from his predecessor on 16 Nov 1982 (when the latter proceeded on pension) could have easily issued the usable garnish out of this, BEFORE the Exercise and Local Purchase quantity could have been reduced! Cassius stated during the trial that at 7.20 p.m. on 28 June *(I like his exactness for this single statement in the whole trial, while his entire evidence was a confused mess!)*...when there was a power break down in entire Gurgaon area...Never-loyal *'found approximately 50,000 to 55,000 M of garnish in sealed bundles which had ordnance markings'*, (with the help of hurricane lanterns?) in a remote corner of the unit perimeter, (where there were two rooms and both had been occupied by luggage of officers, including the first Commander's, his pet(s) and caretaker[s], besides my own surplus baggage, right from the time we returned from the Exercise and I knew of my selection for the Course and the need for shedding unwanted luggage) and reported the same to him! This room suddenly got a name: *Junk Store*! Irrespective of junk or otherwise, any store-

holder is answerable for it and NOT me! I do not know whether because I had handed over command on paper, (though legally I was the CO till 1 July AN) or on coercion by Crass and Cassius, which is more likely, no one told me about this till 30 June 1983, by when Court of Inquiry had commenced and I was awaiting orders to move for the Course. It is interesting to note that all parameters of this allegedly 'recovered' garnish like: sealed or otherwise; contents per bundle 1,500 (normal) or 2,000 M (very unusual); with or without ordnance markings, and most important: the actual quantity itself kept varying a dozen times, from Quarter Master's first and only Summary of Evidence through my three Summaries, the No 3 Court Martial and the Revision:-

50000 to 55000 as on 30 June 1983 by Cassius;

54,500 in just 3 shades as given in a signed statement on 25 July 1984 by Never-loyal, during my first Summary of Evidence;

46,000 to 50,000 in Oct 1985 during my Second Summary, by Cassius;

55000 on 12 June 1986 by Cassius;

63,800 or 63,900 by Cassius again on 11 July 1986;

Tanjore Doll deposed on 18 July 1986 that as CO, he was reported 55,000 to 58,000 by Cassius on 28 June 1983;

finally, 73,300 including 50 MM width garnish in open condition, during Revision proceedings!

(I am mentioning these here for you to build the picture of conspiracy in your minds. But the fact remains that I was not informed till 30 June 1983! Strangely, Never-loyal repeatedly stated on oath during the trial that he had found the 'allegedly recovered' garnish on or around 17/18 June 1983; if so, the conspiracy had started earlier)

(2) Rabbi had directed Crass to accompany Tanjore Doll and me the next day to meet Scraggly at Meerut!

LP Included in Handing and Taking Over Certificate and Court of Inquiry Ordered

After having cleverly manipulated me to include the 'Garnish Local Purchase' point in the Handing and Taking Over Certificate, Scraggly had sent on 29 June itself, a recommendation to the Corps by hand of an officer for a Staff Court of Inquiry, while we were at my Farewell Lunch in the Brigade Officers Mess! He must have gloated that he had me really cornered, as my benefactor the General Officer Commanding Corps was moving as Deputy Chief of Army Staff, which I did not know till that evening. *That very evening was to be my formal Dining Out from my Officers Mess and I declined it, in view of these developments.* (9 years later, when I was a Brigade Commander close by and my old Adjutant was commanding the Regiment, I was dined out in 1992!)

> ***"With foxes, we must play the fox!"***
> Dr Thomas Fuller (1732)

Anyway, I found out that the General Officer Commanding Corps was on joining time at Delhi itself; so I approached him over the telephone with this development, as he was fully aware of Scraggly's "ways". He assured me that *if the Court of Inquiry was not specifically against me but only about the transaction, he will ensure that I give my statement before the Court of Inquiry and proceed on the Course, as scheduled,* (as permitted by relevant Army Orders!) He also wished me good luck on the Course! But, Scraggly convinced the Officiating Corps Commander and A staff at Corps that to save time and expense, he was appointing a Lt Col locally to be the Presiding Officer of Court of Inquiry instead of they having to detail one from Ambala/Hissar etc; they fell for it and approved it. *Who would he detail, but for Shifty Eyes from the other Delhi Regt*; he, despite being my friend till then and having taken umpteen favours from me, had recently become jealous of my detailment on the Course! He arrived promptly the next morning (30 June 1983) and I gave my truthful statement before him.

I was a 'nobody' now; I had handed over command, had been given a *Bara Khana,* had refused a Dining Out and was awaiting further orders to move to Mhow.

I leave for Higher Command Course at Mhow

Only at about 12 noon on 1 July 1983, the orders came over the telephone, after I pestered the General again and he called up his old Chief of Staff. Immediately my successor organized a quick farewell and I rushed home to spend at least 2 hours with my family, as it was the 13th birthday of my elder daughter. *(That would be the last birthday of hers, which we would celebrate as a complete family, till she passed away 11 years later, as a bright young Chartered Accountant).*

I must narrate an aside here, from a Middle titled *"Twist of Fate"* in Deccan Herald of 7 Dec 2006: *"I am to board a train for Khandwa en route to Mhow, after clearly instructing the staff to 'load all 12 pieces'. At the station, I am informed, all 13, including the thermos, have been loaded! Holding 13 to be unlucky, I move to the bogie, to find it numbered 00013 and my berth number: 13! I tell my wife about my apprehensions; she asks me not to be stupid. I land at Mhow and my accommodation number: 13! When I call and inform my wife my further fears, she repeats her words! But fate has other ideas; she has a fire accident the next week and succumbs to it, leaving two young girls behind".*

I learnt later Quarter Master had been recalled but arrived only on 2 July and that the Court of Inquiry continued till mid Aug 1983.

Unfortunate Accident and I lose my Wife

On night 9/10 July 1983, within a week of my departure for the Course, there was an unfortunate fire accident in the kitchen and my wife received 70% burns. (That very morning I had spoken to her over my neighbour's telephone.) I came to know of it only at about 1 p.m. on Sunday, 10 July. There was neither STD nor mobile phones those days. Immediately, Commander of Higher Command Wing, Major General KS

Randhawa, (who as General Officer Commanding Armoured Division had appreciated my Regt's camouflage and concealment 4 months earlier) spoke to the Commandant, Lieutenant General AK Handoo and arranged for a car, with additional petrol and some emergency cash for me from his pocket, to go to Indore, Khandwa or Ratlam and catch any flight or train and get to Delhi the fastest. I had no leave to my credit; but the General said that they would treat me on furlough. I caught the Rajdhani Express from Ratlam and reached Delhi on 11 July and went straight to the Army Hospital. Regrettably, Army Hospital, the biggest and only one of its kind in India, did not even have a proper Burns Ward. Some makeshift arrangements were made after a few days. The doctors admired her will to live and were hopeful but told me to wait for full 10 days and nights; she passed away, at 7.10 p.m. on 19 July 83, Tuesday, the 10th day. I had to worry about the girls' studies (Classes 9 and 4, which they had just joined); I had to take a decision also whether to return to the Course or seek a different posting to another station, where I could look after them or even apply for premature retirement. My aged parents in law, even in their own grief, volunteered to close down establishment at Dehradun where they had been living for 30 years and shift to Bangalore (where two other siblings of my wife stayed) so as to look after my two girls and asked me to return to the Course.

My wife's cremation was planned for 5 p.m. on 20 July 1983 and as if he was waiting just for it, Scraggly sent word to the Regt that I should go at 2.30 p.m. to the Regt for giving additional evidence/cross examination by QM, where provisions of Army Rule 180 had been invoked as his character and military reputation were affected. I could have easily refused, as I was then under Central Command and on furlough. *Only Army HQ could have ordered my presence, for which I had to be on duty! But, any hesitation by me would have meant, I had something to hide.* I decided to finish with the Court of Inquiry once for all, not knowing how wrong I was. 'My friend', Lt Col Shifty Eyes grilled me with many questions; I did not remember nor could I answer, since I was in total grief and many other more urgent matters were bothering me: the first one being my wife's cremation and the future of children. It took place at about 5.30 p.m; *none of the three attended: Scraggly; 'my friend': Shifty Eyes, the Presiding Officer of Court of Inquiry; and my 'younger brother': Crass, all being in station.*

On 25 July 1983, while still in mourning, I sought an interview with Station Commander, Delhi Cantt (*whose Staff Officer I had been in 1969-70 for a year in Deolali and whose wife and mine had been good friends*) for permission to retain for 10 months, as allowed by the rules, the same accommodation at Delhi cantonment which my wife had NOT handed over nor the Regt. As an alternative, he could at least transfer the present accommodation of my friend on my name, for which I had a written consent. This way, my aged parents in law could shift residence temporarily to look after the girls, till I took charge. He dismissed me from his presence in 2 minutes flat, after saying a firm "No" without assigning any reason *and asked his staff officer to tell my friend also to vacate the accommodation*! That is the time I realized the meaning of a saying in the Indian Army that *when you lose your wife, you are an outcaste and when you are a 'disciplinary case', you are an 'untouchable'*: I was BOTH!

How many battles at a time could I fight? Still I didn't give up. But I made a mistake; I handed over my accommodation and then met Colonel BS Garewal, Director (Quartering) at Army HQ, a fellow Gunner, seeking a flat in Bangalore where my spinster sister (who was my foster mother) could shift from Trichy and look after the girls, while I went through the Course! He was kind, gave me a patient hearing and advised me to apply to Government of India, through proper channel as they alone could sanction it, provided Station HQ Bangalore accepted that they could allot one! I got an application typed in his office and he even accepted an advance copy on behalf of Army HQ! He also sent another advance copy of my application to Station Commander, Bangalore in order to save valuable time!

It took me over 10 days to sort out a zillion other matters: I selfishly accepted my parents in law's offer and bade a tearful farewell to my motherless minor girls (13 and 8) on 31 July 1983, after giving them essential luggage; repacked rest of the baggage so as to carry minimum required for me to run my establishment and placed bulk of it in the Regt, *where I had **already** placed non essential stuff in a room as explained*. This fact is important to remember, as later this room comes into prominence in the GCM, with a different name as *'Junk Stores'*!

I am back on Higher Command Course

I left on 4 Aug 1983 and reached Mhow the next day, where two dear friends who knew me for over 2 decades and were on the same Course, received me. I dropped into their arms and cried for a while: unusual for a soldier who had actively participated in ferocious operations in 1965 and 1971; but I was a human being too, whose worlds...both life and career...had suddenly come crashing down. The next thing I did was waiting near the telephone, where I had asked my children to call me up from Bangalore at 3 p.m. on 5 Aug 1983. What a relief it was; yes it was painful too.

The next few months were mostly eventless as I had to concentrate on studies. However, as Direct Dialling had come into Mhow, whereby the clerk at the PCO could directly dial the Bangalore number (though not STD), I made it a routine to call the children at 8 a.m. every Sunday. Half the time out of the three minutes was spent on our crying, out of helplessness, while the elder girl, just turned 13 was braver than me; and would say as to what we would achieve by crying, as *Amma* would never come back! The younger (8), did not even know what had hit her, as once she had asked her grandfather (which I learnt many years later) whether she would never see her mother again!

I was also lucky to spend a day with them when the Course had gone on an all India tour, with Bangalore being the last station in end Sep 1983. Again, Generals Handoo and Randhawa were kind and permitted me to stay back on casual leave at Bangalore, instead of being rule-bound to ask me to go to Mhow and come back on leave! I sought an appointment and met the Station Commander, Bangalore. He was too curt and had only a NO for an answer, despite having received all along the channel, a positive recommendation! How could Government of India help me now?

In Oct 1983, I heard rumours of derogatory remarks against my character and military reputation in the Court of Inquiry; if so, provisions of Army Rule 180 ought to have been invoked and I should have been present for all future recording; this was NOT done; nor were provisions of Defence Services Regulations (Regulations for the Army) Para 518 invoked, whereby the Presiding Officer should have been senior in rank to me and all members at least Lt Col's! I could not even get a whiff of its proceedings, as I was far away! So I felt, there was some hope after all. How wrong I was once more!

In Dec 1983, I heard rumours about disciplinary attachment orders for the QM. *Was mine to follow*? That is the time, when daughters arrived for a few days stay with me at Mhow during Christmas holidays; what a welcome change! My fellow-course-mates made it a memorable stay both at Mhow and in one or two outings. After all, world is not full of just Scraggly, Rabbi, Crass and Cassius; it does have Generals Handoo and Randhawa; 'my benefactor, the Corps Commander', Colonel Garewal and fellow-student-officers, some of whom I had never even met earlier!

J'Accuse! Get Attached!

On *Pongal* day, Saturday 14 Jan 1984, I was told by Major General Randhawa that I had been attached by Army HQ under Army Instruction 106/60 to my old Brigade HQ at Meerut, for discipline, as *'cognizance of my offence had been taken'* and that I should be ready to move in about 48 hours. I asked him if I could meet the Commandant; he agreed to arrange an Interview depending on the latter's commitments. On 15th I had almost packed up to leave, as no information had come about Commandant granting me an Interview! That took place on 16th and Commandant was kind enough to speak to AG's Branch at Army HQ right then and tell them that having attended more than 70% of the Course, I should complete the balance and then go for attachment or whatever. So I was able to complete the Course. But I immediately sought a copy of the Court of Inquiry, which would have been the basis for 'taking cognizance'.

For the next 10 weeks, I poured over military law books and the Court of Inquiry proceedings many times over. I could see how most witnesses had twisted their statements after I had left for the Course: *even the Quarter Master had done 3, 4 times*!

Arrival at Meerut and First Summary of Evidence

The course terminated on 7 Apr 1984 and during the Valedictory Function presided over by Field Marshal SHFJ Manekshaw, everyone's wife and parents were with them, less me: I was all alone! *(It would be so for the rest of my life, except my girls, of whom too, I lost the elder 10 years later).* I was not entitled to even the normal joining and preparatory time (7-8 days) or any leave from now on, except on extreme compassionate grounds; so I left on 10 Apr, as per rail reservation done and reported to the Brigade HQ on 11 Apr 1984. I was allotted a reasonable room in a Regt's Mess and promptly Colonel Rabbi (to be my "CO" shortly) came to meet me. It was, I knew, just to mark attendance as an ex-colleague from the same Regt!

Quarter Master's Summary of Evidence had to be completed where I was a Prosecution Witness. What a joke and a big farce, once the authorities had already made up their mind to try us jointly which is why we both had been attached to the same Regt in the same Brigade and the same Mess! Mine could then begin! But there was a catch, which I had learnt by repeated reading of the Army Act and Army Rules recently.

On 23 Apr 1984, Rabbi called me to his office and over a cup of coffee, handed over my Tentative Charge Sheet (as in Annexure 3, which had to be *'heard'* by him but he did not). Army Rules 22 and 25 lay down clearly that in the case of an officer, where an offence has been alleged, a preliminary investigation is a must and a 'Hearing of Charge' too when the officer demands it; and also that the Commanding Officer alone has the power to order a Summary of Evidence. I put down my 'demand' for it in writing on both the points to Rabbi and got a reply from him, as my "CO" stating that *'Higher HQ had directed recording of Summary of Evidence and that cognizance had already been taken' and so, no hearing of Charge was necessary*. I next wrote seeking a copy of the Summary of Evidence proceedings of the Quarter Master in order to enable me to cross examine the Prosecution Witnesses who may be produced in my case. He replied saying NO provision existed and so I should report for the proceeding. With this ammunition in my hand, I was ready for whatever else they did in future.

A Lt Col 3½ years my junior (who was a very junior battery commander in my time) recorded my Summary of Evidence, which carried on from 26 Apr 1984 to 25 July 1984. I had made up my mind to tear Major Crass to pieces in my cross examination and prove him to be a liar. *Later I felt I had let out my line of defence but it was too late.*

Commander had changed before I arrived at Meerut. Though I had known the new one, he could do nothing except dance to the tune of the A Branch at Corps HQ, as the puppet strings had moved to higher levels after departure of Scraggly. *Still he did give me the deserved dignity and after speaking to me, kept me on full pay during the period of disciplinary proceedings; or else I could not have managed funding the stay of my girls with two different relatives* (though both at Bangalore) and their schooling; my own bills and fee for the Counsel when I appointed one! There was one more good man after all and I was grateful to him!

CHAPTER 7 FIRST GENERAL COURT MARTIAL: A FARCE

A GCM ordered by the Corps HQ was convened on 27 Mar 1985, for the Joint Trial of Quarter Master and me. This was the biggest *'tamasha'* Indian Army's legal system would ever enact in its 38 years of its existence till then in independent India! Sample these:

- The Court was to assemble at 3 p.m. and I was called up to the Brigade Commander and placed under Close Arrest at about 2.50 p.m. (There was no 'marching up' under escort, probably as the Brigade Commander wanted to show his feelings for me in the only way he could. *Very kind of him indeed; I was grateful.*) But the Court assembled only at 7.45 p.m.! While a Court could sit beyond 6 p.m. in the interest of justice, NO regulation permitted the first or any sitting commencing at 7.45 p.m., as per Army Rule 81(3).
- Members arrived piece meal, each not knowing when the others were coming, though all had been detailed from one single station: Ambala Cantonment, where the Corps HQ was also located!

- *NO JA was present, which is obligatory in every GCM*. I raised a Special Plea to General Jurisdiction of the court, telling them *it was not properly constituted in the absence of the JA, which was mandatory*. The presiding officer told me to keep quiet but I refused and raised my voice again, on the same plea.
- *NO Defending Officer was provided to me, despite my written request nine months earlier in July 1984*! I raised my plea on it as per Army Rule 95.
- I said I had NOT been given leave to go to Delhi and find a suitable Counsel, to engage for my Defence; while Prosecution had a Counsel!
- All the members belonging to different religious denominations (Hindus and Christians) took oath on the Gita!
- They read out my name and the Charge Sheet and asked me to plead Guilty or Not Guilty and I refused saying they were not properly constituted.
- I said in the absence of the JA and my Defence Counsel or at least a Defending Officer of my choice, I considered them to be wasting their time!
- I refuted each of their orders including answering to my name and past appointment, telling them repeatedly they were NOT constituted as per law and I would NOT obey them!
- They did not allow any objection to the Charge.
- *The Quarter Master, my co-accused, just followed suit.*
- They appeared to have been ordered by A Branch at Corps HQ to somehow *arraign* us the same night!
- The Court adjourned at about 9.15 PM, after *what they thought was completion of arraignment*!
- I was making verbatim notes of the proceedings, which they didn't realize! After 3-4 days I sent full

details of the above farce to Western Army Commander with a copy to his Deputy Judge Advocate General, *seeking stoppage of such a tamasha as this GCM.* (Years later, this Deputy JAG whom I met as JAG expressed amazement at my phenomenal memory!)

- *I had still not used the 'ammunition', I mentioned earlier of Army Rules 22 and 25! Well that would come in handy another day!*
- The Court was dissolved without any written intimation to me or my co-accused. The only applicable provision of Army Act 117 (3) for dissolution had not been invoked in writing.

The further irony was that the Brigadier from Engineers who presided over that farcical Court did not even get a rap on the knuckles; instead got kicked upwards as a Local Major General and Military Attaché to the USA! No action was taken against the A and JA staff of Corps either! But even a copy of these inchoate proceedings was not given to me on a request!

During Dec 1984, Rabbi left on promotion to the East as a Brigadier and a new Deputy Commander arrived, who would be my "CO". On 6 July 1985 or so, Commander also changed. (Both were non controversial persons). The new Commander had been my student on a course in 1968 and later my staff college course-mate in 1973, besides being a 'valued friend'! He later rose to be Chief of Army Staff. But he could do nothing, as the die had been cast years ago by a predecessor of his and much water had already flown over the infamous *'ganda nala'* (dirty nullah) of Meerut since 29 June 1983. I too did not wish to embarrass him in any way; but fight I would for my very survival; and he knew it too.

Despite many invites from him and his wife, I did not visit his home. What a contrast between my not calling on Scraggly for 2 years due to our differences; and now I am forced to repeat the same to a friend, another commander, for a different reason!

CHAPTER 8

SECOND GENERAL COURT MARTIAL AND THE INTERREGNUM

On The Same Charge and Same Summary of Evidence!

On the same Summary of Evidence and the same Charge, another GCM was convened by Commander, Independent Artillery Brigade, on 26 July 1985, to assemble on 30 July 1985. The scene when I was called in to be placed under close arrest by this Commander, a friend, was poignant. After the ritual was done and I waited with my escort in a veranda to be called into the Court, he came close to me and whispered words to the effect he was confident that being truthful, I would be out of the agony in due course! This is what I call real friendship! Again what a contrast with some of my own Regt officers!

The trial commenced at 11.20 a.m. Luckily I got the Defending Officer of my choice, Major HS Bedi from a local unit, who would also be one for my co-accused, Quarter Master. Before arraignment, he raised 2 points: (1) That the Defence Counsel engaged by us would NOT be available till 7 Aug 1985 as he was committed in a Court Martial at Tezpur, which fact had been given in writing a week earlier and (2) that we propose to raise a Special Plea to General

Jurisdiction of this Court under Army Rule 51, in the presence of Defence Counsel only. The prosecutcr objected that sufficient time had been given for engaging a counsel and I rebutted saying that only at about 7.15 p.m. on 25 July 1985 was the firm date of trial intimated; obviously we could not have retained a lawyer from Mar 1985, imagining that another Court may be ordered. After a lot of arguments, the Court was adjourned till 8 Aug 1985.

On re-assembling on 8 Aug 1985, when the Prosecution sought arraignment first, my counsel raised a point regarding Plea to Jurisdiction under Army Rule 51 and also seeking Colonel Rabbi as my No 1 Witness, to prove my letter seeking Hearing of Charge and his reply on directions from higher HQ to record Summary of Evidence! His words were: *"I do not wish to delay the proceedings of the court further as I am sure on merits, I have got a good case, but the accused persons have been sent to trial without the 'commanding officer' of the accused persons having applied his mind to the case. In this case the 'commanding officer' had acted upon the directions of the superior authorities. It is the right of every accused person subject to the Army Act that his CO, in his discretion, should decide whether the case ought to be proceeded with or not. This right has been denied to the accused persons"* and handed in a detailed written submission on the same. Prosecutor needed time to check with records and the officers concerned; and so under Army Rule 82 (1), the Court was adjourned for 48 hours.

When the Court reassembled, Prosecutor wanted to arraign us and as briefed by my counsel, I insisted that my plea under Army Rule 51 be decided first and I raised it, saying I wanted to call as my witness, Colonel Rabbi, the 'commanding officer' who had ordered the Summary of Evidence; (This was to *'prove'* the two letters on the subject, pertaining to my seeking on 24 Apr 1984, after being handed over a Tentative Charge Sheet on 23 Apr 1984 (see *Annexure 3*), a *'Hearing of Charge under Army Rules 22 & 25'* and 'CO' replying: *"Higher HQ have directed S of E to be recorded against you!"*

Instead of my ex-commanding officer, the Court decided to call the Deputy Assistant Adjutant General, a Staff Officer (Major) at the brigade HQ to check if records existed to check whether provisions of Army Rules 22 and 25 had been complied with or not in respect of both accused. He stated that other than (my) letter seeking it dated 24 Apr 1984 and the *Deputy Commander's reply the next day quoting directions from higher HQ*, there was nothing on record to indicate one way or the other! Availability of Rabbi serving in the East was also not known. After a lot of deliberations, the Court adjourned sine die and informed the Convening Authority. Rabbi was flown in post-haste and the Court reassembled on 12 Aug. He was made to eat a humble pie on many points:

- The exclusive powers of a CO under Army Order 217/72 regarding ordering a Summary of Evidence: *'No person other than a commanding officer has the right to direct Summary of Evidence be taken'*;
- Army Order 251/72 laying down that a formation commander himself shall be the Commanding Officer of officers of his HQ;
- Acting under *'dictation'* of a superior person/HQ and not exercising own 'discretion', in that there was a letter dated 28 Nov 1983 signed by Colonel A at Corps HQ addressed to the brigade HQ, with the words: *"Order S of E against the officers blamed..."*
- Provisions of Army Order 70/84 on "preliminary Investigation of a Charge by Commanding Officer" (of which, a draft had been received in the HQ).

Among many other things, Rabbi stated that: *I was a close friend of his* (ahem! ahem*!*); he had carried out a ***Preliminary*** Investigation on 28 June 1983 till 9 p.m. (i.e., well before he became my "CO"), which till then had been an *"Informal"* one, even according to his letter of 25 Apr 1984; and had reported to Commander that detailed investigation may be required; he had NO previous knowledge of any irregularity in local purchase before that date; Commander in his wisdom had ordered a staff Court of Inquiry and also forwarded the same to Corps HQ, who sent further directions! Arguments in respect of Quarter Master were also advanced.

My Counsel sought time till 16 Aug to submit a written address and as Prosecutor also had another case, the Court adjourned till then. In our address, we again stressed on precedence of Army Order 212/72 over letters within the Brigade HQ; *"hearing" being mandatory, whether an accused demanded the same or not*; and three important citations from Supreme Court: AIR 1952, Page 17 in the Commissioner of Police Vs. Gordhan Das Bhanji; AIR 1965 (Mysore) Page 143 in M Singh Vs. Director I & C; and AIR, 1964, Page 358 in State of UP Vs. Shingara Singh. Prosecution wished to give a written reply and so Court was adjourned till next day, which they did. Then JA gave summing up and advice.

As a number of intricate questions of law had been raised by us, citing case laws, the Court adjourned sine die and decided to refer the matter to the Convening Authority. The latter in his Reassembly Order dated 22 Aug 1985 for the same day, directed the Court to *"apply their mind judiciously and thereafter identify the specific issue or issues on which they are doubtful and then make a written submission to me"*. JA washed his hands off and just drew the attention to his earlier advice! The Court after further deliberations *'decided to make a detailed written reference to the Convening Authority and adjourn sine die'*.

The next we heard on 30 Aug was that the Court had been dissolved on 29 Aug 1985 by the Convening Authority, but *no authority for the dissolution was mentioned in the Dissolution Order*! One more folly in the legal system of the Army.

The Interregnum: Pack Up Now and Move to Ambala

We awaited further instructions, but I wondered why for the second time, NO action was being contemplated against yet another Brigadier, (Rabbi, this time) for having wasted good 17 months of everyone's time and my life and career, despite my written request.

On 12 Sep 1985, we were informed that we should be ready to move to an Independent Armoured Brigade HQ in Ambala Cantonment in a few days! When 16 Sep was decided as the date for departure, I finally decided to go for Dinner to my most recent Commander, as he had nothing more to do with my Case and no one could raise a finger against him or me for this socializing! They looked after me very well; wished me best of luck and offered to drop me/get me dropped back to my room. I refused and went back on my own scooter!

Move to Ambala was somewhat a blessing in disguise for me, as I could lean on a relative and a childhood friend, Colonel (later Brigadier, now a Ph D and LL B) V Ramanan of Assam Regt, who was on staff of the local Sub Area. My period of being ostracized socially was finally over, as I spent bulk of my time, discussing my case with him day in and day out. He, his wife and children were heaven-sent comfort for me! In fact during his stay at Ambala, I was able to get my daughters over to stay with them twice; he also introduced me to golf, a totally relaxing mind game! I did not know how and when I could ever thank him enough for all that he would be doing for me.

NO fresh attachment was issued: only HQ Corps had sent a signal: a major lacuna, as I had originally been moved to Meerut, under orders from Army HQ! I did NOT point it out, as I wanted the rest of Indian Army to know how inefficient and stupid, the A Staff at various levels were; and how they harassed even a senior officer such as a Lt Col with over 23 years service! And, most importantly, how the so-called justice system in the Army was made to function by the inefficient A Staff!

Brigade Routine Order was published on 17 Sep 1985, appointing Deputy Commander of Independent Armoured

Brigade as "CO" for attached officers also! Summary of Evidence recorded in the previous Brigade was received officially on 22nd, which is against all norms of the so-called justice system, as the new "CO" has to independently *"Hear the Charge"*; exercise his mind independently and only, if necessary, order a Summary of Evidence; peruse it and then take further action! Funnily, later in the third GCM when we grilled the Deputy Assistant Adjutant General, the Deputy Commander and Commander of this Brigade, each gave different versions of whether or not the last named two had perused the previous Summary of Evidence before my second one was ordered! One more cover up this time by Commanders!

Another 'Hearing of Charge' and another Summary of Evidence

On 3 Oct 1985, the farce of "Hearing of Charge' was done by this Deputy Commander, who ordered another Summary of Evidence; second one for me! Once again, another Lt Col, 3½ years my junior, from the Armoured Corps was detailed. It commenced on 8 Oct 1985; but in the meantime sitting idle from 16 Sep to now, I had tied up with my motherless minor girls to come during their holidays to Ambala, as Ramanan and family were there. When I asked for just one day's casual leave on 13 Oct to go to Delhi and bring them, it was refused; whereas *the system was playing havoc with my time,* life and career since 28 June 1983! So, my minor daughters who travelled by rail unescorted all the way from Bangalore, had to go to ISBT, Delhi to take a bus and reach Ambala Bus Stand. They called me at the Officers Mess telephone! I rushed there and brought them to my friend's home for stay. (*The next time, my children arrived on 23 Apr 1986, my GCM had just commenced that day and I was under close arrest, with a 2 Lt as escort with a loaded pistol! But, the next 7 days were bliss, despite the trial in progress. Ramanan got posted out in July 1987 and I missed him and the family till I left Ambala)*!

Abrupt Ceasing of Summary of Evidence and Fresh Attachment Order

On 20 Dec 1985, recording of second Summary of Evidence was stopped abruptly, when they realized that I had NOT been attached by Army HQ! It took 3 months and 4 days for the A Staff to realize yet another of their follies! So instead of moving me to another Brigade/station, another attachment order was issued by Army HQ the same day, for me with the same Brigade, with Commander becoming my 4th "created CO" (2 in previous Brigade and 2nd here)! This ensured that the 'biased' A and JA staff at Corps HQ continued to deal LOCALLY and 'effectively' with my case! It took the Staff another 10 days to cancel the Brigade Routine Order appointing the Deputy Commander as my CO!

On 30 Dec 1985, I appealed to the Army Commander (my old benefactor) through a formal application to stop the farce being enacted in the name of *'justice being done'*; no reply was received till 3 May 1986! Within a few days, I was admitted in Military Hospital, Ambala Cantonment for emergency surgery for my old case of *'Fissure in Ano'* which I had been suffering stoically since Dec 1982; I stayed in ICU for a few days followed by Officers Ward. Repeatedly letters were sent to me, instead of to the hospital, by the Brigade, seeking a tentative date of discharge, as if I had any control over my surgery and recuperation!

Yet Another 'Hearing of Charge' and Third Summary of Evidence!

On 13 Jan 1986, as another *Pongal* gift for me, Corps HQ ordered 'fresh' recording of yet another Summary of Evidence, declaring all proceedings so far *'invalid'* and to be sent to them in sealed condition! I was reminded of the proverb: *'locking the stable door, after the horse had bolted!'*, as all of them had read through by now both Summaries of Evidence of mine; and one, of the Quarter Master: what a farce! After another 18 days, on 31 Jan, Deputy Assistant Adjutant General informed me over telephone that 'Hearing of Charge' would commence soon! 8 more days passed and on 8 Feb 1986, it commenced on the same Charge Sheet by yet another created "CO", the Commander! His elder brother, my boss in Army HQ in 1978-79 used to say that his younger brother was a straightforward person; so I decided to take a chance for the first time and produced 4 defence witnesses, all of whom stated that *neither there was any secrecy about the LP, nor deficiency of garnish existed after it was received and distributed.* I had a lot of hope; but this "CO" had to function under the same Corps HQ, in the same station. He had also studied BOTH the previous Summaries of Evidence in detail! How can he now say anything but 'cognizance taken'? Thus I had committed yet another blunder, by revealing my hand once more.

On 13 Feb 1986, the 4th "CO" took cognizance and ordered a Summary of Evidence; the third for me: this time recorded by an officer 5½ years junior to me! Some more regression! On 11 Mar 1986, I sent an appeal, this time to General Officer Commanding Corps on vindictiveness and denial of fair play and justice; I got no reply till GCM commenced, as he was the Convening Authority himself!

Appointment of CO Number 5 for Me in 2 Years!

The legal system in the army believes in Graham Greene, who said: *"Nothing ...ever lost by delay"*. But I repeatedly kept pointing out to the authorities that: *"Irretrievable time is flying!"* On 23 Mar 1986, Commander changed in the Brigade; so yet another 'CO' for me: 5th one; 2 in previous Brigade and 3rd here! On 25 Mar 1986, I submitted a letter that I was NOT interested in getting the proceedings delayed; if they could move things faster! This was necessary, as I heard rumours in the Brigade HQ that I wished to delay matters so that the Case would get time-barred in May 1986, (3 years from the date of alleged offence).

Abrupt Stopping of Recording of Summary of Evidence No 3

On 31 Mar 1986, recording of evidence stopped abruptly in Summary of Evidence; neither information nor reasons were given to me! Cross examination by me of one Prosecution Witness (Major Crass) had not yet been done and reply to a clarification sought from another Prosecution Witness (Major Bandicoot) of previous Brigade had not yet been received! The same day I submitted a Non Statutory Complaint, pointing out the closure of the 3rd Summary of Evidence, WITHOUT WAITING for written replies from a few Defence Witnesses, who had been examined as Prosecution Witnesses in previous Summaries of Evidence (and whom they did not wish to present!) and seeking that the A & JA staff of HQ ... Corps should NOT deal with my case any longer, as I foresaw interference in the course of justice! NO reply was received for 2 months, by when the 3rd GCM (*based on 3rd Summary of Evidence, under 5th CO*) had gone on for a month!

My illness and admission to ICU at Military Hospital

From 1 to 6 Apr 1986, I was placed Sick In Quarters due to '*undiagnosed breathlessness*'; Brigade HQ was kept in picture every day by the Regimental Medical Officer of my 'host Regiment' attending on me. At about midnight of 6/7 Apr 1986, I was evacuated by him to Military Hospital, Ambala Cantonment in a 'breathless' condition and I stayed in ICU till 12 Apr and in Officers Ward till 21 Apr, but GCM still got convened!

On 8 Apr 1986, despite the Doctors' objections, Tentative Date of Trial Commencement as second week of Apr (it was second week already!) and Charge Sheet (*see Annexure 5)* were handed over to me in ICU at 4.40 p.m., *by a Clerk,* against the provisions of Army Rule 34 (another ignominy and humiliation). I was also asked to give the list of my Defence Witnesses and to state whether I would be engaging a Defence Counsel! *Common sense alone would have told them that I could not have done any of it, while at the ICU or even if I were to be in officers' ward.* I replied giving the facts: asking for Major HS Bedi as my Defending Officer and also requested that I may not be subjected to pressure/harassment in ICU, where I was prevented from any physical work whatsoever. (Later, for the first time in my career, I was medically downgraded to 3rd lower level of fitness! This low category continued for 3 stretches of 6 months each!).

On 12 Apr 1986, when I was still at the ICU, I was handed over a copy of Summary of Evidence and another copy of Charge Sheet by a clerk again; but not the firm date of trial! After I was shifted to the Officers Ward, I wrote to the Brigade for 4 days leave to engage a counsel from Delhi, where such counsel would be available in plenty.

On 18 Apr 1986, at 4 p.m. when I was still in Military Hospital, Brigade informed me that the trial would start at 8.30 a.m. on 23 Apr at a mechanized infantry battalion location and gave me a possible list of officers who may be constituting the Court; but NO word yet on my leave for finding and engaging a counsel!

On 19 Apr 1986, I got another letter saying *I had been aware from 13 Feb 1986 of the impending disciplinary process and should have organized a counsel.* It also said: "*In the interest of justice, therefore, especially when the date of trial has been fixed, your request to get away from the venue of trial is unjust, unfair and appears to* (sic) *thwart the process of law.*" That very night, I appealed to their good sense again to allow me 4 days casual leave to engage a counsel, after discharge from Military Hospital.

On 21 Apr 1986, on Corps HQ repeatedly 'bullying' Commandant Military Hospital, I was discharged but felt very weak. The composition of the court which was to be informed at least 96 hours earlier, *EXCEPT ON ACTIVE SERVICE*, as per Army Rule 34(3), was given to me at 8.45 p.m., just 36 hours earlier! *The last time I heard this particular Brigade was on active service was only in 1971, and it was 1986 now!*

CHAPTER 9 THIRD GENERAL COURT MARTIAL AND REVISION

On 23 Apr 1986, my THIRD GCM commenced at 3.07 p.m., despite everything; (my motherless-minor girls who were worried about my hospital admission with undiagnosed illness for so many days, decided to arrive that night, unescorted once again, taking the same route).

As my GCM had commenced, I was under close arrest, with a 2 Lt as escort with a loaded pistol! *As far as possible, an officer of equal rank is to be the escort, except in emergencies; but Deputy JAG and Colonel A at Corps HQ continued to find ways to humiliate me; you will read more and more about it!*

Defence Services Regulations (Regulations for the Army) Para 459 (b) states that: *"When the CO of a Corps is to be tried, as many members as possible will be officers, who have held or are holding command equivalent to that held by the accused"*. Having been CO of a major unit, my objection to the members who were Officers Commanding minor units like Workshop Company and ASC Tank Transporter Company was not accepted! There were over 100 commanding officers of major units in the rank of Colonel/Lieutenant Colonel under that Corps but they found it convenient to detail officers far junior to me from Ambala alone! Only the Presiding Officer was senior in rank and service, as required.

Luckily I had Major (later Lt Col) HS Bedi, my Defending Officer of choice and Colonel Ramanan joined as Defending Officer for the Quarter Master, Accused No 2 (A-2, hereafter).

My basic right to challenge the members of the Court under Army Rule 44 was denied to me, as I insisted on doing so ONLY when I had the services of a defence counsel of my choice, for which I had been repeatedly requesting for 4 days leave right from the Officers Ward of Military Hospital. I gave a written submission of 6 pages and 9 Annexures to the Court on the very first day, i.e., 23 Apr 1986.

Objections by A-2, first, regarding his high BP, which a doctor certified that he had just then brought under control with strong medication; and second, for leave to engage a counsel were rejected, after Judge Advocate gave a lengthy advice quoting Army Rules 95(1) and 56, virtually forcing the court not to do so *'at this stage'*. Thus on day 1, the proceedings ended at 8.20 p.m. under the special provisions of Army Rule 81!

When I needed to go to the Bus Stand (just 2 KM away) that night to bring my unescorted daughters and leave them at my friend's home, the Escort refused as I was under close arrest! Ramanan told him that while he and I went in the former's scooter, the escort could follow in uniform on my scooter. Finally the young officer understood my predicament and came! But after a few days stay, I sent the children back, as I was unable to spend time with them due to the trial.

The next day, third objection by A-2, though unprecedented, to the presence of a particular JA at the trial under Army Rule 39 (2) and Note 3 to Army Rule 102 and Army Rule 105 was also rejected! This was the same person who though detailed, had not attended first GCM on 27

Mar 1985, but had received (*and definitely would have read*) the Summaries of Evidence of both mine and A-2! *Being in Command HQ,* he would have *read my second Summary of Evidence also; all this would sorely prejudice our defence.*

In short, the Court bulldozed its way, as I could watch the Presiding Officer and JA being called to the telephone and *'dictated'* (not only that day but everyday, thereafter) and also in person by Colonel A & Deputy JAG of Corps HQ. *Thank goodness that mobile telephony was not in existence in India then*!

On 25 Apr 1986, Colonel A from Corps HQ directed the Brigade that (Quarter Master and) I should continue under close arrest, throughout! That day, we objected to the illegal appointment of many different Commanding Officers, citing objections. This too was disallowed. Next came pleading to the Charge: Guilty or Not Guilty. Citing Army Rules 49 and 51, I submitted my inability to plead to the Charge and Jurisdiction, except in the presence of my counsel. On Judge Advocate's advice drawing attention to Army Rule 52(1), the Court decided to treat my plea as refusal to plead and entered my plea as 'Not Guilty'; same for A-2.

(Even in the previous 2 General Courts Martial, after the arraignment, I had only been under "Open Arrest"! So, I appealed to General Officer Commanding Corps. *As no action was taken for two months,* I appealed to General Officer Commanding in Chief, Western Command on 26 June 1986; still NO action. *What a humiliation for a Substantive Lieutenant Colonel, with 24 years service, who has been suffering every humiliation, harassment and 'farce' done in the name of 'Discipline' and 'Justice' and had never shown any inclination to 'abscond' or desire to move a High Court!*)

Long Adjournment from 25 Apr to 3 June 1986: All for the Prosecution!

Now that the arraignment was complete, the Court adjourned till 1 May 1986. On that date, my counsel and both defending officers were present; Colonel NS Bains, (Retired) my counsel stated to the Court that he would be amicus curiae for A-2. Prosecutor came late and so the Court admonished the staff officer.

From then on, the Court kept getting adjourned for one reason or the other, but *not of our doing;* they were unable to get the witnesses demanded by us on 1 May, for Plea to Jurisdiction even till 21 May. As the adjournment was long, I sought *'release from close arrest without prejudice to re-arrest'* and some leave so that I could go to Bangalore and spend some time with my girls, *whom I had to send back, just 2 days prior to this adjournment*! NO reply to both requests was received.

In fact, between July 1985 and Aug 1986, all my requests for a weekend pass or just one day's leave each, as applicable, to go to Hardwar (just a few hours from Ambala) to perform the obligatory annual rites for my late mother (2 July 1985 and 21 June 1986); wife (11 Aug 1985 and 14 Aug 1986) and father (15 July 1986) were refused! I was treated as if I had committed a murder and so might abscond, even if I hadn't done so in the past 3 years!

My Plea to Jurisdiction

Returning to the thread, Court then checked on availability of seven witnesses, which I needed for Plea to Jurisdiction, viz,

CO No 1, i.e., Rabbi;

Deputy Assistant Adjutant General of Artillery Brigade;

CO No 4, i.e., Commander Independent Armoured Brigade;

Deputy Assistant Adjutant and Quartermaster General of Artillery Brigade, i.e., Major Bandicoot;

CO No 3, i.e., Deputy Commander Armoured Brigade;

Colonel A at Corps HQ and

Deputy Assistant Adjutant General of Armoured Brigade.

The Prosecutor said most witnesses were serving in far off places and so it would take time. My counsel pointed out that A-2 had retired during the pendancy of the case and in view of Army Act 123 having been invoked for him, he would not be getting any pay and allowances till final confirmation; this fact may please be kept in mind.

After advice by JA, Court was adjourned till 21 May 1986, to enable presence of witnesses to Plea to Jurisdiction.

On 21 May 1986, Colonel ... (Retired), Advocate, Punjab and Haryana High Court arrived as Prosecution Counsel and submitted that he needed time to go through the proceedings so far and so required a day! (He was a *specialist in army prosecutions,* just as Colonel Bains was in defending! Once that Colonel did tell me jokingly that I should *'not have argued with a bulldozer and should have gone with the flow of traffic'*! I thanked him and said: *"My principles and convictions as well as my trust in my subordinates were more important to me than escaping any rap on the knuckle for a minor offence"*.)

The next day, Prosecution Counsel submitted that 4 of the 7 witnesses were available; but my Counsel stated that he would examine CO No1, Rabbi first, followed by CO No 4 (Commander of the Armoured Brigade) and then only decide who else and in what order, *if at all,* he would examine. Interestingly, Command and Corps A Branch staff told the Prosecutor that under Army Rule 137, defence should defray the cost of the witnesses' presence! My counsel rightly pointed out that it was the Court which had directed the presence of these witnesses, though on our request; and it was the Court alone which could order the cost of defraying; further the cost for just 3 outstation witnesses alone would be Rs 15,000 which the accused can ill afford; he also drew attention to Note 5 to Army Rule 137. Judge Advocate advised that cost-defrayal was only an enabling provision and cannot be of binding nature. Prosecutor now requested that the Court be adjourned till 28 May 1986, whereupon the Court expressed displeasure that no proper action had been taken by the prosecution for 20 days till now during the adjournment to get all the witnesses.

The adjournment was extended till 3 June 1986, but at the appointed time, both QM and I were absent as our daily medical examination had not been completed. This was another development to our detriment; Colonel A at Corps had ordered that our daily medical examination which was so far being done by the doctor of the 'host regiment' where we were lodged would henceforth be done at the Military Hospital. This was not only harassment and waste of time, but more significantly, being under close arrest, we had also to travel without our belts, under escort of 2 Lt's for 5 KM each way every day, like common criminals and make a spectacle of our plight for public viewing. This was the reason for my appeal to Corps and then Army Commanders; but in vain.

Once we arrived, my Counsel submitted that a copy of the previous two inchoate Court Martial proceedings which he had requested had not been made available. After some demurring by Prosecution Counsel about entitlement to a copy, Court directed him to make it available for perusal.

Thus after a delay of 42 days (23 Apr to 3 June) by the Prosecution, we were able to commence the examination of the first witness to our Plea to Jurisdiction, i.e., Rabbi.

In the meantime, the following events of importance had taken place:-

- After the GCM had commenced and I had been arraigned, a reply to my appeal of 13 Mar 1986 came on 1 May 1986: "*You will be getting sufficient opportunity to defend yourself on the points mentioned by you in your Appeal, at the trial*"!
- On 3 May 1986, I was informed by a letter regarding my appeal of 31 Dec 1985 that: "*Decision of the General Officer Commanding in Chief will be communicated to you on its receipt*"! (That never happened!)

On 20 May 1986, a reply to my Non Statutory Complaint was given by the Corps HQ itself that: *"Since the trial has commenced by way of a GCM, the case is sub judice and no action can be taken at this stage"*, as if I didn't know. How convenient to delay matters and take this route!

Rabbi when called as the first witness deposed the fact about his preliminary investigations on 28 June 1983 as the "CO" (*which then he was legally NOT*) and which was different from what he had stated in previous trial; there he had said he had NOT done any investigation **after** being appointed as "CO". When questioned by my counsel, he clarified: "...I meant to convey that ***BEFORE**** the preliminary investigations done in the Regiment for which I was detailed, and before calling them on charge sheet, no other investigations were carried out by me as a CO;

(Readers would recall I had started making my own copy in the Court by taking down the dictation being given by the JA, in my own 'private' shorthand, and later cross checking it with the official version, when typed copy was available [though not for the farce of the first GCM] every day. I had pointed out hundreds of mistakes and wrong recordings to every Judge Advocate who attended these trials, while noting down even page numbers, which would be handy for any future petitions! Later I got it typed as and when my elder daughter when present or I got the time. Unfortunately many mistakes in recording were not corrected, as I saw during the Revision proceedings in Nov 1986. I did not want to remind every new JA, as it was his job alone! THIS NARRATIVE IS FROM MY OWN RECORD.)

Rabbi further deposed admitting that A-2 had requested in writing to be attached outside that Brigade and had stated that he did not expect to get justice, but had never asked for compliance of Hearing of Charge.

Deputy Assistant Adjutant General of Independent Artillery Brigade as No 2 witness stated: "... During 1985,

*This was a wrong recording

a court martial... was ordered. ... The court martial... was dissolved under orders of .... *There is nothing on record to indicate* ***under what authority and for what reasons*** *the court was dissolved."*

The third witness was CO No 4 (till recently Commander of Independent Armoured Brigade). He stated on oath that he '...*was not given any documents pertaining to the case.* (*This was later refuted by his own staff officer, Witness No 7 herein*) ... Sometime in Sep 1985, order was published...Deputy Commander would be the CO. ...the said order was cancelled sometime during Dec and then I assumed command, automatically as CO... I did not pass any order in writing regarding the Summary of Evidence (S of E)... Since the attachment order was held invalid, all the proceedings including the S of E also became invalid...' After stating that he neither carried out preliminary investigations, nor ordered S of E against A-2, he added that he 'had perused that S of E, which he found valid and so did not order an S of E'. He further stated that he was NOT successor to Commander Independent Artillery Brigade! (*He was then not entitled to get or read A-2's S of E or even mine*!). His further re-examination was pended for obtaining certain documents. Later, on recall after Witness 4, he stated that *his staff had received the S of E proceedings by hand of 'Bandicoot', without a covering letter on 22 Sep 1985*, and that they were put up to him in Jan 1986, after he became the CO, (which was not the truth, as later brought out by his own staff, Witness No 7 to Jurisdiction)! He also confirmed that he had not formally *'seen'* A-2 and had ordered S of E against me in mid Feb 1986! On a question by the Judge Advocate, he stated that Army HQ had issued attachment order for me alone on 20 Dec 1985, which was received on 26 Dec 1985; hence another Hearing, S of E etc for me.

Witness No 4 was Major Bandicoot, who stated that on 24 Jan 1984, A-2 was called into Rabbi's office, who read out the charge sheet. A-2 had stated that as he did not expect justice from Artillery, he may be attached elsewhere; but had not demanded a Hearing. No witnesses had been called by Rabbi either! After stating that A-2 did not say: *"Mera jo hona hai, so hona hai"* (meaning: *whatever has to happen to me will happen*), he immediately corrected himself: he was not sure if he had said so or not!

Witness No 5 was Deputy Commander of the present brigade who had recently been 'removed' unceremoniously from being our "CO". The main points deposed were:-

- He had got a copy of my Summary by an officer's hand from my previous brigade.
- NO charge sheet was received.
- On 9 Oct 1985, he had written a letter ordering A-2 to attend Hearing of Charge, but withdrew it (There is no written proof for it) as it was not required, as briefed by Deputy JAG at Corps HQ!
- He did not get A-2's (QM's) S of E.
- He had felt that I should get a fresh Hearing on such re-attachment, which is why he had requested the Commander to be CO No 4! (Later we would argue that this *'Bias'* is for me to worry about and not for him)!
- He contradicted himself immediately, saying he was also briefed by the Deputy JAG at Corps not to continue as CO, which was why the Commander had to assume that duty! (Which of the two would you believe?)
- He used to brief the Commander (later to be my CO No 4) "sometimes" about the case!

The next witness (No 6) was Colonel A from Corps HQ who along with Deputy JAG there, had been moving the puppet strings. The very first thing he did was to say he had never seen us earlier! Major points stated by him were:

- He had written a letter dated 28 Nov 1983 with the words: *"Order S of E against the officers blamed..."*

- He had also written another letter dated 4 Dec 1985 to my present unit, directing that *'Regiment's Quarter Master Branch Subedar Head Clerk,* (who was the one who got all Local Purchase papers prepared and had given evidence in one Summary of Evidence each for me and A-2*), be NOT examined as Prosecution Witness '...Accused may summon him'.*
- On 30 and 31 Dec 1985, my present unit had written to him seeking clarification on a fresh Summary for me, as most witnesses had arrived! He had replied on 13 Jan 1986, directing:
  - commence disciplinary proceedings afresh forthwith;
  - proceedings recorded so far rendered invalid;
  - intimate weekly progress report, to reach every Monday;
  - forward all copies of S of E proceedings recorded so far, less original exhibits for sealing and safe custody to Corps HQ forthwith; (*once again, what is the use of locking the stable door after the horse had bolted? Also, one copy each had been retained, as I could see the officer recording my 3rd S of E, referring to it in my presence, during the recording everyday*!)

At that stage, the Prosecution counsel asked the witness to give out his intentions and circumstances which prompted him to write: "*"Order S of E against the officers blamed...*". This was objected to by my counsel and the JAG as *"Contents of a document cannot be supplemented by oral evidence"*. A lot of legal arguments on the Applicability and Relevance as per Sections 6, 93 and 94 of Indian Evidence Act took place. After a lengthy advice by the JA, the Court disallowed Prosecutor's question.

The seventh and the last witness to jurisdiction was Deputy Assistant Adjutant General of Independent Armoured Brigade. He stated the following main points:

- Both Summaries of Evidence were received on or around 22 Sep 1985 from previous brigade.
- *They were with the Deputy Commander, (i.e., my CO No 3), for 10 to 15 days during working hours,* which he, as *Witness No 5 had denied*!
- Later, when Commander became CO No 4, he used to collect *the same* during working hours from him; in Jan or Feb 1986, *which that person had denied*!
- No Hearing of charge took place for A-2; *'I do not know why'*.

Thus without delay, my counsel completed the examination of all 7 witnesses in 2 days and sought a day to submit written Plea Against Jurisdiction; it was granted.

On 6 June 1986, my counsel submitted verbally: *"A-2 has been ordered to wear uniform. He, not being in service, is not entitled to wear uniform. In fact, he would be committing an offence if he wears uniform. A-1 (i.e., me) has been put under close arrest. It is in the discretion of administrative authority to do so but it is an arbitrary discretion. I would be severely hampered in my defence, if he continues to be under close arrest. I would be grateful if these sentiments are conveyed to the convening authority"*.

Thereafter, he submitted Arguments on Special Plea to General Jurisdiction of this Court, besides a verbal address, covering many essential points as follows:

- As far as courts martial are concerned, your decision is almost final. Even though Army Act Section 164 gives the right of petition to the accused, it is a meaningless right; as *an appeal without a right of audience is ineffective*. And, secondly, the *petition is disposed of by non-speaking orders* and one does not know what arguments have been accepted and what rejected. Even though superior courts in the country entertain petitions against the findings and sentence of courts martial, the grounds on which they do so are very limited. Findings of facts, by your Honour, they will not review. Even at the risk of wasting your time, therefore, I have to raise preliminary objections. Because, *ultimately these are the only points the superior courts will review. The accused persons are convinced that they have a good case on merits also and are prepared to fight it out on merit also, if required later.*

- Army Act gives very vast powers to military authorities in disposal of cases. *Courts martial do not have to give any reason for their findings,* nor do their superior authorities have to give any reasons for confirmation or rejection. The right of appeal is a limited one. The only safeguard available to the accused is that ***NO case against a person can go up for trial, unless his Commanding Officer so desires.*** Army Rules 22 to 24 give very vast powers to Commanding Officers. He has the power to dismiss the charge, even though there is evidence, if he considers it inexpedient to proceed with the case... Supreme Court has also held that it is mandatory. Commanding Officer being the only protection against arbitrariness ..., the procedure laid down in Army Rules 22 to 24 should be strictly observed.
- Non adherence to procedure established by law (as elucidated by Supreme Court in Maneka Gandhi case);
- "Cognizance" not defined in Army Act; still it 'had not been taken by the competent authority in case of A-2'.
- No preliminary investigation and Hearing of charge had been held for A-2, whether he demanded it or not, as they were mandatory according to Army Rules 22 to 25.
- 'Trial is based on a Summary of A-2 which is no longer in force'.
- "Who is a CO"? Is Army Order 217/72 correct or Army Order 251/72 or the letter from Army HQ

dated 14 Jan 1982, laying down as to who would be CO? The executive cannot appoint a CO arbitrarily.

- CO not having acted under own discretion, but under *'dictation'*;
- Irregularity in handing over a previously recorded Summary of Evidence on the same charge to another CO;
- In my case, cognizance of offence having been taken by CO No 3, his Commander could not arbitrarily cancel his appointment and assume powers of a CO (as CO No 4); action already started ought to have continued;
- Second cognizance taken on me in the same unit, after a likely fear of a 'Bias' expressed by CO No 3 is illegal, as the accused alone could have decided on bias; (citations were given).
- Dissolution Order of 29 Aug 1985 NOT having been issued under the only applicable section (117) of Army Act, further trial is illegal;
- Second and third cognizance of the same offence by a succession of CO's at different locations was illegal.

After a Prosecution reply in a written address and advice by JA, the Court rejected the Plea to Jurisdiction and adjourned until 11 June 1986. On reassembly, the Court followed the 'Procedure on a plea of NOT Guilty', by asking me and A-2 the following questions: *"Do you wish to apply for an adjournment on the grounds that any of the rules relating to procedure before trial have not been complied with and that you have been prejudiced thereby or on the ground that you have not had sufficient opportunity for preparing your defence?"*

Both of us replied 'NO', after which the Prosecutor handed in a written Opening Address of 3½ pages, just giving out the charge sheet as now signed by CO No 5 on 11 Apr 1986 (contents being the same as in Annexure 4, but with a totalling error of the amount in paise as *40 instead of 20!*); the other ingredients of his address being:

A-2 and I (A-1) had acted dishonestly.

We had acted *'together'* when I had been on leave from 29 Apr to 27 June 1983;

The quantity of scrim garnish received was only 19,500 M while we had submitted bills for Rs 61,526/*40*(sic) P towards 87,000 M which had been taken on ledger charge;

A-1 (that is me) had said that transaction needed to be investigated in Handing Over Notes as well as Certificate to successor, Tanjore Doll;

An *anonymous* (sic) letter had been received and investigations done;

On the basis of separate Summaries, the accused have been brought before the court on a joint trial.

Thereafter, examination of 10 Prosecution and 14 Defence Witnesses commenced on 11 June 86. Details are at Annexure 6; but it may help readers to know in brief as to what was attempted to be proved by both prosecution and defence, before a Revision was ordered.

WHAT WAS ATTEMPTED TO BE PROVED BY PROSECUTION & DEFENCE

What did Prosecution Try to Prove?

1. I was CO of ...Medium Regt and Major... was the QM during Apr-May 1983.
2. My leave dates were 29 Apr to 27 June 1983 only and were not changed (to commence from 5 May) on a letter from Brigade, as well as subsequent telephonic instructions on 4 May on Commander's orders.
3. We fully well knew that only 19,500 M of scrim garnish had been brought by PW-7, Subedar Never-

loyal. Still we prepared and submitted to DDOS ...Corps, contingent bills for local purchase of 87,000 M of it totalling to Rs. 61,526/40 P.

4. I had signed the Contingent Bills and other connected documents while on leave, after 29 Apr 1983.
5. There was secrecy in the whole transaction, (because, Major Crass who officiated as CO in my place during my leave was not given any Note about this deal, while handing over by me in Apr 83, whereas the Exercise was over on 12 Mar 83!)
6. I had acted in concert with my Quarter Master, with intent to defraud the Govt, by claiming Rs 61,526/ **40**P for 87,000 metres of Garnish Scrim, while well knowing that ONLY 19,500 metres had been received. (The figure in the charge sheet was Rs 61,526/**20** P!)
7. Garnish of Ordnance pattern had existed in the unit's 'junk stores' even after we returned from Exercise Dig Vijay!

What Defence attempted to Prove

1. Exercise Dig Vijay was to take place during Dec 1982- Mar 1983 and clear orders had been received for carriage of two camouflage nets for each gun, vehicle etc, against one each as authorized.
2. From Aug 1982 onwards, there was constant pressure on the unit from higher HQ, to prepare two camouflage nets (against one authorized), duly knitted with scrim garnish for 100% vehicles, guns and fieldworks etc.
3. The dependent Ordnance Depot had regretted Non Availability in Nov 1982.
4. The stock, as per ledger of the unit, on 25 Nov 1982, the date of annual stock taking board (less than a

month before the expected date of moving for the Exercise) of the major shade of garnish scrim (MB Green) to be contracted was NIL and so there was an immediate necessity to go in for Local Purchase. The holdings at subunits were 1,22,400 which were part of nets already held plus 99,000 of Undyed which was not of much use! Even otherwise, the requirement of garnish for over 235 nets (2,01,160M) could not be met with the then existing stock of 1,22,400 M in which there was **NO** MB Green garnish at all! There was no holding of the three major shades 75 MM scrim garnish, required for knitting the nets in the Regt, right from Aug/Dec 1981.

5. Sub unit commanders had clamoured for garnish right from Aug/Sep 1982, when PW-9 was officiating as CO in my place!

6. In view of no other go, on QM's well-meaning suggestion, I had ordered local purchase of 87,000 M of scrim garnish 75 MM well before leaving the Exercise, in order to prepare the nets.

7. The fact about the necessity of LP was not only informed to sub unit commanders in unit conferences but also to the Brigade HQ, where Commander himself had agreed to speak to Deputy Director of Ordnance Services, his batchmate at Corps HQ. This was openly announced in a unit Sainik Sammelan and men were asked to directly approach the CO, if still there was deficiency. All this was not secrecy.

8. The amount contracted did arrive on 13 Dec 1982 and was distributed to sub units, besides 7000-8000M to Workshop and 68 knitted nets to Brigade HQ (on 25 Feb 83), which, even at the *minimum* would have needed (68x590=40,120 M); Regt got back only 15,000 from Bde in July 1983.

9. Sub unit commanders had given a written certificate in Dec 1982, just prior to leaving for exercise that all

items for the Exercise had been received, INCLUDING garnish; but the entire file had been destroyed as per security instructions!

10. If local purchase had not been resorted to, the Regt could not have had two nets each.
11. As per Brigade directions, I had been present in office and NOT on leave up to and inclusive of 4 May 1983. The Documents were ready for despatch on 6 May only (PW-3).
12. There was not only a conspiracy between Scraggly and Crass, to 'fix' me for presumed insults but Crass had threatened all concerned to toe his line or else.
13. The driver of the vehicle which went to collect the garnish; the Regimental Havildar Major who had detailed working party with it etc confirmed that '50 to 100 bundles' had been brought. 58 bundles had in fact been received by PW- 7, as confirmed by DW-12.
14. The evidence of PW-7, on which Prosecution had solely relied, was false, as it was a bogus issue record on forged signatures The major prosecution evidence, i.e., so-called Nominal Issue Voucher (NIV) under which ONLY 19,500 M had been issued was a fraud, because:
    - Two of the four signatories stated on oath that they had not signed that voucher; (the Prosecution did not prove the other 2 signatures!)
    - Even the JCO QM in Exercise area, who was stated to have received 'some' garnish out of that 19,500 M said that he did not get any in the Exercise area.
    - The voucher was totally anachronistic in that it had been entered as Serial 601 in the Issue Register, much after many entries of later dates of 1983!

- PW-7 had brought total LP garnish as contracted but was giving evidence under duress (by Major Crass), without having maintained any records.
- PW-7 also stated that he had issued 4,600 OR 46,000 M of 75 MM garnish on 6 Nov 1982, when he was NOT even the Subedar QM and the ledger shows NIL balance on that date.
- He was thus trying to defend himself for not maintaining his documents properly and so, had fallen into Crass' snare.

15. PW-3, 5 and 10 (clerks) stated on oath, they had not prepared the NIV!
16. There was NO junk store in the Regt at all; so the recovery was a fraud too, as the quantity so alleged varied from about 40,000 M through 55,000 M to 73,200 (and finally got reduced to 70,200 during Revision Proceedings)! It was simply garnish Undyed 99,000 M, bulk of which could not be used for Exercise as it did not satisfy the shades required for knitting nets for the Exercise!
17. Many witnesses who had NO knowledge of LP garnish (as per Prosecution arguments) could not have had it in any case, as for instance:
    - PW-1 joined the unit on 4 Mar 1983 when it was away on Exercise and went away on leave for 2 months from 24 Mar to 22 May (but recalled on 14 May)! (Regt had returned on 13 Mar 1983!)
    - DW-7, whom we had produced for other reasons, could not have known either, as he joined the Regt only on 21 Dec 1982 and was committed with duties in another unit in Rajasthan till 16 Jan 1983 and then was attached to yet another unit for the Exercise till 13 Mar 1983! (These persons were quoted by the 'learned' Prosecution Counsel as more proof in his Closing Address, that even Defence Witnesses produced by us were unaware!)

18. We also attempted to prove by the bearing, demeanour, interestedness, motive, inconsistency in testimony and total discrepancies (within the evidence of a single Prosecution Witness; or among that of many, when compared), that PW-1, 2 and 7 were totally unreliable!

Closing Addresses

On conclusion of evidence of PW-14, Lt Col Bedi, my Defending Officer submitted that with this, there were no more witnesses for the defence of A-1 and so the case is closed as far as A-1 was concerned. He also stated that there will be only one Closing Address on behalf of both accused, to enable preparation of which, he requested adjournment till 18 Aug 1986. But Colonel Ramanan submitted that during the course of interview with DW-11, he received information about the persons who had looked after the garnish from the time it reached unit till it was distributed. CO... Medium Regiment has been approached through ...Armoured Brigade to make at least one of these persons available...he was to get back to him today. So this witness will be examined on the morning of 18 Aug and then Closing Address will follow. A minimum of 4 days are required keeping also in mind the intervening holidays.

Prosecution Counsel submitted that if it be so, Defence ought to have got this fact out during the testimony of DW-11. *Any witness ought to have been asked through the Court or prosecution and not direct*! No adjournment should be given on this score. Question of Closing Address would arise only after Defence closes its case.

Colonel Ramanan submitted that no specific person had been indicated by DW-11, but only a group; hence we are trying to find out at least one name. *Prosecution had been saying that Defence should themselves arrange their witnesses and suddenly he is shifting his stand*! Only for saving the time of the Court, I had put this matter and closing address together; only tomorrow, we would know the name if available.

JA drew attention to Army Rule 136 and as for the witness, stated the court should arrive at all decisions based on specifics and not on conjectures; regarding adjournment for Closing Address, he said 'any period reasonable and just' may be considered.

After a decision in closed court, it announced adjournment till 18 Aug 1986, to examine the witness <u>and</u> to deliver the Closing Address.

No witness as stated could be found by Ramanan through CO (PW-9) and so our Closing Address of 27 pages was read out (by my Defending Officer). The main points of our Address are given in Annexure 7, where my counsel put a stake through the heart of all lies by PWs 1, 2 and 7. Then the court was adjourned for a day to enable the Prosecutor to prepare his Closing Address. On 19 Aug 1986, after his Closing Address (gist at same Annexure 7, after Defence's), the Court was adjourned till 21 Aug 1986, to enable the JA's Summing Up. Unfortunately, JA read through his address very fast for **2 hours** and did not also give us a copy to read before or after reading it out. However, *I had made quick shorthand notes as always* and now, I have summarized them also in the same Annexure 7.

At about 1.45 p.m. on Thursday, 21 Aug 1986, the Court found me ***NOT Guilty*** as charged. I felt very relieved, but waited to hear the fate of Quarter Master; he was found Guilty and punished with loss of seniority for promotion and pension for a few years. I rushed to the GPO to call up my daughters with the happy news but had to wait till the evening, as lines to Bangalore were busy!

'Life isn't about waiting for the storm to pass,
it's about learning how to dance in the rain'
(Anonymous)

In the next few weeks, some doomsayers told me that in a Joint Trial, either both should have been found guilty or not guilty; so there might be a Revision. Legal opinions differed but I followed the above quote; and wondered if there was a price to pay for every pleasure?

On Saturday, 27 Sep 1986, GOC-in-C Western Command at Chandi Mandir (former Corps Commander and my benefactor) sent for me to speak from the public telephone in the Officers Mess where I was lodged, to inform me that his HQ Judge Advocate General's Branch was insistent that the verdict of the GCM must be "reviewed" and so, he had no choice; but wished me good luck, as he would be retiring in 3 days and "knew all along" that I would win as I was "not *that type* of a person" !

'When you look long into an abyss,
the abyss looks into you!'
Nietzsche

Revision Ordered

On 3 Nov 1986, QM arrived with the recently retired JAG as his counsel! *That gentleman, having been privy at the highest level, to all that had happened since 1983 in this case, should have had the professional ethic and etiquette not to accept the brief*! Even the Re-assembly Order signed by the Officiating General Officer Commanding was yet to reach us; *but they knew*! I immediately called up my Counsel at Delhi! I knew I had to paddle my own canoe from now on!

On 5 Nov 1986, GCM was ordered to "re-assemble" on 6 Nov 1986. *A JA from HQ Western Command this time, (obviously briefed about his mission...to fix both the accused...) arrived. He had NO clue of the details of the case as would be seen later!*

Salient points of the Reassembly Order (signed by Chief of Staff, officiating as GOC ...Corps given below) appeared to be to ensure that both were punished:

- *'...for the purpose of reconsidering Findings in respect of both the accused persons...**while in no way wishing to interfere with the discretion** vested in the Court to accept or reject any part of evidence before it, I as the Convening Authority wish to point out that it appears* to have erred in appreciating the points of law and the evidence on record ...'.

- 'During Nov 1982, Ordnance Depot Shakurbasti vide ***Issue Voucher*** dated 22 Nov 1982 issued 54,500 M of garnish to ...Regt and marked non availability for 90,000 M'. *(46,500M out of this 54,500 M was UNDYED 75 MM and balance 8,000 M was of 50 MM,* ***both of which were not of much use).***

- It then spoke of the local purchase documents having been signed by QM and me; and said: '... *whether or not the documents were submitted for local purchase with the concurrence of both the accused persons'.*

- The Order then gave out the details of evidence of PW-7: Never-loyal; PW-8: CS of Sphere Corporation and DW-13 Rooster covering the 'delivery' and 'collection' and said: *'The Court should consider whether the transaction was held on the mutual understanding of A-2 and PW-13 or whether in accordance with normal procedures of inviting tenders, opening the same in the presence of all contractors, preparing comparative statements and then placing the order with the lowest tenderer. ...whether such transaction could have taken place without the concurrence of A-1; and if ...with concurrence of both, then was it an innocent deal or with intent to defraud'. (JA had never been under pressure like a CO preparing for the biggest exercise* and executing an illegal order of 2 nets each! The intended purchase as explained by the QM was indeed with my concurrence).

- The Order then spoke about the contingent bills etc and again pointed to *'concurrence of both'.*

- It then talked of the two letters from Ordnance Branch of HQ... Corps (dated 7 and 18 Mar 1983) whereby we should have gone in for collection of 67,500 M of garnish from the Depot and for regularization of ONLY 19,500 M got from PW-8/ DW-13. (*We had functioned under the same Corps HQ that had given the illegal order of two nets and it was also aware, the exercise was over on 13 Mar 1983; what would one do about paying the dealer, who had come to our rescue in an emergency? How else could we have knitted 235 nets needing 2,01,160 metres?*)

- The next para (Para 12 of the Order) is the most important and it refers to Section 34 of Indian Penal Code, which *'lays down the law in respect of acts done by several persons in furtherance of common intention... The dominant feature of Section 34 is the element of participation in action. This participation need not be in all cases by physical presence.'*
- In the next para, it spoke of Sphere NOT being the initial tenderer. (*Again how stupid and ignorant can the JA who wrote the RT be? The letterhead of the company is made stylishly such that the word "Sphere" is spread across its whole heading in a slant and flashy manner; anyone with eyesight would have seen it!*)
- The next two paras (Paras 14 and 15) are other very important ones, dealing with the evidence of Quarter Master Branch Subedar Head Clerk. It traces his evidence and then the arguments from us and the prosecution for his non-production. *'Illustration (g) to Indian Evidence Act, Section 14 provides that the Court may presume that evidence which could be and is not produced would, if produced, be unfavourable to the person who withholds it'*. Then it spoke of Army Rule 134: *'...the Court should consider whether the examination of this witness is material to the defence and if so, whether it is practicable to procure his attendance. ...In case the prosecution is unable to produce this witness on re-assembly of the court and the court is satisfied that it is not practicable to secure his attendance, it should ensure that no prejudice is caused to the accused persons due to the non-appearance of this witness'*. (*What a farce and an eye wash! if in spite of repeated requests, the prosecution or the convening authority* ***had not done so since July 1985, when they had sent him back, how could and would they produce him at 24 hours notice, the next day?***)

- In the next para (Para 16), it asked the prosecution to bring the Appendix of the Court of Inquiry, which had been disallowed during the testimony on recall of PW-9, Tanjore Doll and also wanted Lt Col Shifty Eyes to prove his signature on it.
- In Para 18, it stated: '*After Revision Order is read in open Court, it should call ... Quarter Master Branch Subedar Head Clerk... if he could be made available and recall Tanjore Doll (PW-9) and record their evidence on the points contained in Paras 14 and 16 above. .... Thereafter the Court should afford an opportunity to the accused to address the court. Thereafter,* ***if it becomes necessary to clarify any point or points raised by the accused, the JA may give a further summing up***'. (The JA gave a Summing Up which was longer than what was done after the main trial! More about it follows).

On 6 Nov 1986, GCM re-assembled

- Both Defending Officers serving outside Western Command were absent; counsel for A-2 agreed to do without one; but my counsel said that while he would not wait for one, in case there was adjournment for any reason, he would need the same officer (now Lt Col, HS Bedi).
- Prosecution counsel then stated that while PW-9, Tanjore Doll would be available the next day, Shifty Eyes will only be available on 8 Nov. He repeated the same tune about the former Quarter Master Branch Subedar Head Clerk being in Saudi Arabia and efforts having been made when he was in India etc, but now prosecution was unable to procure his attendance.
- My counsel submitted that while we would not insist on the former Quarter Master Branch Subedar Head Clerk (who was Prosecution Witness No 8 in my first Summary of Evidence), we definitely needed

as Defence Witness at least one Prosecution Witness, i.e., JCO QM who had handed over to PW-7, Never-loyal in Nov 1982 (and had proceeded on pension and whom the prosecution did not produce)!

- Defence Counsel for A-2 submitted that:
- Examination of Quarter Master Branch Subedar Head Clerk was crucial for A-2, as he had been found guilty;
- The Revision Order had also emphasized the same; his non-examination would completely vitiate the trial. He then submitted that no efforts at all had been made by the Prosecution either with immigration authorities or even pension authorities; 'any person of such crucial importance in deciding the fate of two senior officers of the army can certainly be located and expatriated. If not, A-2 should be honourably acquitted'.
- He had requested the Adjutant General at Army HQ and the Convening Officer for a copy of the proceedings so far and the Revision Order, in vain. He may now be provided those and given 48 hours to prepare. 9 Nov being a Sunday, the Court could re-assemble on 10 Nov 1986.
- Prosecution Counsel stated that the contention of Counsel for A-2 was incorrect and that all reasonable efforts had been made in respect of Quarter Master Branch Subedar Head Clerk.

After a consideration in closed court, it decided:

- To adjourn until 0900 hours on 8 Nov 1986.
- The Revision Order be exhibited and the Counsel may refer to it.
- Prosecution Counsel shall examine the feasibility of procuring the attendance of Quarter Master Branch Subedar Head Clerk; and ***if reasonably possible***, to do the same.

On 8 Nov 1986, the Court re-assembled. My Defending Officer on leave arrived in civvies, being on leave; and our request through the Prosecution to permit him to appear was accepted!

PW-9, (my successor was) Re-examined by the Court

- Prosecution Counsel handed over to him a carbon copy (NOT the original) of a letter from the Presiding Officer of the Court of Inquiry dated 1 July 1983 regarding 'segregation and sealing' of the 'seized' stock of scrim garnish in the unit.
- (JA read out the letter correctly with the Remark against Serial 2 only.) But, PW-9 was 'coerced' into stating that a Remark by him made on 1 July 1983, against Serials 7 to 9 bracketed in that letter was applicable to all serials before it, that is, 1 to 6 also!
- There were NO questions to suggest by either Counsel.
- Then the Presiding Officer of the Court of Inquiry, Colonel Shifty Eyes was called as a Court Witness and examined by the JA; (the 'dictated' aim: "*Hang both*"!).

Salient Points of Examination of Shifty Eyes

- During June 1983, he was detailed as Presiding officer of a Court of Inquiry by Independent Artillery Brigade HQ to investigate the case of local purchase of scrim garnish by ...Medium Regiment. He had visited and inspected the stock of scrim garnish in the Regt. Thereafter he wrote a letter to the Regt in this regard. He recognized the exhibit produced by PW-9 as the carbon copy of the letter ibid.
- *"In the Remarks Column of Appendix A, the bracketed Remark 'Ordnance Marking of COD Kanpur to OD Shakurbasti' towards Origin Column pertains to Serials 1 to 6 of the Appendix. The second bracketed Remark towards*

Origin Column 'in loose condition with Ordnance cat/part number marked' pertains to Serials 7 to 9 of the Appendix".

- *'I had seen the stores myself'.*
- *'One of the members of the court of inquiry along with Captain Cassius had taken stock of stores based on gunny bag packing'.*
- *'The figures given in the Appendix are **approximately correct**'.*
- *'To the best of my knowledge, this stock did not contain scrim garnish of non-Ordnance pattern'.*
- ***'However, I wish to add that I had NOT physically checked each bundle'.***

  (*The Court was closed at this stage, as the JA was flummoxed by this 'additional' comment from the witness! His brief probably was: through these two witnesses, HANG BOTH THE ACCUSED*! After 15 minutes, it re-opened and continued).
- *'I tried to link up the stores with the unit record. I could not find any link of these stores with the ledgers etc'.*
- *'By the word **link**, I mean the ground balance did not tally with ledger balances'.*
- *'At this stage, I do not recollect the method which was followed to ascertain the quantity of garnish'.*
- *'I am not in a position to state whether there was any other quantity of garnish in the unit or not'.*

Cross Examination Declined by Prosecution Counsel.

Cross Examination Declined by Counsel for A-1.

Cross Examination by Counsel for A-2:

- *'The quantities of garnish mentioned in the Appendix (to exhibit) are based on the stocks of garnish which were shown to me. As Presiding Officer of Court of Inquiry, I*

> *did not inspect the unit for all the garnish they had, as I was not entitled to visit every place in the unit to locate garnish.'*

At this stage, the Prosecution Counsel did a *volte face* (obviously as briefed by the A and JA staff at Corps HQ) and submitted that he had gone through ALL his statements but *did not (now) find the former Quarter Master Branch Subedar Head Clerk to be a material witness,* due to the following reasons:

- He had not received the garnish himself, thus he has no personal knowledge about the garnish in question.
- He was the Q Head Clerk and had nothing to do with the stock.
- He was himself ***involved*** in preparation of *'false'* documents.

He further submitted, as if the points below had come to his mind just then (as they say in Hindi: *"Dimag ghaas khaney gaya thha" (His mind had wandered off to graze,* **all these years**) :

- (Firstly??) he is not an essential witness.
- Secondly, he is out of India.
- Thirdly, in the absence of his address in a foreign country, Prosecution is unable to procure his attendance.
- Fourthly, he is not also subject to Army Act.

He further stated: "It is admitted that at the Summary of Evidence of A-2, he as PW-7 then, had stated (...in answer to a question, as under...):

> Q: *"Are you aware that Contingent Bills, Certified Receipt Vouchers and other correspondence were prepared AFTER the entire stock of stores were physically received in the unit?"*
>
> He had replied: *"In May 1983, I had checked up with Subedar Never-loyal if the entire quantity of scrim garnish*

as per the six sets of Local Purchase documents had been received. And, on his confirmation of receipt of Local Purchase garnish, I instructed Lance Naik (...PW-5) to prepare the Certified Receipt Vouchers, Contingent Bills and other connected documents".

- After the directions of the Court on 6 Nov 1986, efforts had been made by sending signals as well as contacting ...(unclear), the Prosecution has come to the conclusion that the attendance of this person cannot be procured. (*What a joke it was that they did NOT do anything from July 1985 till now for 472 days; in just 2 days now, they have done all that was required*!)

My Counsel answered that sending signals was not the answer; *has a reply to the signal been received? Whether the witness is material or not is NOT an open question. It has already been decided by the Court and the Confirming Officer.*

Counsel for A-2 answered that the Hon'ble Court is meeting in pursuance of the Revision Order dated 5 Nov 1986 from the Confirming Authority. In Para 14 of the Revision Order, Confirming Officer has highlighted the importance of the evidence of (...this witness); in Para 15 thereto, he has categorically directed the Court: "*Based on the whole evidence on record, the Court should consider whether the examination of this witness is material to the defence and if so, whether it is practicable to procure his attendance... due to non-appearance of this witness*" (as already extracted by me three pages earlier). The witness has made similar statements in the S of E of both the accused persons. The court very considerately gave the requisite direction to the Prosecution. Unfortunately Prosecution did not make due efforts to procure the attendance of this witness, which is clearly evident from the submission of the Prosecution Counsel itself. In fact, the Defence had earlier apprehended that the Prosecution might not produce this witness, as a deliberate attempt to avoid contradictions of PW-7 on the crucial aspects of his statement. The apprehension has come true.

The Defence is unable to produce him. Under the circumstances of the case, the Court may be pleased to draw adverse inference against the Prosecution, that in case he was called, he would have stated what he had stated at the Summaries of Evidence and has been admitted by the Prosecution to have been so stated by him. The order of the Court regarding calling of this witness has not been implemented by the Prosecution. It amounts to contempt of Court.

Prosecution Counsel replied that the Court was pleased to grant him going into the feasibility of procuring his attendance if it was reasonably possible. Prosecution has made best endeavours; it has been informed by A Branch at HQ Western Command that it is not reasonably practicable to procure attendance of witnesses (thus implying former Subedar QM also, whom we had demanded!!)

JA then gave his advice, after which the Court considered it in closed Court.

On reassembling, the Court decided to sit beyond 6 hours in the interest of justice and discipline. It also decided to proceed with the trial. *Just 1½ hours were given to the Defence to prepare any submissions!*

Written cum Verbal Address by Counsel for A1:

We produced a 12-page typed submission within that time; it included two pages of detailed working of the garnish required for knitting 235 nets and covered the following major points:

- Charge against both accused is for *"together submitting"* contingent bills. This imported Section 34 of Indian Penal Code, for having *'acted in concert'*. Major portion of the closing address by the Prosecution and Advice by the JA after the trial in Aug 1986 was on this subject only. Still the Hon'ble court had acquitted A-1, as it must have decided that there was no illegal concert and that A-1 did not carry any responsibility vicariously for A-2.

- Revision Order while asking the Court to reconsider this point has given NO new grounds for it. You all are mature and senior officers and would have come to that deliberate decision and will adhere to the same.
- (He then covered seriatim the **relevant points** from the Revision Order)
- <u>Para 3</u>: Sphere not being the initial tenderer. *The letterhead of the company is made stylishly and printed separately from the other two words such that the word "Sphere" is spread across its whole name (Sphere Sales Corporation) in a slant and flashy manner.* Sphere Sales Corporation in all copies of their letterheads and 'Sales Corporation' mentioned in Revision Order are one and the same and located at the same address as can be seen. There was NO mala fide intention and even if A-1 may have agreed, of which NO evidence exists. So IPC 34 is NOT applicable to this.
- <u>A-1 signing the local purchase documents</u>: In Nov 1982, A-1 had worked out the total quantity of nets, and thus scrim garnish, required @ 2 nets each (details given in an annexure by us to the submission), which was 2,01,160 M. There was NO unused stock held of various colours as evidenced by PW-3 and PW-9 and that held with batteries was 1,22,400 M. The balance requirement was at least (2,1,160 MINUS 1,22,400=) 78,760 M. A-2 when asked, managed to get 46,500 M from Shakurbasti Depot along with a Non Availability Voucher for 90,000 M in the three main shades required for the nets for the exercise. A-1 reported to Scraggly, the Brigade Commander, who asked him to go for local purchase, also saying he would speak to the Brig at Corps HQ Ordnance who was the sanctioning authority and his batchmate. PW-4 has confirmed this. So going in for local purchase was a genuine and necessary act and no inference of guilty intention can be drawn in signing by A-1.

- Signing of all copies of all 6 exhibits on Application for LP, by A-1: The correct position is that only 4 of these had been signed by A-1 as the Administrative Officer, AFTER A-2 had signed them as the Executive Officer; the other two have been signed by A-2.
- Para 6: All actions as per this Para (Sending of PW-7 to collect from DW-13 in Dec 1982; his arrival back and reporting to A-2; *'understanding'* by PW-8, Mr. CS etc) had been done by A-2 alone and A-1 had nothing to do; hence no concert.
- Then he mentioned that though the Revision Order had not brought it to the notice of the Court, the quantity ordered was in fact received, though A-1 cannot say the source of its receipt. If the Prosecution avers and the Court believes it that it was not from Sphere Sales Corporation, the source of its supply isn't known to A-1. But A-1 can say that the total quantity was available in the unit, as he was able to order and get knitted 235 nets of size 10.7x 6 M size, for which certainly 2,01,160 M of scrim garnish was required and which did not exist in ledgers. It is in evidence that on 25 Nov 1982, the date of Stock Taking Board, there was NO surplus of garnish in the Regt. It is common knowledge that proceedings of the Board are put up to the CO and so were they done for this Board also. So, A-1, who was not stockholder of any item was not aware of any surpluses, if held in the Regt. All that A-1 can say is that the required amount of garnish was produced in the unit. A-1 signing Contingent Bills for the same was in the ordinary course of duty and could not be termed 'dishonest'.
- The next point is about the two letters from Corps Ordnance dated 7 and 18 Mar 1983. Your Honours can see from the "SEEN BY" stamp of the unit that A-1 saw them for the first time on 18 June 1983.

However A-2 had acted on them by asking HQ...Corps Ordnance to return the documents; and when received, by sending the same (signed by A-1 in Dec 1982) under a fresh covering letter dated Apr 1983, without intimation to A-1.

- Para 10 of the Revision Order is factually incorrect in that NO FRESH LOCAL PURCHASE DOCUMENTS WERE MADE. (Also, Exhibit and PW-3 at Pages 121 and 122 of the Proceedings refer). On 18 June 1983, the issue had become a live one already, after initiation of ACR of PW-2 Crass on 7 June 1983 and this became a complaint by PW-1 and PW-2 to A-1; the statements of Cassius (Page 90) and Tanjore Doll (Page 214) are pertinent: A-1 had then remarked as to why these two letters had not been put up to him till then. It is in this context that complaint by PW-2, Crass to A-1 and the latter telling him that he, PW-2 as Officiating CO, should deal with it as deemed fit by him may be seen. It is in this context that PW-2 sending a courier on A-1's advice and A-2's letter should be seen. A-1 rejoined from leave on 28 June 1983 and the same day he voluntarily wrote in the Handing Over Notes that the LP of garnish needed deeper investigation. A-1 also reflected the same in the Handing Over certificate in the presence of the Commander. Evidence of PW-9, Tanjore Doll (at Page 216) is relevant. A-1 did this due to complaint by PW-2 and the two letters ibid not having been shown to him till then.

  Paras 11 and 13: A reference has been made to a DO letter and subsequent tampering with dates on documents. It is in evidence that the said DO letter was not shown to anyone at all by A-2, leave alone A-1, who was on leave then. It is also in evidence that PW-3 handed over the said DO to A-2, who asked him to amend the dates on the documents immediately. There is not even a suggestion that

A-2 consulted anyone or took time over it. 'I fail to see how anyone can see dishonest concert, when it was physically impossible for him to consult anyone'.

- Before Closing. There was a question by A-2 to Lt Col... (now A-1) in his Summary of Evidence where the latter was a Prosecution Witness:

  "*Q 56: Why did you mention in your Handing/Taking Over Certificate that the matter of LP of garnish needed deeper investigation, when you knew that the complete quantity has been physically received in the unit?*"

  On 18 June 1983, when he saw various letters, irrespective of his personal knowledge and conviction, he decided that the matter be settled once for all by further investigation. A-1 had no reason to doubt the honesty of A-2 but to settle matters finally, had suggested investigation, for which he directed a courier be sent to A-2 advising him to come back (PW-2 in Page 104). A-2 chose not to come back but sent a certificate instead.

- From all the above, it would be clear that A-1 did not share any intention, guilty or otherwise, with A-2; so no question of *concert* as per Section 34 of IPC. You may therefore be pleased to adhere to your previous finding of "NOT GUILTY" against A-1. I only wish to repeat a few points:

  - Going for LP was an honest, sincere and necessary act in view of the emergent requirement of garnish for the exercise and its non-availability in the unit; and the same was done with the verbal approval of the Commander.
  - Signing of LP documents by A-1 was an honest and sincere act and NO guilty inference should be drawn from the same.
  - The required amount of garnish was made available to the unit by A-2; the source is not

known to A-1; nor did he have any reason to doubt the statement of A-2 that the required garnish was obtained from Sphere Sales Corporation, Jalandhar.

- The required amount of garnish having been supplied, signing of contingent bills was not only an honest and genuine act, but a necessary one, as the garnish received had to be paid for.
- Letters which could have caused suspicion were never shown to A-1, till shown by PW-1 on 18 June 1983, by when the whole issue became alive after A-1 wrote the ACR of Crass, PW-2 on 07 June 1983.
- The conduct of A-1 thereafter speaks for his honesty. He would not like to comment whether documents were sent by A-2 by courier, as the facts and circumstances under which it was done were not known to him.
- The Handing Over Notes and the Handing Over Certificate of which mention has been made by PW-9, Colonel Tanjore Doll speaks volumes of the honesty of A-1.

At this stage, Counsel for A-2 requested 20 minutes for including points from my Counsel's submission which had come to him as a surprise. It was granted, which increased to 40 minutes!

Written cum Verbal Address by Counsel for A2:

Salient points from his submission are listed below:

- Before giving out his written address, he wanted to draw attention to a few points from my (counsel's) address; these were:
  - It was not open to A-1 to say now that he did not know how much garnish and from where it had come.

- Arrival of stores and signing of papers for Sphere Sales Corporation was by A-1 and here, he has denied it.
- After knowing the holdings as nil from Stock Taking board and working out the requirements, unit had gone for LP; it was not open to A-1 to deny it. (*I had NOT done so either!*) 'It is a pity that when chips are down, we tend to pass the blame to the weakest shoulders'.
- Regarding the DO and the other letter(s), it was nothing alarming and so it would have been more becoming of a CO if he had stated 'QM need not have shown me' rather than insinuating that he was on leave and in station; ...so it could have been shown...'.
- The question ibid from Summary of Evidence by A-2 to A-1, is full of pathos, which has been twisted by A-1.
- When 'the heat was on', A-2 had taken all the blame both over the telephone (on 17 June 1983) and subsequently in his Certificate dated 21 June 1983, which NO dishonest person would ever do!

He then shifted to the written address, where he pointed out that the Revision Order had laid down the following 3 questions for re-consideration by the Court:

(a) Whether in the peculiar facts and circumstances of the case, A-1 could be absolved of the culpability, if any, attached to A-2?

(b) Whether the examination of former Quarter Master Branch Subedar Head Clerk is material to the Defence?

(c) Whether the finding of GUILTY against A-2 is at all sustainable, based on the totality of evidence on record.

- Regarding Point at (a) above, there could be no separateness of, or shall we say, lack of understanding, coordination or commonality of interest or approach between the two accused, though it was not 'connivance'.
- Before commenting upon (b) and (c), he stated:
  - The same point (as my Counsel), about Sphere letterhead and the fact that it had indeed tendered.
  - Regarding amendments made to documents, it was only corrections as pointed out by Corps HQ Ordnance of incorrect dates by the clerks and was NOT 'tampering with documents'.
- Regarding Point at (b) above, the fact that former Quarter Master Branch Subedar Head Clerk being material to the Defence, he brought out a number of important (questions by me and) replies by him, as under:
  - PW-7 had reported to him that the complete quantity (approx 90,000 M) had been received; and again after receipt of sanction and before preparation of Contingent Bills etc in May 1983.
  - As ordered by A-2, he had collected 7,000 to 8,000M of LP garnish and handed over to OC, Workshop on 16/17 Dec 1982, when he had personally seen 35 to 40 bundles of LP garnish lying in the veranda of Tentage Stores.
  - In mid-Dec 1982 all the battery commanders had certified in writing that they had received all their requirements for the exercise, including LP garnish. (This was possible only if the full quantity of approx 90,000 M of LP garnish had been received).
  - On his return from casual leave, PW-3 had reported to A-2 that LP documents had been dispatched by him to Corps HQ on 19 May 1983. This would give the lie to the mischievous statement by the

same PW-3 that on 6 May 1983, he had handed over the documents to A-2 for carrying to Corps HQ!

- Quoting Prosecution's words before the Court on 12 July 1986 (at Page 182 of Proceedings) and now those of the Convening Officer in the Revision Order, he submitted that the finding of Guilty against A-2 should be revised to NOT Guilty and he should be acquitted.

- He then went on to Point at (c) above and said he wished to hit at the very crux of the charge, its gravamen being the exact quantity of the LP garnish received in the unit. *It is yet to be proved that only 19,500 M was received*! There is only one PW, No 7 whose deposition must clinch this all important issue, provided he is truthful. All his statements regarding this event have been proved false, eg,
- Detailment with vague quantity to be brought;
- Driver;
- Working Party;
- Loading;
- Collection;
- Documentation: Preparation (cooking up) of a false Voucher: NIV wherein two signatories have denied receiving anything on that NIV (!); NO item called 'Garnishing 75 MM ***Undyed Brown***' exists in Ordnance vocabulary nor authorized to a Medium Regiment (!);
- Making anachronistic entry for this Voucher of Dec 1982 in his Register after entries of 1983 (!);
- Disposal of even 3,000 M out of this 19,500 M (?) etc.
- *He has comprehensively proved himself to be a false and unreliable witness, who has shamefully perjured to save*

himself from not maintaining an account for 87,000 M of LP garnish brought and distributed by him.

He summed up by stating:

- *The deposition of PW 7 falls to the ground and the entire Prosecution case falls with it.*
- *The agony, humiliation, expense and setback to their careers by these two honest, upright and hardworking officers over the last 3 ½ years that this case has dragged on, can never be adequately compensated.*
- *It is quite obvious that this is a case of monumental betrayal, disloyalty on the part of some of their colleagues and subordinates who shamelessly contrived to stoop low to contrive minor procedural infirmities resorted to in the bona fide procurement of a vitally important and urgently required item for use, after these officers were not on the scene.*
- *Members of this Hon'ble Court with their vast experience of men and matters caught in the whirlpool of similar situations will, no doubt, see through their game and vindicate the honour of these senior officers with brilliant and unblemished record of service, with an acquittal.*

The Court was adjourned till 10 Nov 1986.

On re-assembly, the Court found that *both the Defence Counsels as well as Defending Officers were not present*. Both accused persons submitted separately that they have gone with their concurrence and the Court could proceed in their absence. It would be appropriate for me to refresh the minds of the readers regarding Para 198 on Page 77 of 'The Notes on Indian Military and Air Force Law' which states clearly:

"**REVISION**

198. *Should be sparingly used*, as a rule, only with a view to correction of minor errors in the finding and sentence.

Instead of Revision, partial confirmation can often be resorted to."

Now back to the proceedings.

Additional Summing up by the JA

'...I shall, therefore, endeavour *to clarify certain points raised by the defence counsels in their addresses only,* that too in brief to assist you to arrive at a just decision....' (*That is EXACTLY what he* ***did not*** *do, but brought in extraneous matters*.)

- He first read out Army Act Section 160 on Revision of finding or sentence and Army Rule 68 on Revision; interestingly, Note (i) to this Army Rule enables revision of finding of acquittal!
- He then went on to explain '*Value of Extracts of S of E on the Record of GCM Proceedings*' and covered the following:
  - At the S of E, a person makes an unsworn statement. At the trial stage, his previous written statement is used to contradict him during cross examination. Therefore the statement of a witness at the S of E can be brought on record, ONLY during his cross examination, i.e., unless the witness is examined in the Court, his statement cannot be brought on record.
  - In the instant case, Prosecution has admitted ...the question and answer to/from former Quarter Master Subedar Head Clerk:

    Q: *"Are you aware that Contingent Bills, Certified Receipt Vouchers and other correspondence were prepared AFTER the entire stock of stores were physically received in the unit?"*

    He had replied: *"In May 1983, I had checked up with Subedar Never-loyal if the entire quantity of scrim garnish as per the six sets of Local Purchase documents had been received. And, on his confirmation of receipt of Local Purchase garnish, I instructed Lance Naik (...PW-5) to prepare the Certified Receipt Vouchers, Contingent Bills and other connected documents".*

- This admission of the Prosecution had come on record under special circumstances. It is not evidence and you cannot base your finding on it...It can only be used to judge the credibility of the statement of Subedar Never-loyal, PW-7. *Considering the normal and possible conduct of ordinary prudent person under the circumstances, you should see whether former Quarter Master Branch Subedar Head Clerk (not examined) was a link in the chain of preparation of documents...and whether or not he would have had a motive to make a statement exculpating his action/participation, more so when the statement was made without the sanctity of oath or affirmation.* ...(JA then went on to justify all statements of PW-7, the most unreliable witness, as you, dear readers, would have seen right through!)

- Next, he went on to '*Addresses of Counsels*' and stated:
  - Addresses of Counsels are not evidence. These are their interpretations of facts which deserve your careful consideration...you must exclude extraneous facts.
  - Defence Counsel for A-1 has correctly pointed out that LP documents were not made afresh. Only covering letter was changed.
- Next, he stated the obvious: based on fresh evidence taken now, addresses of Defence Counsels, JA's additional summing up, complete proceedings and evidence on record and the reasons given by the Confirming officer in the Revision Order, *court **should** arrive at its **fresh finding in respect of both.*** (This is like dictating to the Court that they ought to arrive at a fresh finding!)

- JA then went on to re-iterate some selected evidence; such as:
  - Sphere was not a tenderer; but the Court may see if a clerical error was possible regarding the Letterhead! (*How stupid one can get?*) He then re-iterated 'knowing that only 19,500 M was supplied, the accused together had submitted the contingent bills for the purchase of 87,000 M!
  - PW-3 stated *A-2 had brought the sanction* (a lie, as PW-3 never stated this) in May 1983 and he prepared and handed over the 6 sets to A-2 on 6 May 1983....Obviously documents were signed between 6 and 24 May 1983...A-1 was on leave from 29 Apr 1983; defence contention is 5 May 1983. ...he was on leave during 6 to 24 May 1983. Where was the need for A-1 to sign backdated?... Why PW-2, Crass was not told in handing over when A-1 went on leave?.. Was it an honest act or...that...DDOS would forward the documents to CDA? Based on this you should conclude whether A-1 and A-2 maintained complete secrecy. The fact that this came to limelight only on receipt of the DO letter in May/June 1983 due to the absence of both A-1 and A-2. (*How much more stupid can a JA get? He does not know anything about the events or even the evidence on record*).
  - Contention of A-1 for having mentioned the need for deeper investigation in his Handing Over Notes to Tanjore Doll, PW-9: was it genuine or for gaining sympathy?
  - JA, once again without knowing or having studied all the evidence on record, then went on about the 54,500 M of garnish received on 22 Nov 1982 and 19,500 having been issued from LP and NO OTHER ISSUES HAVING BEEN MADE. (*Even a dimwit would have known after even a cursory study of*

the Proceedings that two nets [totally unauthorized] per vehicle/gun had been ordered and as to how much garnish would be needed for 235 nets of 10.7x 6 M, as worked out in detail and shown by us. There had been appreciation during the exercise, for camouflage and concealment, ONLY for my Regt!)

- He then pointed out: on the one hand Defence indicated LP of 87,000 M was emergent and on the other had loaned 15,000 M to Brigade and 7,000 M to DW-14. (*One more lack of total understanding by the JA, who had not followed the entire evidence. That is exactly the reason and proof that when there was no garnish in the Regt from 25 Nov 1982, how could we have loaned this quantity.* Also, what loaned was NOT 15,000 M **but** *68 knitted nets with* ***at least*** *40,120 M of garnish*!)
  - While Counsel for A-1 explained how bona fide the actions by A-1 were who signed documents put up by A-2, without even knowing where the stores had come from, Counsel for A-2, on the other hand argued it was joint. *"Both of them must swim together or sink together"* were his words. (It was totally illegal for JA to draw attention to Addresses by the Defence Counsels, as he had himself stated right at the beginning of his additional summing up a while earlier that *Addresses of Counsels are not evidence*!)
  - Intention, individual or common is not subject of positive proof. It must be judged from the proved acts of the accused and from the circumstances of the case.
- He then told the Court that they should now decide:
  - Whether or not there existed a common intention between the accused persons.
  - Whether or not the action of both were within the scope of the charter of duties, responsibilities and

powers in the furtherance of common intention between them. He repeated the words of Counsel for A-2 **once again**: *"Both of them must swim together or sink together". MOST UNETHICAL FOR A JA TO DO SUCH A THING, WHO IS SUPPOSED TO BE IMPARTIAL AND ONLY DO THE ACTS AS MENTIONED IN ARMY ACT 160 AND THE REVISION ORDER, THAT HE HIMSELF HAD READ OUT A LITTLE WHILE EARLIER.* He then explained convenient portions of selected evidence to show common intention.

(Yes, Major..., A-2 and I did have a common intention and that was a genuine one: just to ensure that the Regt got the required quantity of garnish in time for the exercise to knit and carry the unauthorized two nets each.)

-Next, he explained 'good faith' which is defined NEGATIVELY in Section 52 of Indian Penal Code as: *"Nothing is said to be done in good faith, which is done or believed without due care or attention"*; and followed it up with definitions of *'Proved'*, *'Disproved'* and *'Not proved'* . *'Absolute certainty is rarely obtainable in judicial proceedings and neither is required by law. The degree of certainty upon which you as prudent men of the world would act is alone required of you....If you have the degree of certainty... you should convict ....if there exists any reasonable doubt, ...prosecution has failed to establish the case and the accused person(s) is/are entitled to an acquittal as a matter of right'*.

(His entire summing up reminds me of a small anecdote from Tamil: People were at a feast and were praising the cook and were about to partake a sweet dish *'payasam'*. Just then the chef entered and said loudly: *'I must tell you this. When I was making the payasam, a small house lizard fell into it; but I removed it immediately. So you can enjoy it without any hitch'*! Would anyone have continued eating it? That is what the JA's aim was: to poison the minds of the Court!)

Against the spirit of Army Rule 105(8) and despite a clear direction in the Revision Order that: *"if it becomes necessary to clarify any points raised by the Accused,* the JA may give a further summing up", he exceeded his brief on 10 Nov 1986, plainly to support the stand of his two superior officers in Judge Advocate General's Branch who had written the 2 Reports on Applications for Trial for my Joint Trial after 2 Summaries of Evidence, and made a lengthy 3 hour summing up! At one place, he stated: 'addresses of the counsel are NOT evidence', but within a few minutes quoted verbatim, bits and pieces of the address by Counsel for Accused 2, his erstwhile Reviewing Officer: the former Judge Advocate General himself, NO less, to say, *'both must swim together or sink together"* but did not include it in his written one! He also added a fresh point about 'secrecy' by me in not mentioning the LP details in my Handing Over Notes to Major Crass, before my annual leave; I had already brought on record more than ample evidence about the 'openness' of this LP by 11 different witnesses : 7 by the Prosecution Witness and 4 by Defence Witnesses!

The irony is that there is NO provision in the military law, for the accused to rebut anything wrong or motivated or malicious/ tendentious in Prosecution and JA's closing addresses or Additional Summing up by the JA during Revision!

The Court then closed for deliberations for JUST 55 MINUTES! What was the way out with the Court, who, in any case were ambitious officers like everyone else and were locally and directly under the watchful eyes of HQ...Corps, except to punish me also? So, the very same Court, who, after examining 10 Prosecution Witnesses and 14 Defence Witnesses over 120 days, many times sitting beyond 6 hours per day and beyond 6 p.m. (under Army Rule 81, in the *'interest of justice and discipline'*) had found me "NOT GUILTY", now found me also GUILTY after just two days' hearing of statements by 2 witnesses for less than a total of an hour and deliberations for less than an hour now.

But the court did take 1 hour 55 minutes of deliberations to decide the extent of my punishment and then sentenced me to a very minor punishment! *For this, I need not have waited and wasted 5 precious years of my life and career; and undergone all the humiliation, but if left unchallenged, it would seal my career once for all.*

"Whether 'tis nobler in the mind to suffer
The Slings and Arrows of outrageous Fortune
Or to take arms against a sea of troubles,
And by opposing, end them."
– William Shakespeare (Hamlet)

On 29 Nov 1986, I sent a detailed 64-page 'Pre–Confirmation Petition' to Chief of Army Staff, through the General Officer Commanding in Chief, Western Command, pointing out the flaws in the entire justice system. Brief of this is Annexure 8. No action was taken for the next 7 months.

So, on 5 June 1987, frustrated by this inordinate delay, I sent a brief Demi Official letter of just 8 pages (which was even a much shorter gist than Annexure 8) and 2 enclosures (*one of them with two passport size photographs of myself as in May 1983 and June 1987*) to Chief of Army Staff. I came to know later in Feb 1988 that Chief of Army Staff had remarked in red on this Demi Official letter, for speedy discussion by the Complaint Advisory Board and Discipline and Vigilance Directorate at AG's Branch!

In mid-Jan 1988, Chief of Staff ... Corps, who had signed the Revision Order as Officiating General Officer Commanding and was proceeding as General Officer Commanding of another Corps, enquired from me at the golf course, if I was aware of any progress in my case and showed concern (for the first time, in person) about my health, daughters etc! I expressed surprise that he should ask me! He just smiled. That showed me some light at the end of the tunnel!

At about 6 p.m. on 12 Feb 1988, I received a call at the public telephone in the Golf Course from a friend in the

Discipline and Vigilance Directorate that "**Chief of Army Staff *has NOT confirmed the Proceedings*"**. He also advised me that I should reach Delhi at the earliest; get the pending promotion to a Colonel and a compassionate posting and move on in life!

Birds sing after a storm; why shouldn't people feel as free to delight in whatever sunlight remains to them?

– Rose Kennedy (wife of Joseph Patrick Kennedy Sr.)

CHAPTER 10

AFTER-EFFECTS

I do an MBA Course and Stand First in the University

During 1984 and 1987, there was a lot of time at hand with me, between the various courts martial and summaries of evidence; so I had taken up the three-year MBA contact-cum-correspondence course for armed forces officers, which involved attending contact programmes at the university twice a year: once for 14 days and another time for 42 days. This contact programme period is treated as duty under Government of India orders, which allowed a total of six months in service. Being under a disciplinary ban, my leave was highly restricted; but I thought there should be no objection to my attending the MBA course, which was treated as duty and was in a military station close by: Patiala! I did not approach the Corps HQ with so many *'well wishers'* there, but the Command. Friends in Command and Army HQ interpreted it the same way as I did; and helped me; how very kind of them: *there are some noble souls after all, just as there are many who are not so*! In fact, Discipline and Vigilance Directorate issued an attachment order for me to a unit in Patiala for those durations! (Funnily, my

Commander during the first GCM also passed the Entrance Examination in 1985 alongside me; but I had to postpone it by a year due to the disciplinary proceedings intervening!) I completed it during 1986-1989 and got a First Class and the University Gold Medal for standing first, from the hands of General OP Malhotra, then Governor of Punjab in 1991 (when I was Brigadier)!

I get promoted first as a Colonel and then as a Brigadier

One day my fate was hanging in balance tilting towards 'ten years imprisonment' (the maximum punishment for *Intent to Defraud*) and the next day, I got a long pending (since Apr 1984) promotion to a Colonel and a prestigious posting to Defence Services Staff College, Wellington (Tamilnadu) as Instructor! I reported on 18 Mar 1988; and in Apr 1988, I moved the daughters under my care in Wellington, despite the elder one having to reappear in all the First Year's papers for her B Com along with those of the Second Year! She was happy that at least 'the family' (though without my wife) could be together at one place; this was just a very small price to pay, she had said.

On 16 Aug 1988, I got a letter from Military Secretary's (MS) Branch, Army HQ that I had been graded *'Defer'* for promotion to next rank of Brigadier for want of sufficient reports in the rank of Colonel by a Board held in May 1988! Was it my fault? But what to do but wait.

In Oct 1989, I got a Demi Official letter from a Brigadier in MS Branch informing me that I am approved to be a Brig by a Board, as a "First Review Case" (which indicated I had missed it with my batchmates of 1962, in original consideration)! Some questions rankled in my mind:

- *When I had earned NO reports in a Colonel's rank till 1 Sep 1988 (and the next in Sep 1989 was still on its way, up the channel), how could I be a Review Case?*
- *When was the Board that made me a "Reject" held?*
- *Why wasn't I informed then?*

There is many a Slip between the Shoulder and the Pip!

I learnt informally from a friend in MS Branch that it had been in July 1988. Obviously I could have earned NO report in the two months period between those two boards (May and July 1988), when 1 Sep is the due date for ACR **and** a minimum of 90 days physical service under the Initiating Officer is warranted, after I came in from the cold! After the last ACR as a Lt Col in May 1983 (which Scraggly wrote twice on 15 and 16 June 1983), the first one due was only on 1 Sep 1988, which I had got, but my name had been placed before *this Board in July 1988*!

As advised by the same friend, I submitted a Statutory Complaint. No reply was received, but friends advised me not to waste the opportunity but to grab the promotion and move, instead of fighting on and staying as a Colonel! There was a lot of merit in it and so, I moved as a Brigadier to Jammu & Kashmir in Dec 1989; but the girls had to stay back till final exams in Apr/May 1990 (Class 10)/(B-Com); as I did not want a third migration for the elder daughter for her degree. But, another separation for us and so soon; how sad. Earlier, I had to leave them alone on two occasions to attend the contact programme for MBA in July 1988 and July 1989; (I missed the shorter contact programmes in Mar 1988 and Mar 1989). I thought I would move them with me in 1990; but that was not to be, as the elder girl Anu, wanted to pursue Chartered Accountancy once the results came out and that would not have been possible in those troubled times in J & K.

I got only 10 days leave in May 1990, for the whole year due to 'Operation TOPAC' by Pakistan; I visited the children in Wellington and shifted them back with my in-laws at Bangalore, before returning. In July 1990, Vandana (aka Anu) passed B Com in First Class and stood first in Bharathiar University, Coimbatore; but was not eligible for the prize, as she had 'migrated' from elsewhere after first year! I arranged for her Chartered Accountancy in Bangalore itself; but I took Vinita, who got a first class in Class 10, to do her class 11 in a Kendriya Vidyalaya close by, in troubled J & K! *That was yet another stupid decision by me,* as subsequently when she did class 12 from Bangalore, Government of Karnataka had insisted on presence for both Classes 11 and 12 in Karnataka, for her to be eligible for Army quota in MBBS. Thus despite 98.8 % in the three required subjects (Physics, Chemistry and Biology) she could not get a seat for MBBS! She joined B Sc (Microbiology), due to her father's folly (of affection)!

On 7 Nov 1990, one year after my complaint, I got a letter from Government of India, that my statutory complaint was rejected as *"no injustice has been done"*! It was not a speaking order, just as no Government letters ever are; and no reasons were mentioned!

On 1 Feb 1991, I wrote a Demi Official letter to Chief of Army Staff, who was also the Senior Colonel Commandant of Artillery, responsible for welfare of Gunners. Unfortunately, the reply was drafted by the same person, who had committed the mistake of placing my name before a Board in July 1988 (within 60 days of having been graded *'Defer'* by the May 1988 Board **and** without my having earned a report as required). So what justice would I get, even if it was the Chief whom I had addressed? *Yet another grave mistake by me.* On 24 Mar 1991, I received a reply from Senior Civilian Staff Officer on behalf of COAS. My fears came true; the former only justified his actions! So, I decided to seek an interview with the Military Secretary, to 'exhaust all available remedies' within the Army and if still unsuccessful, file a Writ petition in J&K High Court at Jammu!

MS Interview and Writ Petition

On 5 June 1991, I met the MS in an Interview to put forward two requests: fixation of my correct seniority for a Brigadier so that I did not miss out further promotions and a compassionate posting to Bangalore, *except in Recruiting,* as it was a stressful job with dozens of frivolous anonymous letters floating right up to the President and PM and being passed down for comments or even investigations sometimes! MS gave me a patient hearing and said that he could not help me with the seniority as a Brigadier, as it was a Government decision; but he would certainly post me to Bangalore when a vacancy arose and he could not forecast where it would be; *if I wanted Bangalore I couldn't be choosey about the appointment*!

(I must share something interesting with you: the same MS who is settled in Bangalore after retirement, told me in Feb 1995, before I retired that I should never have chosen the Courts-route, as the Ministry and the civilian officers in MS Branch dealing with higher promotions of Army 'frown' on it. I asked him two simple questions: why then did he not tell me this on 5 June 1991, even informally, he being from my own alma mater, though 7 years senior? What other avenue did I have? He had no answer! But I do not hold it against him, as he obviously would have had his reasons.)

Thus finally having exhausted all the avenues open for redressal within the Army and the Government, I filed a writ petition regarding fixing of correct seniority for promotion, in J & K High Court, in June 1991: *another big mistake, this time on the place*: the lawyers there were frequently on strike! I would be 2500 KM away at Bangalore, when the hearings take place! But what to do? *It may sound a paradox to any reader that an officer who suffered for five years in so many courts martial in so many places did not move the Courts but now does so for his promotion. The logic is simple: I had to exhaust all available avenues within Service first, before knocking at the doors of a court!*

I was in Bangalore, Fighting a Seesaw Legal Battle in J & K High Court

My Writ petition was admitted, as WP .../91 in Aug 1991 and notice was issued to the opposite parties. In end-Feb 1992, I moved to Bangalore on posting. The first hearing came up on 11 May 1992 and the Government counsel wanted two months for reply. On 28 Aug 1992, the case was listed; but there was total 'bandh' in Jammu! However, Court directed listing in 2 weeks! But, objections were filed by Government only in Oct 1992.

The case was listed again on 12 Nov 1992 but Government counsel had just changed; so another six weeks' delay! On 9 Feb 1993, two months for Counter and one for Rejoinder were directed by the HC. A mention was also made for early hearing; still it didn't come up!

As No 1 Selection Board to decide on Major Generals was due from 19-23 Apr, I submitted on 8 Apr 1993, an application to the HC for speedy hearing. The case got listed only on 16 July 1993; but didn't come up whole day!

On 19 July 1993, Anu (Vandana) got *16th All-India rank in CA (Finals)* but funnily had to wait for three more months of 'Article-ship' till Sep 1993 to get her Certification! She began getting congratulations and dozens of offers for employment from many!

The case came up at Serial No 1 before Justice RP Sethi on 27 July 1993; but there was another strike by lawyers! I volunteered to argue my own case, but there was NO Government counsel! On 16 Aug 1993, it was listed before Justice AM Mir; but Government counsel was committed elsewhere. So it was not taken up!

Getting restless, I requested my lawyer to file a CMP (2331/1993) on 23 Aug 1993 for direction to Government to consider me in No 1 Selection Board (for Major Generals) due on 17 Sep 1993, at least along with officers of 1963 seniority, with inter-se seniority to be sorted out later. CMP was listed in Serial 8 of Supplementary List 2 days later; but did not come up! Two more days later, on 27th, it was listed at Serial 1 in Supplementary List before Justice RP Sethi; I appeared in the absence of my counsel! He directed listing on 30 Aug 1993 with the Main Petition .../1991, as Government counsel sought 24 hours more! The next day, objections were filed by Respondents; but they were willing to consider in No 1 SB in Sep 1993, also averring that there had been NO delay on their part! Justice RP Sethi directed on 30 Aug 1993, consideration of my name *"along with... batchmates of 1962 (backlog/fresh cases)"*. He also directed the Registry to *"expedite the hearing of the Main Petition"*. To my bad luck, he moved soon as Chief Justice of another High Court, leaving the case "part-heard"!

In Sep 1993, Vandana (Anu) became a full fledged CA and wanted to join ISEC (ICICI Securities) at Bombay. I was reluctant but let her go for the interview. She was selected and was asked to join as a Management Trainee (MT) for a year, on 19 Nov 1993. On 18 Nov 1993, we saw her off to Bombay. As I couldn't afford a telephone with STD even as a serving Brigadier, nor was one authorized by the Government, I got to speak to her once a week on Saturdays, very early in the morning through army channels via Madras and Pune! Communication was not very good, but at least we could shout and assume the other heard it and all was well at both ends! I heard frequent reports from her bosses who visited Bangalore from time to time that she was doing extremely well and was slated to go for training abroad, after her training there was over in Nov 1994 or soon thereafter.

In June 1994, my lawyer in Jammu got elevated as a Judge in a High Court, the youngest so far in Indian judicial history! His younger brother, another lawyer would represent me in future!

During a visit to Delhi in July 1994, I learnt from a friend in MS branch, that I stood approved by No 1 Selection Board for a Major General (with 1963 batch and not my own 1962 Batch) but the case was shuttling between Military Secretary and the Government, as Ministry of Defence was not keen to promote an officer with a *'blemish'*. *I could not understand the ways of the Babus (I am sure, no one does!)* : when I had been cleared of the case and could pick up two ranks and now have been found acceptable by a Board consisting of the seven senior most Generals of the Army, where was the hitch? He advised me to file a case in any High Court to get the result declared! On 19 July 1994, I filed another Civil Miscellaneous Petition (CMP) for result to be declared. It came up before Justice VK Gupta on 5 Aug 1994; he ordered that *'the result in a sealed envelop will be delivered to the Court in 10 days'*. On 10 Aug 1994, results were made public but not my name, as it was sub judice!

On 24 Aug 1994, Original Writ Petition (OWP) was listed before Justice BA Khan, but as Government counsel was not available, it was not heard! In Sep 1994, Respondents filed objections to CMP stating that 'directions of 5 Aug of the Court were received by the MS only on 16 Aug; and as the date has expired, the matter may be dropped'!

I lose my Daughter and withdraw my Writ Petition

On 1 Oct 1994, Vandana passed away at a young age of 24, in a traffic accident at Haji Ali Circle, Bombay. *What more sufferings could I bear*? I was now more worried about Vinita, who needed parental care. What was the use of fighting for a promotion, if I was going to be separated from my only daughter, as I would surely be moved to a non-family station? I discussed my problem with the Adjutant General, who was an old friend and said I wanted to seek premature retirement; he advised me not to do so, but promised help, provided I applied for continued retention in Bangalore. I was aware, having served in MS Branch that I would have to give an 'Adverse Career Certificate' for such a retention (meaning: I was willing to *seal my fate against further promotions*), along with that application! I did so. Within a few days, I decided also to withdraw my Petition, but friends and well wishers advised me against it. So, on 15 Nov 1994, I made one last trip to Jammu to see if I could pursue my Writ Petition within a reasonable time but only met with yet another hartal/strike/bandh, whatever by the lawyers! I requested my lawyer to withdraw my Original Writ Petition. As I heard nothing from him for four months, and in view of the Adverse Career Certificate given by me to MS Branch for retention in Bangalore, reminded him on 24 Mar 1995 to withdraw my WP.

On 19 Apr 1995, it was withdrawn and HC *'dismissed it as withdrawn'*. I informed the MS Branch as I felt it was my duty to do so. In any case, having submitted an adverse career certificate, I was not looking forward to any promotion now.

In May 1995, Vinita decided to do MA in Social Work from Tata Institute of Social Sciences, Bombay and was successful in the Entrance Exam and Interview; and she joined the 2-year course! In Sep 1995, I collected her "gold" medals when she has stood first, from the university in all subjects. What 'Gold'; the university gave just Rs 100 per subject and neither gold nor any medal, with a promise to send a Certificate each, which hasn't reached us in 13 years!

I Retire Peacefully

I was left alone in Bangalore, and soon to retire! That day arrived and on 30 Nov 1995, I retired peacefully and settled in my own flat.

CHAPTER 11 SOME LESSONS THAT I HAD LEARNT

1. **I Should Not Have Taken Over My Regiment's Command:** Though I had been offered by the higher ups to stay as a Lieutenant Colonel on promotion at Army HQ, with a promise to take over command of my own parent Regiment, I should have declined it and moved out on promotion in Aug/Sep 1979, to any other Regiment or I should have at least done so, when it was decided in Apr 1980 that my Regt would come to Dundahera Camp, near Delhi under a normal Relief Programme. My five continuous years at Delhi/close by had caused jealousy in many. Even after taking over my Regt in Nov 1980, I should have sought a move out, once when Director General Artillery had called to tell me in late June 1981 that Scraggly would shortly arrive as my new Brigade Commander! If I had said so, the General could have moved me by Sep/Oct 1981. Well, as they say, who knows what Fate has in store!
2. **I Ought to Have Been a Good Judge of Human Beings or Listened to Those Who Were:** Despite

knowing Major Crass for 7 years and Scraggly for 5 years and their nature, I failed to judge them and their process of thinking. If Crass (on 28 June 1983) and Scraggly (in Nov 1983, as told to me by a common friend) were 'willing' to close the case after an apology from me, I should have known their minds earlier. I had had enough warnings from my late wife about Crass, which I had ignored only at my peril. The first ACR from Scraggly had lulled me from being alive to his ways.

3. **Planning of Annual Leave Prior to Posting/Course:** Knowing that Scraggly had been waiting to 'catch' me right from 1981 and Crass had developed animosity, ill-will and rancour from 15 Mar 1983 (through 9 and 22 Apr 1983, 7 and 11-12 June 1983), I should have planned my leave from mid-Mar to mid-May 1983, to have been present in the Regt for at least 6 weeks before proceeding on the Course. This would have ensured that there was no loose talk, developing into 'doubts' in some minds that something must have been wrong in the innocuous deal for local purchase of garnish. Or irrespective of the back-ache, I should have rejoined voluntarily from leave on or about 15/16 June 1983, when I had made two trips to Brigade HQ at Meerut. Or I should not have been ambitious for the Course but withdrawn voluntarily citing personal reasons, even on 18 June 1983 and sorted this matter out once for all, as Army HQ would have needed at least a month to issue a new posting for me. Yes I might have lost out on the Course; but not on my honour for those 5 years!

4. **Trusting beyond Limits:** Despite seeing at Army HQ, his below average ACR in character qualities for two continuous years, I had placed absolute trust in Crass and continued to have it, in spite of hints from many to the contrary. I should have nipped his attempts at canards at the bud.

5. **Ensuring Publication/Retention of Certain Documents:** The instances were many:

   a. While the message-log on appreciation by General Officer Commanding of the Armoured Division to my Regt for excellent camouflage and concealment during Exercise Dig Vijay was classified being part of the exercise documents and was destroyed, I could have published a Special Part One order of my Regt the same day, congratulating them for this achievement, which would have stayed in the records! Similarly, I should have insisted on the Commander/staff for the compliment he had paid for physical efficiency.

   b. Similarly, I should have ensured that the minutes of the conferences at Brigade HQ had included both: my expressing difficulties on getting garnish and Scraggly not only suggesting local purchase but volunteering to speak to his batchmate at Corps HQ, the sanctioning authority.

   c. I should have photocopied my first ACR by Scraggly on 15 June 1983 (though it would have been a mean act) so that when he wrote again and I signed again on 16 June 1983, it would have proved his evil intentions.

   d. When commencement of my leave was delayed till 5 May 1983, I should not only have got the Regimental Part 1 Order regarding assumption of command by Crass amended, but I should have also sent a letter to Brigade HQ seeking an amendment of dates as 5 May-27 June 1983. I could and should have done it in person even on 15/16 June 1983, when I had gone to Brigade HQ.

   e. The Regimental Police Gate Register and the Message Log Book containing the details of the working party; the Board Proceedings of the

Stock Opening Board for Dec 1982 etc ought to have been impounded and called for during my very first Summary of Evidence.

f. **I Should have Rejoined from Leave Voluntarily on One of These Occasions:**

Irrespective of back-ache, I should have done so on any of the following dates:

- Having seen Crass' mischievous writing on two signals on 11/12 June 1983.
- After he had acted funny about recall of QM on 18 June 1983, while he had himself told me the previous day over the telephone that he had satisfied himself and that any point remaining could be clarified on QM's rejoining.
- Or even on 25 June 1983, after the Promotion Conference when he was not recalling QM himself but telling me.
- Or on 27 June 1983, after Rabbi had visited me on 26 June 1983, in my new flat and sown a doubt.
- Or even that very night, prior to my Bara Khana, when the pseudonymous letter had arrived.

6. **Recall of QM:** This again had not been handled well by me. I should have stopped him on 17 June myself or ordered Crass to do so, when there had been long telephone calls to me from him and Crass. I could have insisted on 18 or 25 June 1983. I did not do it as I didn't want to impinge on Crass' powers as officiating CO. I did it only on 27 June at the Bara Khana when the Bde letter with pseudonymous letter had arrived.

7. **Welfare and Facilities for Officers:** I had probably 'pampered' my officers by giving them a vehicle to

commute daily to and fro Delhi/the Regt and by excusing Games/PT on alternate days, so that they could work from 6 a.m. to 2 p.m. on 3 days a week and 8 a.m. to 6 p.m. on the remaining 3 days, as they had all just arrived from a field/non-family area. This way I was probably taken to be weak and soft, despite a tough exterior on parade.

8. **Not Calling on Scraggly etc:** Much against the customs and social norms of the Army, I had not called on Scraggly and wife, with my wife. I had even sent him the bills for the *'atta'* and eggs he had taken; may be he had genuinely intended to send the money subsequently. All these probably were incorrect acts, which aggravated his vengeful spirit!

9. **I Should NOT Have Retained Crass as 2IC At All:** Having had endless experience of his immaturity, I should have got him moved out the moment he was passed over finally.

10. **Strictly Following ACR Norms:** I could have ignored them and graded all Majors as Above Average, thus playing safe. Well, it was not in my blood either to grade to please or to disobey instructions from Army HQ.

11. **Premature Retirement:** I probably should have stuck to my decision to seek premature retirement with 20 years service and at age 40+, in Aug 1982, despite pressure from my wife and advice from her brother!

EPILOGUE

ABOUT MYSELF AND THIS BOOK

Getting into the series of trials was, to me, plunging with boulders tied to both my ankles right into the depths of a marsh! The humiliation was beyond the painful: pulling a tooth without pain killer would have been easier! As I lost my wife too almost at the same time as the start of this long and painful saga, real friends became harder to find and most doors of social circuit were banged shut on my face! Once it was over, I felt relieved at being spared the ordeal any longer, more than the thrill of getting out free. I must request you to bear with so many details in the narrative; but those are essential to understand the agony I was put through for 5 long years, and while I had NOT delayed the proceedings nor moved a Court.

A number of my friends and relatives have said that any lesser man would have *either gone mad or committed suicide or absconded,* for all the tragedies suffered and the trials and tribulations heaped on me over those five years. But what then about both my motherless minor daughters? That thought and the strong will to vindicate myself were the motivators to fight back. Today this saga reminds me of Norman Vincent Peale's anecdote. He once asked his huge audience: '*Do you have any problems*?' Everyone raised hands. He then asked them: '*How many of you would like to solve your problems?*' Again every one raised hands. His next question was: '*On my way here, there was a place where I saw some people were relaxed and had no problems; how many would want to be like them?*' Again all hands went up. Now he said: '*A little distance from here is a cemetery, and these people with no problems at all are there, at peace with the world. How many would like to be so?'* NO hands went up now! He then said: ***'Problems are a sign of life. As long as you live, you will have problems. The day you don't have them, you are dead**!'*

Why did I delay writing this thus far? The idea did strike me in 1988 but I had to pick up the threads of my life as well as career. By then, professionally, I was left way behind in the 'rat race' as it were; so had to work harder, leaving no time for anything else. Successive personal tragedies in life delayed it. One General asked me even when I was serving, to write it, to benefit posterity and the Army itself. I argued with him that it would be taken as mud-slinging. After being goaded by him more than once, I finally began 25 years later, using verbatim notes taken down by me in 'my own shorthand' during the trials; and the phenomenal memory my parents have injected in my genes! My late elder girl, Vandana, aka Anu had helped me in re-writing in full-hand from my 'shorthand' notes and in typing out! There were other catalysts too: Lieutenant General Raj Kadyan a batch-mate; and, of course my (younger) daughter, Vinita, who was under 8 when it all started but is now a committed social worker and a young mother!

I wish to assure you that it was no fun writing this, as old wounds were pierced repeatedly; but stoicism was my lodestar, so that others benefit. I believe that not only I am the only officer to have faced 4 Summaries of Evidence (including QM's), 4 Courts Martial and a Revision, over 5 years in 3 stations, for a single allegation and to have come out unscathed but also to have got 2 more promotions! *I believe my case is a case study in Judge Advocate General's Branch for new inductees*!

Serving any nation through its army is a noble profession; and serving the Indian Army is the noblest of them all. Whatever little I have achieved in life: a gold medal in MBA and a University first in M Sc (Defence), both while serving; and after retirement, modelling assignments in the print media and consultancy as HR and Interviewing Professional:

all of them, I owe it to the Great Indian Army. How can I forget all the humour and poignancy I experienced in my 35 years in uniform that today gives me the ingredients for writing Middles in *Deccan Herald* and *The Tribune* regularly!

Now, about the Others

Scraggly: Hoodwinking the system further, he rose to be a Major General.

Rabbi: Last known to be working in a dubious financial company in Central India.

Shifty Eyes: Rose to be a Major General and now settled in Delhi.

Tanjore Doll: Did invite me for the wedding of one of his sons. He retired in 1990. During the Silver Jubilee of my Regiment in 1991, we had stood shoulder to shoulder, receiving the guests. We did speak about how the whole thing was a trumped up case; was totally avoidable and how he too had fallen into the machinations of Crass; but that could not have come into this book. I heard he is now doing a noble job for the physically challenged in his home state. I wish him best of luck.

Crass: Had reached his ceiling even while serving with me. When I was at a military station in Mar 1989 with a special train full of Staff College student-officers, he and his wife tried their best to meet me; but I avoided them like plague, throughout those two days. Good luck to them, wherever they are.

Cassius: Became a time scale Lt Col and retired. Was breeding dogs and selling them, even while in service. I learnt recently that unfortunately he and wife have been afflicted with paralysis and are recovering. I wish them good health and luck.

Today, I do not carry any ill-will against any of them and that is the truth. At the same time, I do not wish to meet any of these 5, ever: Scraggly; Rabbi; Shifty Eyes; Crass and Cassius, as my trust in them has evaporated like alcohol over a flame! I do follow the advice given to me the moment I came out unscathed, by many friends in very senior ranks; one I remember very distinctly *"Do not harbour any ill-feelings towards those who tried to harm you. Let the past be past...Rise like a Phoenix from the ashes; I am sure you will"*. When I retired, a number of very senior officers wrote to me saying: *'While every one does have his share of problems in life, God has been unduly unkind to you, such a bright, straight-forward and honest man; else you would have risen far higher'* etc. That was heart-warming but just a consolation.

Subedar Head Clerk of Quarter Master Branch: Had probably gone away to Middle East, after giving evidence in our Summaries of Evidence. I got a real surprise, when in 1992, I got an air mail letter from him out of the blue, congratulating me for coming out of the clouds and rising to be a Brigadier; (obviously he had read my name in a news report on a Recruitment Rally in Kerala in the *'Khaleej Times'*). I wanted to write back and thank him, but no idea of his address or where he is now.

My Adjutant: *'The man who knew too much'*, rose to be CO of the same Regt, (when he 'dined me out') and later, a Brigadier. After a brief stint in a private firm, has moved to home station, Amritsar. He, his wife and daughters keep in touch with me regularly with New Year Cards and invitations for major events and telephone calls.

All Others in the Regiment: Officers, both of my time and later, keep in touch regularly by e-mails, telephone calls and greeting cards! Some officers, JCOs and men came all the way to attend the wedding of Vinita in 2001! They approach me for any advice they need! The men do call or meet me when any of them comes to Bangalore. *I do visit the Regiment often too*. They are indeed very kind and hospitable to me, even though not even 1% of them had been there when I had commanded 25-28 years ago!

That is what is great about the Indian Army, which is the cause of envy of all other non-uniformed services!

ANNEXURES

ANNEXURE 1: ORGANISATION OF INDIAN ARMY (IN OUTLINE)

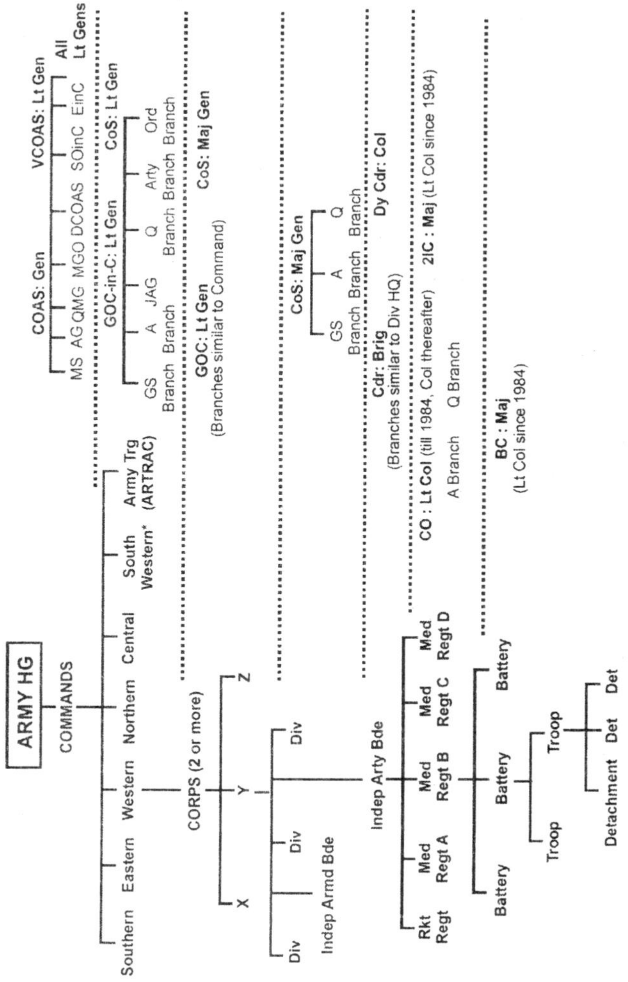

* recent addition

ANNEXURE 2 : LAYOUT CHART OF MY 'MEDIUM REGIMENT'

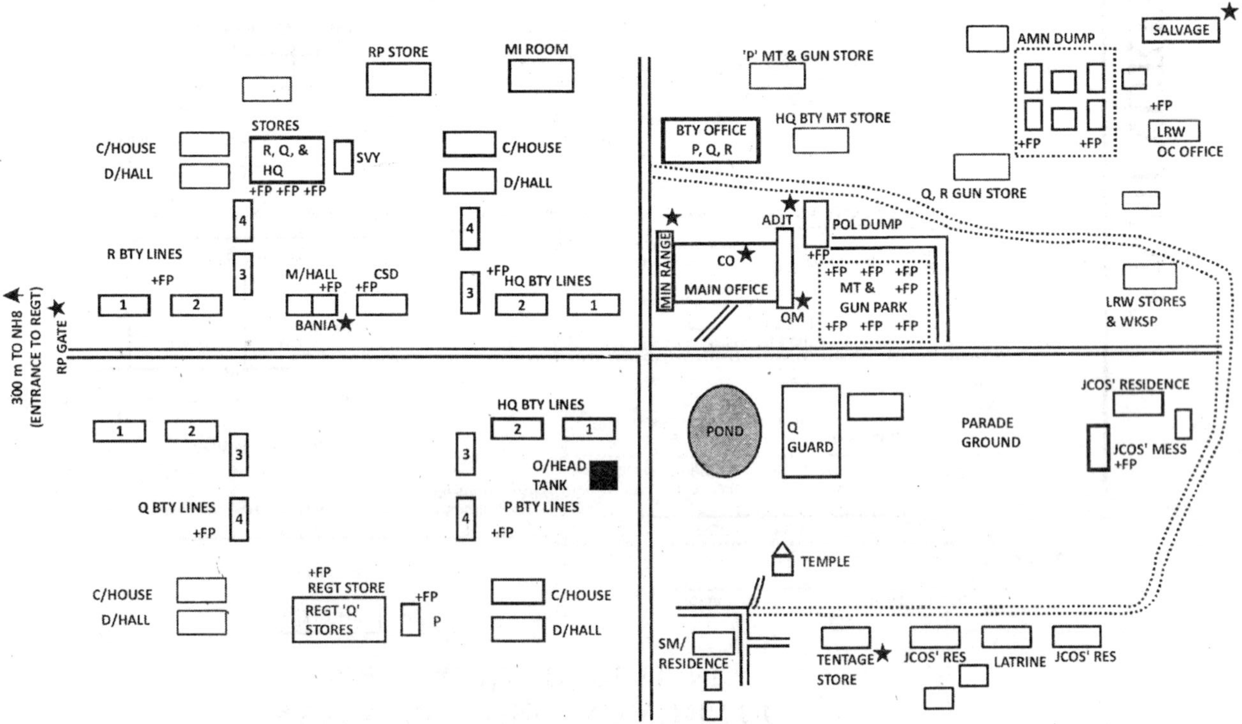

NOTES

(1) This is a presentable version of a clumsy Chart deposed by PW-7, Never-loyal and later authenticated by the 'maker', Colonel Tanjore Doll. To enable ease in understanding, I have placed a STAR next to some locations.

a. SALVAGE STORE is at the right hand top of the chart; even PW-7/9 had NOT written JUNK STORE anywhere on it! Notice it is out on a limb and the Regt had NEITHER a compound wall NOR a fence!

b. Regimental Police (RP) Gate is at the Entrance, between the Other Ranks Living Barracks No 1 of Q and R Batteries and close to them.

c. National Highway No 8 is about 300 M West, from the RP Gate running NORTH-SOUTH. (NOT seen on the Chart).

d. Miniature Range and Offices of CO, Adjutant and QM are in the Main Office building.

(2) TENTAGE STORE marked wrong was changed to the correct inter-se location, by PW-9 next to Subedar Major's Residence, after I pointed it out. Note its inter-se location vis-à-vis Salvage Stores as also distances given out by witnesses.

(3) There was NO electric connection to the Ammunition Dump (safety requirement) and thereafter to the Salvage Stores.

(4) (a) It was an old, unused and 'fit for demolition' barrack at the Northeast corner of the unit's unfenced perimeter, with two rooms approx the sizes being 15'x 12' & 10'x 10'. On arrival in Nov 1980, we earmarked it, as Salvage Store. A salvage store is a place where stores which are to be condemned are kept segregated, so that they could be readily inspected by Brigade Ordnance Officer who carries out the Monthly Condemnation Boards; thus the

unserviceable stores that are to be back-loaded to Returned Salvage Stores Depot (RSSD) in Shakurbasti were kept.

b. When our first Brigade Commander requested in July 1981, to accommodate his car and some valuable/fragile items at my home and the rest of it, along with his pets in my unit, our choice fell on this. Some gaping holes in its roof were covered with bitumen sheets to prevent leakage to the extent possible. It was cleaned up and colour/ white-washed in July 1981! His luggage remained till after Dec 1982, (both at my home and) in the unit: (where too it had been divided into two lots: one with the helpers and pets staying with heavy baggage in these 2 rooms and the rest outside the Miniature Range in Main Office Building).

c. After he vacated, the rooms were to revert as Salvage Store but the luggage of some officers who had smaller houses in Gurgaon was placed there; later the luggage of DW-7 was placed there from last week of Dec 1982 and till I was to leave for the course. In view of my decision to leave my family behind at Delhi for the children education and not being permitted to retain the same house in Delhi, I planned shifting to a small unoccupied flat of a friend. But I could not accommodate my baggage in that flat; so when I was just recovering from back ache in mid June 1983, I got my bulk baggage shifted to the bigger of the two rooms between 15 and 18 June 1983, the day when I had visited the unit (for the first time after 4 May 1983). This was well before I shifted to the smaller flat on 26 June 1983. (Three weeks later, after I lost my wife, my entire baggage was shifted there. I collected it only in Mar 1988).

d. *Thus there is NO way, any other Govt stores could have found a place in those 2 small rooms where luggage of a few officers, besides mine had been stacked upto the leaking roof!*

ANNEXURE 3: TENTATIVE CHARGE SHEET

(This is the tentative Charge Sheet given to me, by Rabbi ***WITHOUT*** Hearing of Charge!)

IC ..., Ex- Commanding Officer... Medium Regiment attached with Headquarters .... (Independent) Artillery Brigade, an officer holding a permanent commission in the Regular Army, is charged with:-

Army Act Section 52(f)	SUCH AN OFFENCE AS IS MENTIONED IN CLAUSE (f) OF SECTION 52 OF THE ARMY ACT, WITH THE INTENT TO DEFRAUD,

in that he,

at Dundahera Camp, while performing the duties of Commanding Officer .... Medium Regiment, with intent to defraud signed the following contingent bills of approx Rs 61,520-20 (Rupees sixty one thousand five hundred and twenty six and paise twenty only) for payment of garnish scrim quantity approx 87,000 metres while on Annual Leave during 1983 when the entire quantity of said scrim garnish had not been received:-

1. ... dated 09 April 83 for Rs 9900.80
2. ... dated 12 April 83 for Rs 4243.00
3. ... dated 23 April 83 for Rs 9900.80
4. ... dated 28 April 83 for Rs 9900.80
5. ... dated 04 May 83 for Rs 9900.80
6. ... dated 10 May 83 for Rs 17680.00

Signed…
(Rabbi)
Colonel
Commanding Officer
HQ …. Independent Artillery Bde

Place: Meerut Cantt
Date: 23 April 1984

Summary of Evidence to be recorded

Signed…
(Rabbi)
Col
Dy Cdr ….
Independent Artillery
Brigade

Meerut Cantt
23 April 1984

ANNEXURE 4: CHARGE SHEET

(The Charge Sheet given to BOTH: Quarter Master and me from Mar 1985 onward)

	The accused, (1) ... Lt Col (Substantive) ..., of... Medium Regiment holding a permanent commission in the regular army and (2) SL- .... Maj (Substantive) ....of ... Medium Regiment holding a special list commission in the regular army, both attached to Headquarters .... (Independent) Artillery Brigade, are charged with:-
Army Act	SUCH AN OFFENCE AS IS MENTIONED IN CLAUSE (f) OF SECTION 52 OF
Section 52(f)	THE ARMY ACT, WITH THE INTENT TO DEFRAUD,
in that they together,	
	at Dundahera Camp during May 1983, while being Officer Commanding and Quarter Master respectively of .... Medium Regiment, with intent to defraud, submitted to DDOS HQ ... Corps, the undermentioned contingent bills pertaining to the purchase of 87,000 metres of scrim garnish valued at Rs 61,520-20 from Globe Sales Corporation, Jullundur, well knowing that only 19,500 metres of scrim garnish was supplied by the said firm:-

Sr. No	Bill No's	Nomen-clature	Qty	Rate	Amount Rs.
1.	...dated 9 April 83	EC scrim garnishing 75 mm MB Green	14000 M	0.68 Per meter	9900.80
2.	... dated 12 April 83	-do-	6000 M	-do-	4243.00
3.	... dated 23 April 83	-do-	14000 M	-do-	9900.80
4.	... dated 28 April 83	-do-	14000 M	-do-	9900.80
5.	... dated 04 May 83	-do-	14000 M	-do-	9900.80
6.	... dated 10 May 83	EC scrim garnishing 75 mm Lt Green	14000 M	-do-	9900.80
		EC scrim garnishing 75 mm D/ Brown	11000 M	-do-	7779.20
		Total (Including sales tax 4%)			61,526.20

Signed...
(Name)
Colonel
Commanding Officer
HQ .... Independent
Artillery Bde

Place: Meerut Cantt
Date: 23 July 1985

To be tried by a General Court Martial

Signed...
(Name)
Brigadier
Commander ....
Independent Artillery Brigade

Meerut Cantt

25 July 1985

(Note: In Apr 1986, another Charge Sheet was given where the amount was shown as Rs 61,526/40 P and the name of the unit to which attached was changed; other details remaining the same. Of course signed by Commander...Independent Armoured Brigade, both as CO and as Commander!)

ANNEXURE 5: SOME PROVISIONS OF ARMY ACT, 1950 AND ARMY RULES, 1954 AS THEY EXISTED IN 1983-86

*(These are extracted from my handwritten copy of Proceedings and may **not** be authentic)*

Army Act

Section 52 (f): Offences in respect of property

Any person subject to this Act who commits any of the following offences, that is to say,

...

(f) does any other thing with intent to defraud, or to cause wrongful gain to one person or wrongful loss to another person, shall, on conviction by court-martial, be liable to suffer imprisonment for a term which may extend to ten years or, such less punishment as is in this Act mentioned.

Section 117: Dissolution of Courts-martial

(1) ...

(2)...

(3) The officer who convened a court-martial may dissolve such court-martial if it appears to him that military exigencies or the necessities of discipline render it impossible or inexpedient to continue the said court-martial.

(4) Where a court-martial is dissolved under this section, the accused may be tried again.

Section 124: Place of trial

Any person subject to this Act who commits any offence against it may be tried in any place whatever.

Section 129: Judge-advocate

Every general court-martial shall... be attended by a judge-advocate....

Section 130: Challenges

(1) At all trials by general,...court-martial, as soon as the Court is assembled, the names of the presiding officer and members shall be read over to the accused, who shall thereupon be asked whether he objects to being tried by any officer sitting on the court...

Section 131 Oaths of member, judge-advocate and witness

(1) An oath or affirmation in the prescribed manner shall be administered to every member of every court-martial and to the judge-advocate, before the commencement of trial...

Section 153 Finding and sentence not valid, unless confirmed

No finding or sentence of a general...court-martial shall be valid except so far as it may be confirmed as provided by this Act.

Section 160 Revision of Finding or sentence

- Any finding or sentence of a court-martial which requires confirmation may be once revised by order of the confirming authority and on such revision, the court, if so directed by the confirming authority, may take additional evidence...

Section 164 Remedy against order, finding or sentence of court-martial

1. Any person subject to this Act who considers himself aggrieved by any order by any court-martial may present a petition to the officer or authority empowered to confirm any finding or sentence of such court-martial and the confirming authority may

take such steps as may be considered necessary to satisfy itself as to the correctness, legality or propriety of the order passed or as to the regularity of any proceeding to which the order relates...

Army Rules

(It is learnt that Army Rules 22 to 25 were amended by SRO of 6 Dec 1993 and again by an Act of Parliament in 2003; and so were NOT applicable during 1983 to 1988).

Army Rule 22

Hearing of Charge:

(a) Every charge against a person subject to the Act, other than an officer, shall be heard in the presence of the accused. The accused shall have full liberty to cross-examine any witness against him, and to call any witness, and make any statement in his defence.

(b) The CO shall dismiss the charge brought before him if, in his opinion, the evidence does not show that an offence under the Act has been committed, and may do so if, in his discretion, he is satisfied that the charge ought not to be proceeded with.

(c) At the conclusion of the hearing of a charge if the commanding officer is of opinion that the charge ought to be proceeded with, he shall without unnecessary delay-

i. dispose of the case summarily under section 80 in accordance with the manner and form in Appendix III or

ii. refer the case to proper superior military authority; or

iii. adjourn the case for the purpose of having the evidence reduced to writing; or

iv. If the accused is below the rank of warrant officer, order his trial by a summary court martial;

Provided that the commanding officer shall not order trial by a summary court-martial without a reference to the officer empowered to convene a district court-martial or on active service a summary general court-martial for the trial of the alleged offender unless either:-

(1) the offence is one which he can try by a summary court-martial without reference to that officer; or

(2) he considers that there is grave reason for immediate action and such reference cannot be made without detriment to discipline.

Army Rule 25 *(as it existed then)*

Procedure on charge against officer

- Where an officer is charged with an offence under the Act, the investigation shall, if he requires it, be held, and the evidence, if he so requires, be taken in his presence in writing in the same manner as nearly as circumstances permit, as is required by Rule 22 and Rule 23 in the case of other persons subject to the Act.
- Where an officer is remanded for the summary disposal ....

(*Note: Subsequently an Army Order 70/84 was published after Supreme Court laid down that Hearing of Charge is a must in all cases, in PPS Bedi Vs. Union of India. My demand made to Colonel Rabbi in Apr 1984 pre-dated this judgement!*)

Army Rule 34 *Warning of accused for trial*

(1) The accused before he is arraigned shall be informed by an officer of every charge for which he is to be tried and also that on giving his names of witnesses or whom he desires to call in his defence, reasonable steps will be taken for procuring their attendance, and those steps shall be taken accordingly. The interval between his being so informed and his arraignment shall not be less than 96 hours or where the accused person is on active service less than twenty-four hours.

(2) The officer at the time of so informing the accused shall give him a copy of the charge-sheet and shall if necessary read and explain to him the charge brought against him. If the accused desires to have it in a language which he understands, a translation thereof shall also be given to him.

(3) The officer shall also deliver to the accused a list of the names, rank and corps (if any), of the officers who are to form the court, and officers in waiting are named, also of those officers in court-martial other than summary court-martial.

(4) If it appears to the court that the accused is liable to be prejudiced at his trial by any non-compliance with this rule, the court shall take steps and, if necessary, adjourn to avoid the accused being so prejudiced.

Army Rule 36: *Suspension of rules on the ground of military exigencies or the necessities of discipline*

Where it appears to the officer convening a court-martial, or to the senior officer on the spot, that military exigencies or the necessities of discipline render it impossible or inexpedient to observe any of the rules 23, 24, 25, 33 and 34 and sub rule (2) of 95, he may, by order under his hand, make a declaration to the effect specifying the nature of such exigencies or necessities, and thereupon the trial or other proceedings shall be valid as if the rule mentioned in declaration had not been contained herein; and such declaration may be made with respect to any or all of the rules aforesaid in the case of the same court martial:

Provided that the accused shall have full opportunity of making his defence, and shall be afforded every facility for preparing it which is practicable, having due regard to the said exigencies or necessities.

Army Rule 39: *Ineligibility and disqualification of officers for court-martial*

(1) An officer is not eligible for serving on a court-martial if he is not subject to the Act.

(2) An officer is disqualified or serving in a general... court-martial if he—

(a) is an officer who convened the court; or

(b) is the prosecutor or witness for the prosecution; or

(c) investigated the charges before trial, or took down the summary of evidence, or was a member of court of inquiry respecting the matters on which the charges against the accused are founded, or was the squadron, battery, company or other commander, who made preliminary inquiry into the case, or was a member of a previous court-martial which tried the accused in respect of the same offence; or

(d) is the commanding officer of the accused or of the corps to which the accused belongs; or

(e) has a personal interest in the case.

(3) The provost marshal or assistant provost marshal is disqualified from serving on a general ... court-martial.

Army Rule 49: *Objection by accused to the charge*

The accused, when required to plead to any charge, may object to the charge on the ground that it does not disclose an offence under the Act, or is not in accordance with these rules. The court after hearing any submission which may be made by the prosecutor or by or on behalf of the accused, shall consider the objection in closed court and shall either disallow it and proceed with the trial, or allow it and adjourn to report to the convening authority or, of it is in doubt, it may adjourn to consult the convening authority.

Army Rule 51: *Special plea to the jurisdiction*

(1) The accused, before pleading to a charge, may offer a special plea to the general jurisdiction of the court, and if he does so, and the court considers that anything stated in such plea shows that that the court has no jurisdiction it shall receive any evidence offered in support, together with any evidence offered by the prosecutor in disproof or

qualification thereof, and any address by or on behalf of the accused and reply by the prosecutor in reference thereto.

(2) If the court overrules the special plea, it shall proceed with the trial.

(3) If the court allows the special plea, it shall record its decision and the reasons for it, and report to the convening authority and adjourn; such decision, shall not require any confirmation, and the convening authority shall either forthwith convene another court for the trial of the accused, or order the accused to be released.

(4) If the court is in doubt as to the validity of the plea, it may refer the matter to the convening authority, and may adjourn for that purpose or may record a special decision with respect to such plea, and proceed with the trial.

Army Rule 60: *Summing up by the judge-advocate*

(1) The judge advocate (if any) shall sum up in open court the evidence and advice the court upon the law relating to the case.

(2) After the summing up of the judge-advocate, no other addresses shall be allowed.

Army Rule 68: *Revision...*

(4) ... If necessary, the judge-advocate may sum up the (additional) evidence and advise the court upon the law relating to the case. ...

Army Rule 81: *Hours of sitting*

(f) A court martial may sit at such times and for such period between the hours of six in the morning and six in the afternoon as may be directed by the proper superior military authority, and so far as no such direction extends, as the court from time to time determines but no court shall sit more than six hours in any one day.

(g) If the court considers it necessary to continue the trial after six in the afternoon or to sit for more than six hours in any one day, it may do so but if it does so, should record in the proceedings the reason for so doing.

(h) In cases requiring an immediate example or when the convening officer certifies under his hand that it is expedient for the public service, trials may be held at any hour...

Army Rule 82: *Continuity of Trial and Adjournment of Court*

(1) When a court is once assembled and the accused has been arraigned, the court shall continue the trial from day to day, in accordance with Rule 81, unless it appears to the court that an adjournment is necessary for the ends of justice or such continuance is impracticable.

(2) to (5) ....

Army Rule 95: *Defending Officer (and friend of accused)*

21. At any general...court martial an accused person may be represented by any officer subject to this Act who shall be called "the defending officer"...

22. It shall be the duty of the convening officer to ascertain whether an accused person desires to have a defending officer assigned to represent him at his trial and, if he does so desire, the convening officer shall use his best endeavours that the accused shall be so represented by a suitable officer. If owing to military exigencies, or for any other reason, there shall in the opinion of the convening officer, be no such officer available for the purpose, the convening officer shall give a written notice to the presiding officer of the court-martial and such notice shall be attached to the proceedings.

Army Rule 134: *Calling of all prosecutor's witnesses*

The prosecutor ... is not bound to call all the witnesses for the prosecution whose evidence is in the summary or abstract of evidence of whom the accused has been informed he ... intends to call, but he ... should ordinarily call such of them as the accused desires, in order that he may cross examine them, and shall, for this reason, so far as practicable, secure the attendance of such witnesses.

Army Rule 136: *List of witnesses of accused*

The accused shall not be required to give to the prosecutor or court, a list of witnesses whom he intends to call, but it shall rest with the accused alone to secure the attendance of any witnesses whose evidence is not contained in the summary ... of evidence and for whose attendance the accused has not requested steps to be taken as provided for in sub rule (1) of rule 34.

Army Rule 137: *Procuring attendance of witnesses*

(1) In the case of trial by general ... court martial, the commanding officer of the accused, the convening officer, or after assembly of the court, the presiding officer, shall take proper steps to procure the attendance of witnesses whom the prosecutor or accused desires to call, and whose attendance can reasonably be procured, but the person requiring the attendance of a witness may be required to undertake to defray the cost (if any) of their attendance.

Army Rule 138: *Procedure when essential witness is absent*

If such proper steps as mentioned in the preceding rule have not been taken as to any witness, or if any witness whose attendance could not be reasonably procured before the assembly of the court is essential to the prosecution or defence, the court shall—

a. take steps to procure the issue of a commission for the examination of such witness; or

b. if it is a general..., adjourn and report the circumstances to the convening officer; or

c. ...

Army Rule 146: *Preservation of proceedings*

(1) The proceedings of a court-martial (...) shall, after promulgation, be forwarded as circumstances require, to the office of Judge-Advocate General, and there preserved

for not less, in the case of a general court-martial, than seven years....

Army Rule 180: *Procedure when character of a person subject to the Act is involved*

Save in the case of a prisoner of war who is still absent, whenever any inquiry affects the character or military reputation of a person subject to the Act, full opportunity must be afforded to such person of being present throughout the enquiry and of making any statement, and of giving any evidence he may wish to make or give, and of cross examining any witness whose evidence in his opinion, affects his character or military reputation and producing any witnesses in defence of his character or military reputation. The presiding officer of the court shall take such steps as may be necessary to ensure that any such person so affected and not previously notified receives notice of fully understands his rights, under this rule.

Army Rule 182: *Proceedings of court of inquiry not admissible in evidence*

"The proceedings of a court of inquiry, or any confession, statement, or answer to a question made or given at a court of inquiry, shall not be admissible in evidence against a person subject to the Act nor shall any evidence in respect of the proceedings of a court, be given against any such person except upon the trial of such person for wilfully giving false evidence before that court.

ANNEXURE 6: GIST OF EVIDENCE DURING THIRD GCM

Prosecution Witnesses

Between 11 June 1986 and 24 July 1986, Prosecution led 10 witnesses:-

PW-1: Captain Cassius, Officiating Quarter Master, from 14 May 1983 onwards.

PW-2: Major Crass, the 2 IC and officiating CO during my leave and about whom I have written enough earlier.

PW-3: Ordnance Clerk of Quarter Master's Branch of Regt, who prepared the LP documents on the orders of Quarter Master through Quarter Master Branch Subedar Head Clerk.

PW-4: Ex Deputy Director of Ordnance Services of Corps HQ, who had sanctioned the Local Purchase.

PW-5: Assistant Stores Clerk of Regt Quarter Master's Branch, who alleged that he amended the LP documents in June 1983, as ordered by Prosecution Witness No 3.

PW-6: Control Clerk from Corps HQ Ordnance Branch.

PW-7: Never-loyal, Junior Commissioned Officer Quarter Master who claimed he had brought *'only 19,500 M of LP garnish'* from a transport agency's office and distributed 16,500 M on a Nominal Issue Voucher (NIV), which was undated, unnumbered and self-made and with forged signatures!

PW-8: Manager of the Company that provided the LP Garnish.

PW-9: My successor CO, Lt Col (later, Colonel) Tanjore Doll.

PW-10: One more clerk of Regt Quarter Master Branch.

Despite repeated requests, the Prosecution did not want to produce two of their witnesses *who had earlier given evidence, in a Summary of Evidence each of mine and A-2*, quoting one excuse after another. These persons were:

-the Quarter Master Branch Subedar Head Clerk, who had ordered all work relating to preparation of Local Purchase papers; and had gone on pension.

-the Junior Commissioned Officer Quarter Master, who had handed over charge to Prosecution Witness No 7 in Nov 1982; and had gone on pension.

Salient points of the evidence by each of them are summarized below.

(PW-1) Captain Cassius (examined on 11 to 13 June 1986)

In the Direct Examination, he stated the following:

-Joined Regt on **04 Mar 1983 at Gurgaon**; went on annual leave on 24 Mar; recalled by Crass to take over as officiating Quarter Master from 14 May; **took all correct certificates from all store holders and clerks**.

-Sent Branch Subedar Head Clerk on leave from 4 June and PW 3 took over, who told him *the same day* that private mail of Quarter Master had accumulated; so requested PW-2 to send a courier. Crass refused; but asked about 'big envelop'! (Witness did not say what he answered; nor did Court ask!)

-After 10 days (!), the clerk put it up on 14 June 1983 and he found one of them: an *'ACR–size'* big envelope from HQ Corps Ordnance Branch and *'had words like LP written on it'*! So he asked for and saw 6 sets of Local Purchase documents (dated from 25 to 30 Dec 1982) returned 'earlier' by Corps Ordnance. He identified them now. Also saw two letters from Corps Ordnance in the file, one dated 7 Mar 1983, asking for *re-floating of tender enquiries* and another dated 18 Mar 1983 asking *to liaise with Depot as the item was now available*, (both he produced subject to proof). Neither had been seen by anyone in the Regt, (except the first one by Branch Subedar Head Clerk alone)!

-On 16 June, he told PW 3 to put up all documents. In the meantime, A-2, while on leave, came to the Regt. (*Wrong date*!) On his request, A-2 showed him six sets of documents, dated from 2 to 9 Apr 1983 (1st set) to 2 to 4 May 1983 (6th set). ALL THESE DATES HAD BEEN AMENDED as per later testimony; so, his authentication of any of the dates was meaningless! A-2 also showed him the three pages of ledger where these three shades of garnish had been taken on charge; these again had been amended as per later testimony! (My counsel asked to see the ledger which was not available: 45 days after commencement of trial!) He asked A-2 about the whereabouts of the items who told him that they had been distributed to batteries and used in the Exercise; however, after rejoining from leave, he could show the proof. So the witness took him to Crass, who called '*someone*' (meaning me, at home!), when A-2 told that person: *"Sir, I am entirely responsible for this local purchase. You need not worry. If it will be anyone's GCM, it will be mine and not yours"*. (But I was away at Meerut to meet Scraggly for the second consecutive day, to sign my ACR; I returned only late in the evening! So, this entire alleged telephonic conversation of that day, is incorrect, as proved by me later!)

-On 18 June 1983, PW-3 told him that A-2 had got the documents amended and carried the originals away with him on 16 June. (This was disproved by Adjutant who stated that he, Crass, PW-1 and Sub Maj had seen off A-2 on 17 June, the only day he had come to the unit; and he had left empty-handed!)

-That same day, 18 June (when I had gone to work on the data for next Saturday's conference on promotions), I had asked him as to what his doubt was. He had replied that while A-2 stated he had got 87,000 M and distributed it, Subedar Quarter Master, PW-7 had stated he had brought only 19,500 M and showed an UNDATED and UNNUMBERED Nominal Issue Voucher with 4 signatures for 16,500 M!

(This voucher was disproved later: with two signatories swearing they had NOT signed it; nor was their Army No correct! It had anachronistic entry, i.e., after entries of 1983! 2 years after the Revision, I came to know the reason for this).

-On 21 June, he received a letter from A-2 absolving A-1 and PW-1 from any wrong doing etc. (See Chapter VII *Mischief by Crass starts*).

-On 28 June when Rabbi had come to the unit, PW-1 had ordered PW-7 at about 1500 to 1600 hours, to check all stores for unused garnish. (Why suddenly now?) At about 1920 hours or so, the *latter had 'found' 50,000 to 55,000 M of garnish in sealed bundles in...junk store. When I saw it, I found dispatch details from one ordnance depot to another; railway receipt numbers and cat/part numbers etc'*!

During Cross Examination, he fumbled for answers to all questions; the gist, however, is:

-He did not know me or A-2, before Mar 1983, while he knew most others.

-<u>Before going on leave, he was in the unit-rear for only 14 days</u>.

-He neither knew the number of camouflage nets in his battery, where he was Bty 2IC nor how many took part in the exercise!

-Had taken a certificate from PW-7 and PW-3, while taking over as offg QM!

-Ledger was in the custody of PW-3.

-Private mail is supposed to be redirected to officer on leave, but he did <u>not ask</u> the clerk why he had not done so on 4 or 14 June 1983; but 'he told me registered military mail cannot be redirected'! Besides it was bulky and needed postage stamps! He did not tell me either on 4 or 14 June as to why he was showing me the private mail of A-2; nor did I ask him'. (Regt had

Service Postage Stamps and it could have gone by civil Registered Post!)

He did **NOT**:-

- see the words 'LP' on the big envelope on 4 June.

-find out as to who had signed for that registered military letter!'

-check, when Crass asked, *'from other files except one*'.

-count the number of bundles in the junk store but they were 30 or so in number'.

-care to see the type of marking on the bundles (...'but they were ordnance markings with cat/part number...').

-see the other items lying in the junk store.

-ask PW-7 as to who took them out.

-try to find out if a particular bundle is on charge or not'.

-check up as to how much garnish was on charge that day and how much was held on the ground (other than the bundles) as on that date'.

-He informed Tanjore Doll about it, (when I was the CO still!).

-He informed Tanjore Doll about it, (when I was the CO still!).

At this stage my Counsel wished to see certain documents; so further cross examination of this person will be done after that.

PW-2 Major Crass (examined on 13-14 June 1986)

During his direct examination by the Prosecution Counsel, he stated the following:

-Posted to the Regt in Apr 19**83** (…Wrong, it was May 19**76**!) and officiated as CO from 29 Apr to 27 June 1983.

-A-2 also proceeded on leave on 16 May 1983. (He had sanctioned it against the military norms)

-On 14 June 1983, PW-1 approached him about a courier to A-2 with his private letters. (Did not talk about 4 June). The same day, he saw the Local Purchase papers, *the ledger pages* 64, 66 and 67 of Unit Equipment Ledger No 36. When the exhibits were shown *'the page numbers are not there'*; still he recognized them!

-Regt participated in exercise from 25 Dec 1982 to 13 Mar 1983.

-*'To the best of my knowledge, the unit had collected approximately 2 Lakh metres of garnish* ***till*** *1982 and 55,000 metres in Nov 1982; till I saw the ledger, I did not check up how much was on charge. I cannot say how much garnish was held on charge'.*

-On 18 June during *'investigations'* Subedar Quarter Master (later PW-7) *'told me that he had collected 19,500 metres from a firm in Kashmere Gate, Delhi'... he also showed me an undated, unnumbered NIV in which details of distribution of 16,500 metres of garnish was given.'*

-Neither A-1 nor A-2 *'had told ... about LP'*. (A white lie, disproved later).

-On 16 June, he had asked me over telephone (when I was away at Meerut!) if any local purchase of garnish had been done, when I apprised him that *'some LP has been done; but the details would be given by A-2 during one of his visits to the unit'*! On 16 <u>and</u> 17 June, A-2 had come and had said *'LP was done and distributed to batteries'*. So the witness had called me up and told me that A-2: *"... had come to the unit and that I was not satisfied with the explanation given by him...and he should speak to A-2"*. Subedar Major (now deceased) and Cassius were present then. *"On being told by A-1, he handed over the telephone to A-2, who spoke on the following lines:*

> *"These chaps are making mountain out of mole. I shall explain you everything when I come back from leave. I am responsible for any irregularity/ discrepancy if there is any*

GCM it will be mine. I have got pressing problems at home therefore I shall explain everything once I come back."(sic)

-A-2 also told A-1 he was coming to his house.

-He was told by Cassius on 17 June that A-2 had got two forwarding letters to Corps Ordnance typed, by backdating them and that brigade had not been kept in the loop!

-On 18 June 1983, after a discussion and some investigation, A-1 did not tell him to send a courier to recall A-2; (but in Cross Examination says: *I had sent the courier on 18 June 1983 on the advice of A-1)*. On 25 June when this was again discussed, 'I requested A-1 to send a courier again, but he said A-2 may have gone to his village to attend *'shradh'* ceremony (obsequies) for his mother. *A courier was sent after about 2 days* (Because I had ordered it on 27th night, after seeing the pseudonymous letter!) *but A-2 did not come'.*

-*"I had seen **two bundles** of scrim garnish lying in the veranda two days after the visit"* by Rabbi. Then he voluntarily added: *"These were **machine rolled** having **white chit containing•cat/part number** and contract number"*. (The Court did not ask him as to how he knew the contents inside a bundle: machine rolled etc)!

His Cross Examination may be read in detail, (specially the *'NOT's'*!).

-On 23 May 1983, I attended the marriage of son of A-2 at Dehradun, but did not ask him when he was visiting Delhi. (Note that he had met him but did not ask, whereas I was bed-ridden at home since 10 May and I knew, as he repeated ad nauseam, *'CO said A-2 would come during leave'*!)

-I *do not remember* if Cassius spoke to me about private mail of A-2 on 4 June 1983...he may have mentioned the urgency...I did not feel the necessity of sending a special courier. (*Then he added voluntarily*)... *A-1 told me that A-2 may come to the unit during leave...I cannot say I was expecting* A-2 to visit the unit despite the *above information by A-1.*

-I *cannot say, if* the letters "LP" were written twice. The letter "LP" conveyed to me it concerned Local Purchase.

-A-2 did not confess before me about his responsibility of local purchase nor did he write me a letter. He wrote a letter addressed to ... Medium Regiment. I was the officiating CO. From the letter addressed to the unit I understand that overall it is meant for commanding officer... it is meant for the regiment... I saw it. I do not know if the appointment rubber stamp was affixed on it. I do not remember if I had initialled it. (*He was shown the letter and asked to identify his initials*)!

-I do *not* remember if it was put up before me...I do *not* know to whom the letter was given by the courier. I know that it was brought by a courier, because the courier went on 19 June and returned on 21 June and so I presume.

-I am aware that an officer can be recalled from annual leave only on the permission of army commander.

-I did *not recall* A-2 from annual leave but had sent a request note for him to *return in his own interest*. His return was in his own interest as investigations were being conducted and no one could answer. Investigations were being carried out by me, A-1, Tanjore Doll and Cassius. A-1 was the senior most amongst us. *I had sent the courier on 18 June 1983 on the advice of A-1*.

-Cassius had shown me the Ledger as a whole and three sheets in a loose form. These were not removed with my permission; I am *not aware* as to who took these out. *"I was neither Commanding Officer nor Quarter Master so my permission was not required"*. I officiated as CO till 26 or 27 June 1983. I *did not* order the impounding of the ledger till I officiated as CO, while the investigations were in progress. The Ledger was the first document produced before me by Cassius. I had seen the contingent bills on 18 June for the first time. *I did not order these to be impounded.* I do not remember if these came to me loose or in a file.

-Perhaps sanction for the local purchase is the only document prepared outside the unit.

-No one told me local purchase of garnish was done during Exercise Dig Vijay, irrespective of the quantity or the amount involved.

-Never-loyal told me during investigations that 19,500 M of garnish was collected before move of the unit for the Exercise. *I cannot say if it was for the Exercise*; during the investigations, I think, Never-loyal told me that this was local purchase garnish. I had *not seen* the sanction for this local purchase of 19,500 M. I did not see the contingent bill also for this 19,500 M.

- *Not aware* if Corps Commander was due to visit the unit during May 1983... if

A-1 was told to adjust commencement of leave pending visit of the corps commander to the unit.

(From this stage, Major Bedi carried out the rest of the cross examination)

-I do *not remember* if I was present in the exercise location on 25 Feb 1983. (That was the day when 68 knitted nets were loaned to Brigade HQ). It is true that *some* garnished camouflage nets were handed over to brigade and *some* garnish and nets were returned to the unit in lieu. I am *not sure* of the figures suggested to me that 68 nets and 15,000 M were so exchanged.

-*Even on seeing a letter shown to me* ...since I do not deal with Q matters..."not aware if this happened or not". Then he was asked to produce Brigade letter of 7 July 1983, (received after I had left for the Course) and *asked to identify his own signature and remarks on it*!

-It is incorrect to suggest that no garnish was received in the unit between 18 Feb and 21 Nov 1982.

-As *"I have no access to the documents, so I cannot produce anything in support of the fact that about 2 lakh M and 50-55 thousand M was received during Aug 1982 and Nov 1982 respectively".*

-It is incorrect to suggest that I have deposed falsely without checking documents; "...during **my** *preliminary investigations, I had found out about the mentioned quantity of garnish".*

-"I had checked either the ledger or the voucher received from the depot"... "I do not offhand remember as the incident is 3 years old".

-"It is incorrect to suggest that I had started officiating as CO sometime during the first week of May 1983 and not with effect from 29 Apr 1983". During Summary of A-2, I may have mentioned that I started officiating from the first week of May 1983 but I do not recollect it...my attention is now drawn ...wherein I had stated that I took over as officiating CO of ...Medium Regiment at Dundahera Camp while "CO" proceeded on annual leave in the first week of May 1983. I now say that I have so stated. I might have made that statement without checking the leave certificate etc which I later checked and so gave correct details before court.

-I had been normally signing against the column of 2IC in the "Seen By" stamp (for the mail) even if was officiating CO. After getting the extract of message log book, I can state that ***on 2 May 1983, I had signed against the column of 2IC and A-1 has signed against column of CO****.*

-I do not remember the outdoor training events from 1 Nov 1980 till Exercise Dig Vijay. I do not know if the unit was maintaining a Training Diary. (One of the main duties of a 2IC *is Training—besides Security, Institutes and Accounts! Training Diary and Draft Training Report are his jobs! He had been 2IC since 1979, i.e., 7 years till the date of this deposition*! The Court would have understood the man by now!)

-After perusing the ledger, I can state that 60,000 M (This again is wrong recording: it was only 6,000 and NOT 60,000)*, 51,000 M, 27,000 M and 99,000 M of 75 MM garnish had been received in the unit on 30 Dec 1981, 18 Feb 1982, 30 Dec 1981 and 2 Mar 1982 respectively. Of these, 99,000 M was UNDYED.*

Cross examined by Colonel Ramanan:

-*I think there was a letter from the Brigade telling A-1 to adjust the leave depending upon the visit of corps commander, which was otherwise approved. But I was not aware of the visit, when I took over.*

-I am aware **A-1 had gone from the unit to meet GOC,** Delhi Area on **4 May 1983.**

I do not:

-remember if Adjutant was also present in my office on 16 June 1983, when A-2 spoke to A-1, and if I had given the telephone to him. The conversation by me took place at approx 1200 hours. (I was away at Meerut!)

-remember if I had sent Tanjore Doll to see off A-1 to Meerut at 0745 hours on 16 June 1983.

-remember if I checked ground balances of garnish from Store Hands General Duty; but I had checked from Never-loyal.

-remember if I had checked about the quantity of garnish received from Battery Quarter Master Havildars but I had checked from Battery Commanders.(3 out of 4 were away on leave!)

-remember in which veranda I had seen the two bundles.

-know if Brigade had issued any "SOP" for local purchase. I feel the papers should have been routed through brigade.

I did not:

-verify the stock position and ground balance of unused garnish at the time of my investigations.

-<u>see</u> all the documents of the batteries but concerned ledger.

-<u>visit or verify</u> the record of the agency supplying the materials.

-<u>inspect</u> the Bin cards of Never-loyal's stores but checked his register.

-<u>not verify</u> the stock position from Ordnance Depot, Shakurbasti regarding garnish 75 MM Dark Brown.

-<u>attempt to find out</u> the quantity of ordnance pattern garnish which ought to have been held as per the documents.

-A-2 had asked me to recall Quarter Master Branch Subedar Head Clerk, who had proceeded on pension; but A-1 did not ask me so between 18 and 25 June 1983.

-I had submitted a reply to a letter addressed to me by name from brigade HQ received by hand on 27 June 1983, the same night at 2200 hours by an officer courier, and addressed it to Rabbi.

-<u>I cannot give the procedure</u> for issue of stores from Regt to batteries. Either CO or QM can order issue.

-I am <u>not aware</u> of the life span of scrim garnish. I am aware that orders were issued by brigade HQ to carry 'sufficient'/two nets per gun and vehicle participating in the Exercise.

-I am <u>not aware</u> if A-1 had announced during a durbar or conference that I attended that local purchase of garnish is being resorted to.

-There was a junk store in the Regt.

To questions from the Court, he further answered:

-Whole Q Mail was not passing through me.

-Cassius had informed me that he had taken over by taking all correct certificates from the store-holders. <u>I did not tell him to check</u> the stores once taken over.

-No monthly stock taking of stores was done in the unit except for Petrol, Oil and Lubricants.

The Court now wanted to complete the pending cross-examination of PW-1. But the Prosecution Counsel submitted that *"Bundles have not been brought so far. The documents specified have also not been fully brought. It would require 3 to 4 days...".*

Major Bedi submitted that he has been briefed by the counsel to continue with the cross examination of other Prosecution Witnesses, but not for PW-1.

The Court then directed that documents and other evidence required by the Defence be fully specified. The Court was adjourned till 04 July 1986, i.e., 20 days! (A-2 wished to look up his ailing wife, as the Court was to be adjourned.)

On 4 July 1986, a Judge-Advocate (JA) newly appointed was present; my Counsel was absent. I submitted that he would only be available on 8 July as per a call received by me just then; but Major Bedi could carry on. However, cross examination of Witness 1 would only be done when he arrived and all bundles and documents were present. A-2 re-iterated the same. Just then, Colonel Ramanan submitted a written objection to the presence of the new JA, on the grounds that he was from the same Corps HQ; his presence would deny natural justice, as he had 'personal interest' in the case by rendering periodic advice to CO's 3 and 4; and he is subordinate to the JA who gave the pre-trial advice, etc. A lot of arguments took place and the submission was rejected.

PW-3: Ordnance Clerk of QM Branch of Regt (examined on 4-9 July 1986)

Salient points from his Direct Examination:

-Posted in July 1980; does *'ordnance'* clerk; officiated whenever Head Clerk was away, eg, 18 days from 28 Dec 1982; 14 days from 7 May 1983 and from 3 June 1983 when latter proceeded on pension: (*all dates linked to LP documentation!*)

-On 28 Dec 1982, Head Clerk informed him about local purchase (LP) and handed over 3 quotations given by A-2; later A-2 told him to prepare 6 sets of LP documents, which he did. A-1 had signed in second week of Jan 1983, but the dates are 25-30 Dec 1982. (*Witness was on leave from 28 Dec 1982!*)

Then the Prosecution Counsel asked him: *"The quotations pertained to which month? If it is within your knowledge, you tell the Court"*. Major Bedi objected saying: *'the contents of document cannot be brought on record unless either the document is produced or the Prosecution undertakes to produce it at a later stage'*. The witness was asked to withdraw. Prosecution Counsel answered that *'the question does not relate to the contents of the documents but pertains to the circumstances in which different dates were put. He as a dealing clerk may be permitted to answer'*. Major Bedi read out the definition of a "Document" from Section 3 of the Indian Evidence Act; *'... moreover, since more than one set of quotations were received, it cannot be said as to which of them the question relates and so it should not be allowed'*. JA referred to Section 59 of the Indian Evidence Act. After a consideration in closed court, it decided to disallow the question. The witness was called and continued:

-As directed by A-2, they were sent by Registered Scheduled Despatch Service to Corps Ordnance: 3 in Jan 1983 and 3 in Feb 1983. Two sets were received back in Mar 1983, whereby Corps Ordnance asked *'to re-float tender enquiries'*. That letter was only initialled by Quarter Master Branch Subedar Head Clerk. On 16 Mar 1983, Regt wrote to Corps Ordnance to send back the remaining 4 sets also. On 18 Mar, they were returned with the remarks: *"Garnish is now available at the Depot. Please liaise..." This letter does not bear initials of anyone in the Regt.*

-On 15 Apr 1983, A-2 asked Head Clerk to prepare 6 sets of covering letters to carry personally! *"I was on casual leave from 16 to 30 Apr 1983*...seen these and I produce them: dated, 01, 03, 05, 07, 10 and 13 Apr 1983".

-'*In first week of May 1983, A-2 handed over to Head Clerk in my presence six sets of sanctions from Corps Ordnance along with contractor's bills and forms D'*, who asked him to produce the documents, which he did. As Subedar 'was proceeding on casual leave from 7 May, the witness handed over the documents to A-2 *on* <u>*6 May 1983 itself,*</u> *ready for despatch'*. (The date is important, as I would have obviously signed on/before 4 May, my last day at work before leave).

-On 3 June 1983, Head Clerk handed over a Registered envelope from Corps HQ addressed to A-2, (which he had received on 31 May 1983 in his presence) as he was proceeding on pension. This letter was closed with gum and tied with twine. (*At 0900 hours*) on 14 June, I put it up to Captain Cassius along with a few personal letters, for disposal, who asked for 'Local Purchase: General' File to be put up along with connected documents of correspondence. He returned these at 1300 hours, saying he would inform disposal of personal mail <u>*later*</u>.

-At 1330 hours on *16 June*... (Wrong date)...he handed the letters over to A-2, in the presence of Cassius. After about 10 minutes Cassius left the office and 10 minutes later, A-2 opened the envelop, as PW-3 could see from the telephone-recess; read through and by the same recess, handed them over to the witness in the presence of PW-5. He then saw A-2 reading through a paper and saying: *"The dates in supply orders, contingent bills, and vouchers were the same as were in sanctioning letter. In one voucher, 1,400 M was written in place of 14,000 M"*.

The witness was asked to withdraw as Major Bedi objected 'to the manner in which contents of a so-called paper/letter/DO had been brought on record'...'*as per Section 64 of Indian Evidence Act, documents can only be proved by Primary or Secondary evidence. Provisions of Section 5 come into play when conditions mentioned therein are satisfied. Since none of these conditions had been met, this piece of evidence is improper and will prejudice my client. Secondary evidence cannot be given without accounting for the original. The Honourable Supreme Court have ruled in Seetal Das vs. Sant Ram in AIR 1964, Page 606 that when no foundation is laid for reception of secondary evidence, such evidence should be excluded from consideration.'*

The Prosecution Counsel countered that no document had been brought on record but this piece of evidence was admissible under Section 60. Major Bedi argued further and drew attention to Sections 61 to 63, failing which he said the entire Chapter 5 of that Act would be worthless! After advice by JA on 'Fact' and 'Evidence' etc, the Court disallowed our objection.

The witness continued:

-*'A-2 told me to amend the dates in documents ...giving a gap of 2 to 3 days from the sanctioning letter of Corps HQ. The documents included all of the above plus the Ledger and Unit Equipment Control Register. The amendments were made by me and PW-5 (who) erased the old dates, I then put the fresh dates in pencil and thereafter he put them in ink...Besides these documents, their office copies were also amended...Thereafter on the directions of A-2, PW-5 typed two letters in my presence addressed to Corps HQ: one as Apr 1983 and the other as May 1983'.*

- On 17 June, he amended the dates on Pages 64, 66 and 67 of Unit Ledger No 36, Volume-I to correspond with the amended dates in vouchers; also in Unit Equipment Receipt Control Register. At 1000 hours the same day, Witness handed over all documents to A-2 through the recess, in the presence of PW-10. A-2 then signed the letters as 30 Apr and 12 May 1983 and then gave back office copies of both and *kept the originals and six sets of documents with him.*

-On 18 June, he informed PW-1 about the amendments carried out on both days and that A-2 had taken the rest of the documents; also showed him the office copies.

-'On 27 June 1983 I was called to CO's office, when A-1 asked me if the documents have been sent to Controller of Defence Accounts for payment; I told him that A-2 had taken away the six sets. PW-5 and 10 were also present'; *(but I had NOT gone to the Regt on 27 June 1983 and would disprove this imaginary query!)*

Cross Examination by Major Bedi:

-Witness gave the three types of nets; their sizes and scrim garnish required for each, i.e., 16x11 M; 11x8 M and 8x5 M, needing 2,360; 1180 and 590 M respectively.

-Regt took part in Exercise in Dec 1982, but he didn't know if road column left on 26 Dec.

-After denying the shades mentioned in the documents, he read out the three shades when shown the documents, as Light Green, MB Green and Dark Brown!

- *The last Date of Receipt of 75 MM garnish of these three shades from Ordnance and the Quantity, prior to 26 Dec 1982 (the date when road column left):*

MB Green, 27,000 M, ***30 Dec 1981***;

Light Green, 13,500 M, ***10 Nov 1981***;

Dark Brown, 13,500 M, ***10 Nov 1981***.

-He was then asked to read out Ledger balances of the three, which he did and they were the same as above.

-The Annual Stock taking board for 1982-83 was held on 25 Nov 1982 and the ground balances were: *NIL in Regt Stores for all three;* and NIL of MB green; *10,900 M of Light Green; and 2,500 M of Dark Brown in Battery Stores.*

-*NO scrim garnish was received from Ordnance between 25 Nov 1982 (date of Stock Taking as above) and 30 June 1983*.

Cross Examination by Colonel Ramanan on 7 July 1986:

-Stock taking is held once a year.

-Stores issued to batteries are supported by Nominal Issue Vouchers (NIV) to support entry in Ledger.

-(On being asked to identify all signatures on Ledger Pages, he identified the last entry of Page 67 [local purchase] as that of Cassius!)

-In June 1983, Ledger was taken by Capt Cassius to office of A-1 for a reply to an anonymous letter; on a query by the Court, he added that prior to that A-1 had asked all clerks in a *Bara Khana* about an anonymous letter received.

-In the documents in Jan 1983, but dated as Dec 1982, the Witness had filled the dates as per orders of A-2, for those not filled by A-1!

-There is no time stipulation from the date of Non Availability Voucher/Certificate and the date of quotations, within which documents have to be sent.

-'It is incorrect to suggest that I had already put the dates, before the documents were sent to A-1; I had put 18 Dec 1982 against my initials but I had prepared the documents in Jan 1983 ... Since I had received the quotations in Dec 1982, I put the date 18 Dec 1982 for A-1 to put the same date. (He had just said he prepared the documents on 28 Dec before his leave!)

- 'I cannot say whether the courier to collect the documents back from Corps for re-floating tender enquiries was otherwise going for collection of binoculars and compasses'.

-'I cannot say if any SOP dated 20 Nov 1980 for local purchase of ordnance and other stores signed by Crass was existing or not, as I have not seen it. I am not aware of any SOP vide which all local purchase stores are to be produced before the CO or an officer detailed by him'. He added: *'Such stores were produced before the Quarter Master. However I am aware that a unit board of officers used to be detailed every month for stores received from outstation ordnance depot and for dispatch of stored from unit'.*

- 'Although I have made a statement *before the Court of Inquiry in June 1983, I do not remember if I had stated there*

that the unit board used to check local purchase stores also'. When that was read out, he said:" *...now I say ... no particular board was there and the unit board used to do the same".*

(*Regimental Order No 420A of 27 Nov 1982 detailing a Monthly Board for opening of consignments in Dec 1982 was produced* through this witness!)

-*'It is correct to suggest that in Summary against A-2, I had stated Quarter Master Branch Subedar Head Clerk told me on 28 Dec 1982 that although local purchase of garnish had been carried out by the unit, he has not completed the documentation and I should complete it'.*

-*'In the second Summary for A-1, I had stated: 'Since I had proceeded on casual leave thereafter, I had not seen any covering letter. So I cannot identify any'.*

-He used to put up Unit Equipment Control Register but cannot say why QM did not sign. That Register had been audited for quarter ending 31 Mar 1983...Quarter Master signs the vouchers as per serial numbers allotted in it; and again after taking on ledger charge. Serial Nos 202 to 219 pertaining to different years were wrongly entered by PW-10. On seeing it, witness told him to cut and re-enter for 1983-84. But Serials 203 to 207 could not be so done, as Serials 1 to 18 for 1983-84 for next year had already been entered. Witness did not remember if these cuttings and erasures were brought to the notice of A-2; but voucher bearing amended serial when put up was signed by him.

-Never-loyal *'did not approach me on or after 13 Dec 1982, for preparing a NIV for the LP garnish'.*

-*A-2 had told me to retain his mail except that important letters should be put up to Captain Cassius'.* After receiving the "LP" letter on 3 June 1983, he had informed Cassius about it on *6/7 June* when he had told him to wait.

-He was then queried about the actual layout of the office, the relative seats of all clerks and the Quarter Master etc.

-'It is incorrect to suggest that I had opened the DO letter between 3 and 14 June 1983 or carried out the amendments etc to implicate A-2'.

-'I am not aware of leave dates of A-1; so I cannot say he was on leave from 31 Dec 1982 to 6 Jan 1983'.

-"When A-1 called me to his office ***on 27 June 1983, he was alone and it was 9 a.m****.... I am not sure about the exact time; it was* ***during parade hours only****..."*

-When amendments i.e., dates etc were made, signatures of A-1 existed on them. But he made them on orders of A-2, knowing it was an offence; he did NOT also obtain initials of A-1 on the amendments made!

-On 21 Nov 1982, 31 bundles of 1,500 M were received...*NO bundles of 1,000 M or 2,000 M of scrim garnish 75 MM were received in the unit from Nov 1980 to Nov 1982*; all the scrim garnish received in that period was in 1,500 M bundles.

Re-examination By Prosecution Counsel

-Addressee in the first 3 sets of documents was changed but not in the other 3.

-To the best of his knowledge, NO unit board was held in respect of LP garnish.

-In Aug 1982, total 90 nets of mid size 10.7 x 6 M camouflage nets were issued to batteries. NO issue was made till June 1983.

My Defending Officer, Bedi now desired to further cross examine this witness as a new matter had been introduced, i.e., camouflage nets. The witness was asked to withdraw; then the Prosecution Counsel submitted that as the nets are interlinked with garnish, no new matter had been introduced. Bedi pointed out that the new matter is permitted in Re-examination which is why he did not object then; but the right to further cross examine should still be there. JA gave his advice drawing attention to Section 138 of Indian Evidence Act, after which the Court decided to allow our re-cross examination.

Re-cross Examination by Bedi

-Balance of 10.7x6M camouflage nets on 10 Aug 1982 was 235.

Now the Prosecution wanted to re-re-examine, for which Bedi said that if the Prosecution introduced further fresh matter, he should then have the right to further re-cross examination. JA once again explained the same Section with specific reference to the last bit of evidence just received on record. Based on the same, the Court decided to disallow the Prosecutor's submission. The examination of PW-3 was over, at last!

The Prosecutor then raised the point of unnecessary delay in the balance cross examination of PW-1 (Cassius) saying the Defence Counsel who was to be present by 8 July had still not arrived, while the bundles and all required documents had arrived; he also drew attention to the only exception under Army Rule 135 for cross examination of fresh witnesses. JA then gave a summary of the sequence so far and his advice along with a reading of Section 138 of Indian Evidence Act. The Court decided to adjourn till next day (10 July) to enable the Defence to examine the bundles and documents and then PW-1.

On 10 July, immediately on assembling, Prosecution wished to produce a formal witness, the former Deputy Director of Ordnance Services from Corps HQ, as PW-4.

This gentleman, the ex-DDOS was also a Batchmate of Chief of Staff of the Corps, as also of Scraggly. But the Witness had apparently not had good relations with the General for some reason. There had also been a CBI enquiry against the witness, which resulted in his cashiering/dismissal. Unfortunately for us, the Chief of Staff, who virtually runs the Corps on behalf of the GOC, had thought that my QM and/or I must have had some deal with this witness! That was another reason for our being kept under continued

Close Arrest and frequent change of stations, endless Summaries and Courts Martial! Fate was conspiring and I had no choice but to fight.

PW-4: Ex Deputy Director of Ordnance Services of Corps HQ (examined on 10 July 1986)

-He was DDOS at Corps HQ from 5 Aug 82 to Mar 1985.

-He explained the procedure for Local Purchase and the assessment and evaluation in his office of the requests received for it.

-When shown the office copies (Exhibits), he stated that as they neither bore his signature nor his office stamp or initials of any of his officers, he was unable to say if they were ever received at his office and/or seen by him. Even if received, he stated, he could not remember now after 3½ years, *"as thousands of such applications were received there"*.

-When shown a letter from his office signed by a Major dated 18 Mar 1983 ibid (regarding *stores being available at Depot and to liaise*), he identified the signature.

-He was then shown the sanctions signed by him and he identified those too.

Cross Examination By Colonel Ramanan:

-He produced the originals of covering letters of all the contingent bills sent from the Regt, with his initials dated 23 May 1983, (obtained from Corps Ordnance)!

-After examining the office copies of covering letters from the Regt, which were exhibits earlier produced by Cassius, he stated he could not say, the two bills with the same No and date of Contingent Bill (.../.../Q) but different dates in covering letters (e.g., 2 Apr 83 in the Regt copy and 9 Apr 83 in his office copy; and so on) were the same; he could not also say: *"how many contingent bills dated 9 Apr 1983 were received in my office and from whom".*

-He then produced and identified five more covering letters with same Contingent Bill Nos but dated 05, 17, 22, and 27 Apr 1983 and 2 May 1983, **bearing his initials**. (These were the original dates of my signature, as received in his office!)

-Comparing the two sets of exhibits, he stated: *"Since all the contingent bills attached with [*—existing—*] exhibits bear different dates from the ones now appearing on these exhibits [*—now produced—*], I can say these are NOT the contingent bills which were received in my office along with [*latter*] exhibits. ...I cannot say if contingent bills bearing these dates have been received or not from any other unit in my office or not."*

-It is correct to say that a demonstration relating to use of scrim garnish was held prior to Exercise Dig Vijay on orders of HQ ... Corps.... The general demand for scrim garnish ... was tremendous...Brigadier Scraggly ... was my course-mate ...from the same company also. As all formation commanders used to ... he also used to come and ask for various stores and I used to accommodate all his requests and afterwards their requests used to be submitted to my office which were sanctioned. He used to ask for local purchase of scrim garnish but I don't remember if ...specifically for any unit at Gurgaon. I do not remember if he had come to me or not after Exercise Dig Vijay for ex post facto sanction of local purchase of scrim garnish during the exercise. He had however obtained my concurrence about it sometime in Nov-Dec 1982, before the exercise. I was not in my office from 3/4 Mar to 31 Mar 1983."

-He said letters dated 7 and 18 Mar 1983 were never put up to him.

-He confirmed that *Corps Troops units (such as those of Independent Artillery Brigade) used to deal directly with his office.*

Cross Examination by Bedi:

-Witness confirmed that throughout May 1983, he was present at work.

Re-examination was declined by Prosecution.

I submitted at that stage that a few most essential documents out of the list given by me on 26 June and 5 July 1986, which were vital for cross examination of PW-1, had still not been made available. Prosecution Counsel countered that we should give a list once for all. JA gave his advice and we were forced to re-start the cross examination of PW-1.

Cross Examination of PW-1, Cassius Resumed

Cross Examination by Colonel Ramanan

-He was first asked to read the page numbers of the three ledger pages 64, 66 and 67 (already removed and) placed as exhibits. He was unable to do so. Then he was asked to take out pages numbered the same as these, from the ledger of 1984. When asked to read out the additions and deletions of pages from the Index Card of the ledger; it was blank! He once again confirmed that there is NO entry by any authority for removal of these 3 pages. He had removed them and handed over to the Court of Inquiry in the last week of June 1983. He pointed out that there was no Index Sheet in the Local Purchase (General) File; ... could not say if any pages other than the exhibits already produced have been removed from it or not. The file contained enclosures from 75 to 103, less 79, 84 to 92 and 94.

-Verbatim question and answer:

"Is it correct to say that this file was in your personal possession from 0900 to 1330 hours on 14 June 1983?"

"This file was put up in my office along with other files by the clerk that day."

-The presence of enclosures of 1982 in the file of 1983 was then brought out; also that the file of 1982 had also been put up that day. *"It is correct that I had access to this file till I handed over charge to my successor"*.

-The witness then stated he saw only the 1982 file on 16 June 1983. *"It is incorrect to suggest that I have tampered with these files"*. File on Claims General (opened in Apr 1983) was shown; he stated it was not put up on 14 June 1983 to him.

-He was then confronted with the conflicting statements he had made before the Court of Inquiry (in June 1983) as well as Summary of Evidence of A-2 (in Jan 1984) and now before the Court. He tried to say the officer recording had done it wrongly! (But he had 'signed...*as correct*'!)

-He was asked to produce a chit with the figure of 'recovered garnish' as given in my No 3 Summary, signed by Never-loyal (indicating 54,500M) subject to proof. When asked to explain the anomaly between this and his statement of 63,800 M (actually 63,900 M) to the Court of Inquiry; he replied that the latter figure included all garnish held in the Regt on that date! He then produced the latter state as an exhibit.

-He stated he *was not aware of any instructions by the Court of Inquiry for safe custody of the 'recovered garnish'. He did not, as officiating QM also, take any precautions for its safe custody;* nor did he know where it was on this date.

- Further anomalies in the figures given out by him at 5 different places were brought out through him, as follows:

> -In Court of Inquiry, Never-loyal having told him the figure of <u>50,000 to 55,000 M</u>. In the same Court of Inquiry, a figure of <u>63,800 M</u>, which ought to have *'actually totalled to <u>63,900 M</u>'* according to him!
>
> -In my No 1 Summary, the same Never-loyal having told him a figure of <u>40,000 to 45,000</u> M.

-In my No 2 Summary as 46,000 to 50,000M.

-In my No 3 Summary, first verbally as approx 55,000 M.

-In my No 3 Summary, again, as per the chit ibid as 54,500 M.

-He was then asked if he had replied in the Court of Inquiry (when asked about whether he had checked the state of garnish in the unit between 14 May and 16 June 1983), about *ordering Never-loyal to check the state of garnish on 6 June 1983 and the latter having reported to the Witness: "Garnish was lying in Salvage Store in sealed bundles. On being asked to check, he reported, 55,000 Metres approximately of garnish being held"*. The witness denied it and was then confronted with the recorded statement. He volunteered and stated that he 'had clarified it as 6 July; and not 6 June in the Summary of Evidence'! (There is NO record of this, as the question by the Court of Inquiry was specific: *"Did you check the stock of garnish in Quarter Master Stores between 14 May and 16 June 1983?"* The question of July or a mistaken reply does not arise at all)!

-*"It is incorrect to suggest that all transactions relating to A-1 and A-2, as deposed by me here, in fact, occurred on 17 June 1983 and not on 16 June 1983"*.

Cross Examination Declined by Bedi.

Re-examination by the Prosecution Counsel:

-When he was officiating as QM, Regt kept reminding the Brigade HQ for the ledger pages 64, 66 and 67, for getting the audit completed. Subsequently on CO's orders, fresh pages were inserted.

-*"On 28 June 1983, the bundles which I saw were in a sealed state with ordnance markings. Bundles were approximately 30 to 35 in number, although I had not counted them. The unit junk store is also called salvage store"*

PW-5: Assistant Stores Clerk of QM Branch of Regt (examined on 11 July 1986)

Direct Examination by Prosecution:

-Posted in 1978; working in QM Branch of Regt; returned from annual leave some time in Apr 1983.

-Once he was told by Quarter Master Branch Subedar Head Clerk to prepare formal documents for a local purchase, after sanction was received. He did and handed them over to Head Clerk.

-During second week of June 1983, when PW-3 was officiating as Head Clerk, told him about amendments of dates on all those documents. When he asked him for authority, he was told Quarter Master (A-2). He erased the dates; then Witness No 3 put fresh dates in pencil as had been directed to him by A-2 and he inked them; he then identified such dates, except in one case where 4 May appearing now was not in his hand. He had also amended one figure which was wrong (1,400) as 14,000 M. Then he had prepared the covering letters; he added then that he was told to type one of them as Apr and the other as May.

-Once they were ready, PW-3 handed them over through the telephone recess to A-2 at about noon; but not sure of the time.

Cross Examination by Ramanan:

-Signature in Non Availability Voucher/Certificate of 21 Nov 1982 was not his.

-There was no local purchase for unit MT (about which PW-2 had deposed!)

-While at Exercise location, he was the 'Q' clerk *and he used to put up the Q branch mail between that location and main location to Major Crass through the officiating* QM at exercise... went on leave from exercise...7 Feb to 10 Apr 1983.

-He neither consulted Quarter Master Branch Subedar Head Clerk nor PW-3; nor any one told him to add: *"...locally purchased in Dec 1982"* in the vouchers.

-He did not recollect as to in what form the documents had been handed over to him for the erasures etc: loose; tied; or in file/envelope.

-He neither remembered if office copies were there or not; nor whether he amended them nor not, even after his answer to Question No 21 in Court of Enquiry on the subject and his answer as follows was read out: "Office copies were **not** amended by me". *At the Court of Inquiry, he had been unable to identify any of the documents* as having been prepared by him, *"...as at no place does it have my initials or handwriting"*; but he did now!

Cross examination by Bedi and Re-examination by Prosecution Declined.

PW-6: Ordnance Clerk at Corps Ordnance Branch (examined on 11 July 1986)

Examination by Prosecution Counsel:

-Though from Northern Command Ordnance Branch, officiated as Ordnance Clerk at Corps Ordnance Branch ***"from 3/4 May till about 25 June 1983"***.

-During the third week of May 1983, he had gone to the office of PW 4, and was handed over a folder containing some contingent bills; on checking he found that the date of sanction; date of supply order; and date of voucher—all the three were the same in all of them. Also in one 'contingent bill' (wrongly stated so here, later corrected by the witness as 'Voucher'), the figure was wrongly written as 1,400 M in place of 14,000 M.

-The next morning he brought it to the notice of PW-4, who ...asked for the name of the CO of ... Medium Regiment... could not find...As the name of A-2 existed in the covering letters, *Major from Branch prepared the draft of a Demi Official letter* and asked the witness to type the same on the name of A-2.

(The JA in his Summing Up in Revision twisted this drafting as that by PW-4!)

-The witness then produced the office copy of the said letter and identified it.

-After being shown the copies of all documents, he perused them for 8-10 minutes and then said: *"I can identify these documents only when originals are shown to me"*, as his observations about dates and quantity (in one voucher) did not match.

-I did not receive the documents any time after they were returned by me.

Cross Examination by Defence Counsel:

-After Major's signature, he put the DO and the documents in one envelop and placed it for dispatch on the rack marked: 'Other units'. He did not know what happened to that envelop afterwards.

-Verbatim Question and Answer:

"These documents are not the ones received by you at HQ...Corps"?

"I cannot say so unless I am shown the originals"... 'However I feel ***these are the same...however I cannot say so firmly. These are not the original documents received at HQ Corps'****...'I mean these are only copies.*

I did not receive the documents at any time after they were returned by me.'

Re-examination by Prosecution Counsel:

-The original documents if they are complete in all respects are forwarded to Controller of Defence Accounts (CDA), under the stamp and signature of DDOS at Corps HQ, with a copy of the covering letter to the unit for information.

(This clerk was on this job till 25 June 1983 and documents were not received back in his office, during his tenure)

(Next witness Subedar Never-loyal would be examined on next assembly of the Court, on 14 July 1986)

PW-7: Subedar Quarter Master Never-loyal (examined on 14-17 July 1986)

(Judge Advocate arrived late due to late arrival of vehicle and the Court directed the Prosecutor against such incident again.)

Direct Examination by Prosecution Counsel:

-Serving in the Regt since 1966; took over as Subedar Quarter Master on 16 Nov 1982 from the previous one who left on retirement. *During handing over everything was properly checked and was found correct.* A-2 was the Quarter Master at that time.

-During first or second week of Dec 1982, A-2 told him to go to one ABC Industries at Kashmere Gate, Delhi and collect *some* garnish from one person *Rooster & Co, ...* attached with *ABC Industries.* When he checked with A-2, on quantity of garnish; need for working party; vehicles required and authority for collection, he had told him: no need of working party; to take the already attached vehicle to the witness; and *"to collect whatever quantity of garnish ...given"*. He also told him that a Sikh person from Rooster & Co would meet him at ABC Industries and deliver the item. Accordingly, he left at about 0900/0930 the same day in a Shaktiman 3 ton, driven by *Naik PC* and reached ABC Industries at 1045/ 1100 hours... ***NO OTHER person went with them!*** He met the owner of ABC Industries and told him the purpose, who told him to wait for the representative of Rooster & Co. The person (Sikh) came, (whom he had seen earlier in the Regt, *supplying plastic jerricans*) and led him to a transport Co *"½ to 1½ KM away"*. He asked for the unit and was told ... Medium Regt and the name of A-2.

-'He then showed me a few bundles and asked me to take them. I asked him as to how many bundles are there. He told me to count myself. ...I counted 13 ...and 1500 M in each, totalling 19,500 M. Bundles were packed in thin Hessian cloth and could be seen through that it was UNDYED (khaki) (NO such shade exists in Ordnance Vocabulary!) ... no marking... driver and I loaded in vehicle. ... Each bundle weighed approx 15-20 kg.'

-After loading when asked for need to sign, voucher, challan etc, he was told the person had spoken to A-2 and no need of anything. He reached back at 1245-1300 hours. Reported to A-2 he had brought 13 bundles totalling 19,500 M of garnish. A-2 ordered him to issue it straightway.

-'When I asked him any NIV to be prepared, he told me to issue the garnish first. ... equal quantity to each battery, a little to HQ battery and keep rest with me. Since I was not satisfied about this method of distribution without any receipt or NIV of the material ... I straightaway went to Quarter Master Branch Subedar Head Clerk.... I told him that I had brought 19,500 M of garnish.'

My counsel immediately objected to *'any evidence being brought in record of a conversation between this witness and Subedar... , unless the Prosecution undertook to produce Subedar ... also, as, in a conversation what is said by both parties should be recorded; and what is said by one without bringing on record what the other said is meaningless and unintelligible. Apart from this it is insisted that Subedar... be produced by Prosecution as he is an essential witness, who had earlier been examined in two Summaries of Evidence, by the Prosecution. The statements of Subedar... at the summaries contradict the testimony of PW 7 here. I am making the submission at the earliest stage now for the prosecution to have enough time to procure the presence or take other steps to bring his evidence on record. It is also felt that Subedar ... whose evidence is not favourable to prosecution, and he having attended the proceedings thrice earlier, is not being brought intentionally by the Prosecution.'*

Prosecution Counsel countered saying: 'Hearsay' is permitted under certain circumstances... (He) cannot be compelled to produce any witness. ... *In case ... any lacuna left ... by Prosecution not examining a witness, the benefit of any doubt arising from the matter will certainly go to the Defence. All efforts will be made to procure the attendance of all the witnesses whose evidence is recorded in the Summary of Evidence... and if the Prosecution does not examine any witness whose evidence is there in the Summary of Evidence, he would be surrendered for cross examination to the Defence under Army rule 134. There is ample provision in the law for the procedure... where a witness is dead or cannot be found or his attendance cannot be produced without undue delay or expense. When the proper stage arrives, this question will then be thrashed out.*

Defence Counsel submitted that '*While it is agreed that the request is premature but the same has been made to provide ample opportunity to the prosecution to procure presence of this witness or to support my plea of mala fide at a subsequent stage. Regarding admission of evidence of conversation, the only section I can think of is Section 7 of the Indian Evidence Act, vide which, occasion, cause or effect of what a party has done in consequence of something conveyed to him or his conduct under Section 8 is admissible. But what is stated is the conversation by one of the parties is not covered by any authority of Section 7 or 8 or any other places.*'

JA then gave advice on both points: *Regarding procuring the attendance of Subedar... there is no controversy*. Regarding admissibility of the evidence of alleged conversation ...Section 5 of the Indian Evidence Act.... He then went on to give a gist of many Sections and concluded: '*...if the object is only to prove that the other person indeed asserted something to the witness and not to prove the fact of that thing or event, the witness is competent to speak about it and it may be received in evidence if it is otherwise relevant to the case.*'

The Court considered it in closed court and decided to disallow our objection. The witness was called.

Direct Examination Continued:

-Requested Subedar ... to prepare NIV for issuing garnish to batteries. As there were no documents from the dealer, he was advised by Subedar to issue and keep a record with himself. He then collected a blank voucher form from clothing stores; *got signatures of battery representatives* against the quantity shown on their batteries; and issued the material the same day.

-*'The remaining bundles were kept in the veranda of the tent stores where other stores were also kept'.*

-*'As NIV is prepared in the office, this document was for own record and I had written NIV on it'.* He then showed the distribution of 3 bundles (4,500 M) to each battery and 2 (3,000) to HQ battery.

-*'NIV is prepared by me and it is in my hand and I had written digits 601 in my hand. It is the entry serial number of NIV Register maintained for my own record. If the Register is shown to me, I shall identify serial 601'.* He was shown *"Issue Register, 1983'* and indicated 601; (But *the date was second week of Dec 1982, as he had collected and issued "the same day")*

-He had handed over the NIV and the Register to Subedar ....

-*'I was called to the office of QM in June 1983, but I can't remember the date now'.* At that time, ...Major Crass, Captain Cassius and Major Tanjore Doll ...were present. Crass asked him whether he had brought any local purchase garnish; he gave the details of the quantity, NIV and distribution.

-*'After that, I was not given any instructions by Captain Cassius. I have never checked the quantity of garnish in the Regt. After their enquiry, I was told* **... to** *check all stores in the Regt. I was also instructed to lay outside the respective stores all the unused garnish available in the unit.* (Obvious it is on or after 18 June, as Tanjore Doll and I had visited the unit during our leave for the first time that day; whereas all others say it was 28 June, when Rabbi had come!)

-'I could locate 8 to 10 bundles in tent stores where ordnance, mechanical transport and salvage items were kept; approx 30 such bundles from junk store... the officiating Quarter Master told me to get these bundles placed in front of the clothing stores. Certain other gunny bags etc which were unserviceable were also found underneath the garnish bundles. This entire garnish was approx 54,000 M. All this garnish was ordnance pattern. All the bundles were bearing ordnance markings, such as 'from Calcutta factory to central ordnance depot (COD) Kanpur'; COD Kanpur to Ordnance Depot Shakurbasti, Delhi, cat part numbers and railway receipt numbers, etc in ink.... Subsequently those bundles were inspected by ...(them). (Cassius says, he never ordered Subedar Never-loyal for garnish to be taken out; the latter says he did!)

-Afterwards around middle of June 1983, A-1, who had come to the unit during his leave had asked witness, outside own office, in the veranda, if he had brought any LP garnish and witness told him the quantity.

(This sequence indicates that the so-called recovery of garnish at about 7.20 PM on 28 June is a cooked up event, as my only visits to the Regt in June were on 18 and 25 June, before *Bara Khana* on 27 June and rejoining on 28 June 1983, as brought out by many witnesses from both sides, with the exception of PW-3 who talked of 27 June, 0900 hours! The only doubt is how Tanjore Doll could have got involved so early into the plot and if he knew about any 'alleged recovery' BEFORE 18 June 1983, as he returned to Delhi from leave only on 15 June 1983 and had met me at home on 16 and 17 June and been briefed about the Regt?)

-'The garnish which was taken out from the junk store was not on ledger charge. I cannot say from where this garnish lying in the junk store came'; he then clarified: *'This can be clarified*

from Subedar... who was my predecessor'. (This is the statement AFTER he has obtained certificates from ALL store-holders in Nov 1982 AND STB had been done on 25 Nov 1982!)

-Thereafter on instructions of A-2, he had sent the remaining two bundles to exercise location from where a demand had come for garnish.

-He identified the signatures of the 4 recipients as per the "NIV".

Cross Examination by Defence Counsel:

-'I do not know the full form of ABC Industries. I had earlier gone there in Nov 1982 to collect plastic jerricans for the unit. This ABC... is behind the railway station on the main road. 3 ton was parked just in front of this ABC.... I do not know where the office of Rooster Co was. But I was told as well as I have always found the representative of Rooster Co in ABC Industries. I have been there during the course of my duty 2,3 times. I do not remember the purpose of all my visits except these two specific ones. As and when I visited, I waited and the representative of Rooster Co came there and met me. The plastic jerricans, like the garnish, were collected from elsewhere other than ABC building. I do not remember about other transactions whether delivery was at ABC or any other place. Garnish and jerricans were both got from Rooster Co. I do not remember, I had not collected any other item from Rooster or ABC.'

-He was then asked about the route he had taken both ways and the time taken; as also the parking of a Shaktiman 3 ton in those narrow lanes; and the layout of the office of transport company. Witness was confused about everything!

-'It is incorrect to suggest that each bundle in fact weighed 40 kg, and not 15-20 kg as stated by me. I did not pick up any bundle alone but these were handled by me along with the driver... we had to make 13 trips to load 13 bundles. I had never seen local purchase garnish earlier than this although I had seen ordnance pattern bundles earlier'.

-'I do not know when I had made entry No 601 in the Issue Register, 1983, on the day of issue or later... made in the month of Dec 1982. I can also point out PRIOR to this entry, the following entries of 1983: 489 to 501 of 14 Mar 1983; 502 of 2 Mar 1983; 8 entries of 19 Jan 1983; 503 to 505 of 19 Jan 1983'.

-He then volunteered to say that the <u>Register was for his personal record and it was not accountable</u>. Many NIV come without dates and he enters ***as per directions of Quarter Master***.

(JA fell sick for next 2 days; so the next sitting was on 17 July 1986)

<u>Cross Examination continued</u>:

-A sketch of the unit area (from my No 3 Summary) was shown to the witness and he was asked to identify the 'junk store', after counsel undertook to prove the same through a witness later. *'I point out the junk store which is also known as salvage store. I also point out tent store'.*

(The Court observes that the witness has to be pointed out now and then to answer specifically to questions put to him and not to reply in a vague manner.)

-'I got 30 bundles of garnish removed from the salvage (junk) store to the front of clothing store in a vehicle with the help of some men on the order of... Cassius. I do not remember the driver of the vehicle or any member of the working party. It was around 1930-2000 hours on 28 or 29 June 1983. There is no electricity in the junk store. I do not know if two orderlies of Brig ... and ... were staying in salvage store, as I did not see them...There are two rooms: one big and one small... I do not know the dimensions...the time given by me 1930-2000 hours is the time bundles were removed from the junk (salvage) store. However the bundles were taken out during daylight after which they were shown to Cassius and finally removed at 1930-2000 hours'.

-Handing/taking over done by me while I took over in Nov 1982 was done as per ledgers...Although I maintain bin cards,

in this case, I have not …As far as I remember I have not shown any stock register to Major Crass'.

-'On 06 Nov 1982, I issued 4,600 or 46,000 M , I am not sure, of scrim garnish in the unit. However this issue has been recorded in NIV dated 22 Nov 1982 by someone in the office…When shown the NIV, he accepts,: 'I have prepared and signed this NIV in my own hand'.

<u>Cross Examination Declined by Colonel Ramanan</u>.

<u>Re-examination by Prosecution Counsel</u>:

-'This garnish 4,600 or 46,000 M, which I do not remember is of ordnance pattern. I cannot recollect the colour of this garnish but I can state after seeing the NIV'. In the NIV, Serial 5 relating to Apparatus Camouflage Net 35x20' had been scored out because items were not of correct size and a few, unserviceable. As told to him by his predecessor, when the items had been sent back, they had been returned with a suggestion that these may be placed before the condemnation board. Batteries were told to accept it.

<u>Questions By the Court</u>:

-'I do not know the distance from unit to ABC Industries; it may be 30 KM. The traffic was not very heavy but normal, it being morning hours'.

- 'I could see through the thin Hessian cloth …each of the bundles had 15 small bundles…smaller bundles had 100 M hence bigger ones 1,500 M. Accordingly I distributed the bundles…They opened these before me and checked the same'.

-'When I took over in Nov 1982, <u>I had checked the ground balance of garnish also'.</u>

-'I have never been to the junk store prior to 28 June 1983…store-man used to go there if and when required'…Since no item in the junk store was handed over to me by (the predecessor), who only handed over the keys to me, I did not visit…

- In reply to a question suggested by the Prosecution Counsel: *'When I took over in Nov 1982, I checked up garnish on ledger charge and all of it was ordnance pattern... because it bore ordnance markings'.*

- In reply to a question suggested by the Defence Counsel: *'Serial 5 of the NIV of 22 Nov 1982, which had been scored out did not bear the signature of anyone. I have written US to denote unserviceable. I do not remember if the item was put before condemnation or not'.*

PW-8: Mr. CS, Manager, Sphere Corporation (examined on 17-18 July 1986)

Direct Examination by Prosecution Counsel:

-Manager of Sphere Corporation, Jalandhar since Sep 1980; only an employee and not a shareholder. Firm, since being established in 1978, dealing with supplies to the Army, except food stuff: deals in motor parts, tarpaulins, batteries, clothing and garnish. We always aimed for maximum sales...dealt with ... Ordnance Depots and units and formations (implying from Secunderabad to Rajasthan, Pathankot).

-During Nov Dec 1982, one person 'Rooster' was our representative at Delhi... came to know of need for 87,000 M of garnish for a Medium Regiment at Gurgaon. ... The deal was for 87,000 M.

The witness was asked to withdraw. Prosecution Counsel then submitted that as there was no deal for 87,000 M nor supplied, *witness be treated as adverse* under Section 154 of Indian Evidence Act...the Court has enormous powers. He would like to put questions as if in cross examination.

Defence Counsel submitted that he opposed the request. While the power is vast, it is not arbitrary, but should be judicious and exercised with all established norms of justice. The question the Honourable court is to consider is the actual quantity of garnish supplied. The prosecution argument is that only 19,500 M was supplied. Court cannot determine by an interlocutory order the very question which is to be determined. Hence giving permission at this stage will mean that the Prosecution story has already been believed and the Defence version which is that full 87,000 M was indeed received has been disbelieved. This does not require an interlocutory order but a final decision.

Prosecution Counsel said that it is legally incorrect to call any decision of this court as interlocutory... the permission sought is only to elicit the truth.

JA then gave a lengthy advice drawing attention to a number of provisions including Sections 138 and 154 of Indian Evidence Act and concluded: '... your discretion should be used with interest of justice in view'. The Court was closed...decided to allow the submission for cross examination.

<u>Examination by Prosecution Counsel in Terms of Section 154 of Indian Evidence Act</u>:

-After consulting the firm's record, he stated: total deal was for 87,000 M in three shades, i.e., 62,000 M of MB Green; 11,000 M of Dark Brown and 14,000 M of Light Green; the rate being 68 paise per meter, total value was Rs 61,526/20 P. Then he gave out the details of Bill Nos and amounts of six bills totalling to Rs 61,526/20 P.

-Firm is owned by a Sikh person (and his two lady-relatives) but he has neither ever gone to the Regt nor met anyone.

-When the deal was struck, witness did not know the CO or QM. But had met A-2 at Meerut ...before (the aborted No 2) GCM in Aug 1985.

-'It is correct to suggest that the deal was finalized through Rooster, who generally went...did not inform us about this deal in writing...but on telephone'.

-'We receive tender enquiries for quotations...send the quotations...If rates are approved, we send the supply order and then send the goods along with the bills.

However in this case, as we were informed by Rooster that the unit had not yet got the sanction, but they need the garnish as part of their scheme and officers in the unit are alright and the Govt money will go nowhere. Therefore we told Rooster to give his assent to the unit and that we would supply the material. At the same time it was impressed upon Rooster that the sanction should be obtained at the earliest so that we could send our bill early'.

-They have only one godown of the Firm in Jalandhar. As 3 ½ years have lapsed, he was unable to say what all material was kept there during Nov-Dec 1982. *'However, we do keep garnish in a substantial quantity there'*. Depending on the urgency of need and availability at the godown, the item is sent from there or got from local market and then sent. For this deal, the supply from the godown, was booked with ... Transport Corporation for Delhi. Rooster would collect and deliver. But unfortunately ... I neither remember nor do I have the record of the date of booking. As per my recollection it was in the first week of Dec 1982. Receipt given by ... transport was sent to Rooster but neither he nor we kept a photocopy. Receipt was sent by ordinary post.

-Supply order was received by us in May 1983. From Dec 1982 to May 1983, while we did not write to the Regt for payment, we told Rooster to keep going to find out. We had complete faith and were aware formalities take time, so we knew supply order would be received. *Also we had supplied like this to many units.*

-*Unlike Govt, we don't retain records like supply order for a long time,* after a supply. We had sent 2 out of 6 Supply Orders to ...Independent Armoured Brigade in reply to their questionnaire, as the other 4 were not traceable. An Army courier had brought the questionnaire and taken the reply. I do not have it with me, but I hope I am able to trace it in my office.

-Rooster confirmed the bills have been sent for payment.

-Transport Co at Delhi is *just one furlong* from ABC Industries.

-First request for payment was made vide our letter of 17 June 1983; but do not remember whether by ordinary or registered mail. Thereafter on 12 Aug 83, 6 Oct 83, 9 Dec 1983, 25 Jan 1984 and going on. Only one reply has been received on 04 Jan 1986.

-Do not recollect if supply order was received through Rooster or from the unit.

-We have not served legal notice for payment.

Cross Examination by Defence Counsel:

-(When shown the exhibits of supply order, he said he) did not remember if dates in these were the same as in the ones they had received which were 'similar'; however, quantities and rates are the same and were also reflected in subsequent correspondence with the unit.

-'It is correct that the procedure followed by us is that our representative goes to various units, finds out their requirements of local purchase, collects tender enquiries and after consulting with the Firm...gives quotations to the unit and either collects supply order by hand or the same is received by dak, after which supplies are made, either through our representative or direct...'

-'In dealing with Govt agencies maximum time taken for payment is 2-4 months at the most. Keeping this in mind, allowance is made in rate quotations. To the best of his knowledge, many other traders follow the same procedures.

-100 M of garnish supplied by them weighs over 2.5 kg; (he had no knowledge of the Ordnance one). They buy from open market as well as manufacture garnish; these 87,000 were partly manufactured by them and partly from market

-Questionnaire was received in May 1984.

-Transport Co was paid its charges (by weight and not volume), only after goods were received by Rooster, for which the Firm sends the money every time. He did not remember now but can verify from Firm's records and give it later. They have had and still have lot of dealings with ... Transport Co.

-Rs 2,366/40 P was paid as Sales Tax by Sphere Corporation in July 1983, as the same had to be paid within 30 days of close of the quarter when sale is done.

Cross Examination Declined by Colonel Ramanan.

Re-examination by Prosecution Counsel:

-*'We did not receive tender enquiry for (sic) the unit, as our representative asked us directly for quotations'.*

-*'I have not signed any quotation for this deal quoting 68 Paise per Meter as it was verbal between me and Rooster'*. Rate was only given on telephone to Rooster by him and he would not know who, if any, from Sphere Corporation may have signed any quotation. It was verbal only over the telephone between him and Rooster. Normally the procedure explained is followed, but in the instant case, due to the urgency for exercise indicated by the unit, they had dealt verbally.

-*'In the Summary of Evidence recorded earlier*...(A-2's...), *although we were not asked to produce the receipt from Sales Tax Dept, however we had forwarded our Sales Tax Return for the first quarter of 1983-84 along with bank certificate of payment of tax to sales tax Dept and Chartered Accountant's Certificate'*.

My Counsel withdrew and will be available when we/ Court needed him. Prosecution Counsel pointed out a mistake in entry of a date in an exhibit; the same was accepted.

PW-9: Lt Col Tanjore Doll, My Successor (examined on 18 to 23 July 1986)

Direct Examination by Prosecution Counsel:

-Commanding Officer of ... Medium Regiment since 2 July 1983; was Battery Commander of HQ Battery, when A-1 was CO.

-Unit participated in Exercise Dig Vijay from Dec 1982 to Mar 1983. Initial orders for 100% guns and vehicles to take part were later changed to 6 guns from Regt. Each gun/vehicle had to have two camouflage nets...HQ Battery had carried.

-In Dec 1982, his Battery Quarter Master Havildar reported that some garnish had been received. He could not say, despite having seen if LP or Ordnance type.

-*'During the Exercise in a conference at Brigade HQ, A-1 had mentioned to a Commanding Officer, in my presence about huge quantity of scrim garnish having been contracted. Also during the Exercise, during one of the routine Battery Commanders' Conferences, which I also attended, A-1 had mentioned that local purchase of garnish had been contracted'.*

-He was on annual leave from 26 Apr to 24 June 1983; however was back in station on 15 June 1983 itself.

-*'On 16 June 1983, I met A-1 in his new house in Pratap Chowk area, where he was to shift at a later stage. He told me that presently he was going to Brigade HQ and that on his return he would call me to his house for handing taking over notes relating to the unit. In the evening through a message, we mutually fixed 17th evening for a meeting. I went to his house on 17 June 1983'.*

-Major Crass who was otherwise the 2 IC was officiating as CO then.

-On the morning of 17th, before Physical Training parade, Major Crass went to his house and asked him if he knew about local purchase of garnish. *'I told him that except for the mention made by A-1 during the Exercise, I was not aware about the arrival of this local purchase garnish. In the evening, A-1 and I discussed various unit matters. Thereafter he told me that Major Crass has raised some doubts about local purchase of garnish to him on telephone... also that though Major Crass and A-2 were required to see him about this matter, and give progress report, however, none of these two had reported to him till then. We then decided to visit the unit the next day, to find out the details and accordingly we went to the unit on 18 June 1983'.*

-On reaching the unit, A-1 went to his office, while I went to QM's office, I found Major Crass present there. Subedar Never-loyal (...PW-7...) *was then called by us. When we enquired from him whether he had brought any local purchase garnish, he told us that in the month of Dec 1982, he had brought 19,500 M of garnish from one transport Company at Kashmere Gate....also showed us a voucher for distribution of 16,500 metres of garnish. He also showed us a Register where this distribution of garnish was recorded...* (He identified the exhibits)...*he told us he had dispatched the balance 3,000 M to exercise location...Thereafter in the office of A-1, in his presence, a discussion on the matter was held, in which, Captain Cassius, Major Crass and I participated'.*

-A-1 was briefed about what Never-loyal had said, of which there was no record about 3,000 M said to have been sent to exercise location; A-1 was then shown the file with correspondence in which two letters from Corps Ordnance (07 and 18 Mar 1983): about 're-floating tender enquiries' and 'liaising with depot'. (I saw them for the first time and initialled as per my habit with the date, whereas NO ONE else who had seen the letters so far, had initialled/ signed!)

-A-2 was away on leave; so a courier was sent to him perhaps the same day for some clarifications, and this courier returned around 21 June 1983 with a certificate from A-2 addressed to the Regt, with a copy to me also.

-He then brought out the events of 25 June 1983 and stated that Crass told A-1 that the matter should be sorted out before he left on the Course. *'Since I was to eventually take over from A-1, I also stressed that A-2 should come back to explain the matter'*. When Crass also said so, A-1 stated that A-2 may not be at Dehradun and may have gone to his village somewhere in Uttarkashi. Crass asked again; so A-1 told him to *'do whatever he felt proper, as he was the officiating CO till 27 June 1983'.*

-Major Crass *'also said at that time that* ***someone may write anonymous letter to the brigade HQ on the matter.*** *At this A-1 asked as to who can write.* Crass then said, *since the whole Regt knows about it,* ***anyone can write****'.* In fact A-1 had told Major Crass after the above conversation, in my presence again that *'he could do whatever he felt proper as Officiating Commanding Officer about recalling A-2'.*

-On 27 June 1983, a *Bara Khana* was arranged in honour of A-1. As per a message received, he and Crass had reached ½ hour in advance and Crass told him that all Battery Commanders had also been called ½ an hour earlier. There in CO's office, Crass showed a pseudonymous letter with a covering letter from Brigade addressed to him by name as offg CO, with instructions to reply the same night.

-*'After a few days, I saw a reply addressed to brigade HQ, signed by Major Crass'.*

-He explained the visit of Rabbi with two officers, who *'left after it was dark'.*

-On 29 June, he and A-1 had gone to brigade HQ, *'as per instructions left by Colonel Rabbi; Major Crass, however, did not go to Brigade HQ with us, although he too had been asked by Rabbi to be present'.*

-After Rabbi and party left on 28th evening, Cassius informed the witness *that he has found out* (sic) *about approx 55,000 to 50,000* (sic) *metres of unused garnish. Then I asked him if he has physically checked the garnish; he replied in the negative. I then advised him to layout the garnish next morning and to carry out a physical check. However I am not aware if this garnish was physically checked by Cassius, as he did not get any report regarding this from him.*

-At the brigade HQ on 29 June morning, A-1 explained the handing over points to Scraggly in my presence, when all

points were read over one by one; one of these was concerning local purchase of garnish. Scraggly said it should be in the Handing Taking Over Certificate itself. A-1 told Scraggly that we could come back on 1 July, after clarifying the same from A-2 (likely to arrive on 1 July 1983), though his leave was till 14 July. However, on Scraggly's direction, it was retyped at brigade HQ only and we both signed it. He asked us however to continue with handing/taking over. The certificate was then countersigned by the commander.

-Lt Col Shifty Eyes and two other officers came to the unit on 30 June morning as the Court of Inquiry.

-On 18 June when Cassius showed A-1 the ledger, I also saw the entries in ledger at pages 64, 66 and 67.

Verbatim Question and Answer:

'After having seen those pages, as the commanding officer designate, did you check up the connected documents?'

'In fact when we did not find out (sic) *any challan or convoy note or the railway receipt from the dealer, from which* (sic) *this garnish had come, then only a courier was sent to A-2 for clarification.'*

-Until I took over the unit or even upto today, I have not seen this stock of local purchase garnish in the Unit. (sic)

-It was on 30 June that I was called and directed by the Court of Inquiry to safeguard the garnish which was then lying before the Court. This garnish was of ordnance pattern. This garnish was put under seal and lock (sic)*'. After this garnish was sealed and locked, I did not see any other garnish laid out anywhere in the unit at any time thereafter, except for the fresh consignment of garnish which came during my command tenure.*

-The first letter I saw from Sphere Corporation was on 16 Feb 1984, dated 25 Jan 1984. (He produced both and identified them). After this, as he did not see either the garnish or earlier letters, he sent a reply by registered post on 24 Feb 1984.

-He stated that ledger pages ibid were taken out for producing before Court of Inquiry, Summary of Evidence etc; and after fresh stock started arriving, he ordered PW-1 to put new pages with the same numbers; (then added that he had also sough permission for brigade HQ for the same, as they had informed him that the removed pages will not be returned till finalization of the case).

-No reply was received from Sphere Corporation but another letter came in Dec 1985.

-In June 1986, he received instructions from both his brigade and Armoured Brigade to despatch the bundles as they were required by the Court. They were dispatched under a JCO on 18 June 1986, who handed over ...on 20 June 1986.

-As he had got them sealed, looked after safe custody, dispatched and had seen the markings...he identified the following as Material Evidence (ME):

32 bundles, as ME1 to ME-32.

62 loose rolls of Light/MB green with markings, together as ME-33.

8 loose rolls *Undyed Khaki* (??) with markings, together as ME-34.

12 loose rolls (normal size??) and 2 small loose rolls in various colours of Green with markings, together as ME-35

2 loose rolls *Undyed Khaki* (??) without markings, together as ME-36.

The Court made the following observations:-

-"Of ME-1 to ME-32, *stitching of only 4 (ME-1 to ME-4) is in tact*. The remaining are either partly open or loosely stitched. Garnish seen in all the bundles, except the stitched ones were in various shades of Green.

-26 bundles addressed to Commandant, Central Ordnance Depot, Kanpur...3 bundles have vague markings...2 bundles bear no addresses or markings...1 bundle had Ordnance Depot, Shakurbasti markings.

-ME-33 and ME-34 bear black ink print marks and all of them have white cloth strips bearing factory markings indicating cat/part numbers; length as 100 metres and width as 75 MM".

Direct Examination of PW-9 Continued:

-Before dispatching, he had ordered a board of officers to ascertain the quantity; and produced the board proceedings and identified the signatures.

Cross Examination by Defending Officer of Accused No 2:

-JCO who was member of the board was the same who accompanied the bundles here; *he had been asked to amend certain colours by the receiving unit, so he had done*. However there was no difference in the overall quantity. Board proceedings were accordingly amended and a letter had also been received from receiving unit.

-He had officiated as Commanding Officer during Sep-Oct 1982.

Verbatim Question and Answer:

-*"Is it correct that A-2 had reported about misuse of transport by Major Crass?"*

-*"A-2 told me that Major Crass (...while on leave...) was asking for a vehicle. I told him as far Crass is concerned, he is a senior officer and 2IC of the unit, the matter should be referred to A-1 who was in station."*

-*'Orders to carry two camouflage nets each were passed down to sub units'.*

-*'I cannot say of (sic) hand as to what are the scrim garnish camouflage nets authorized to a Medium Regiment'.*

-*'I cannot say if any policy was laid down by Army HQ in June 1981, vide which 16x11 M size nets for guns and tractors; and 11x8 M nets for jeeps, jongas, 1 tons and trailers was authorized'.*

-At the request of the Defending Officer, he then produced Page 57 of Unit equipment Ledger; and stated, vide which a total of 295 camouflage nets had been received in the unit between Jan and Aug 1982, of which 60 had been issued in the same period. These 295 nets were received in 5 batches: 100 (on 27 Feb 1982); 90 (on 2 May 1982) ; 25, 20 and 60 later.

(At that stage Court adjourned...to re-assemble on 21 July 1986. When re-assembled, JA was late; same vehicle problem! Court directed the Prosecutor to bring the matter to the notice of the Convening Authority for action and intimate the action taken.)

<u>Cross Examination By Defending Officer of Accused No 2 Continued</u>:

-On 25 Nov 1982, the ledger balances of scrim garnish 75 MM were: Grass Green-56,500 M; and Undyed Khaki-99,000 M.

-The following statement of witness is put on record as relevant, on the assurance of the Defending Officer:

"The road column for Exercise Dig Vijay moved on either 25 or 26 Dec 1982 and the rail column, after the departure of the Road column."

-'On 16 or 17 Jan 1983, on return from my casual leave, I went back to Exercise location with A-1, Quarter Master Branch Subedar Head Clerk and a few others'.

-'Although I cannot say if a conference was held in the last week of Nov 1982 or not, as I do not remember the date in particular, but <u>there were a number of conferences of sub unit commanders, during Sep-Oct 1982 onwards, in which shortage of garnish was discussed'</u>.

<u>*-'It is correct that* ***while I was officiating as CO (...in Sep-Oct 1982...) I gave a progress Report to Brigade HQ***</u>

***that efforts are being made to carry two camouflage nets, for each vehicle and gun'*.**

-'After checking unit records, I can say that *57 jeeps, trucks 1 ton, 3 tons and 2 plants and 15 Kraz's and 6 guns participated in the Exercise'*.

Verbatim Question and Answer:

-"Is it correct that apart from the above vehicles, 3 B-vehicles and 5 Kraz's were given to Brigade HQ and other units for the exercise?"

-"I do not remember but some vehicles were given to Brigade HQ and other units".

-'It is correct that on 25/26 Feb 1983, during the exercise, some garnish and camouflage were given to two officers from Brigade HQ in lieu of some camouflage nets and garnish, however I do not remember the exact quantity'.

-'The main Exercise Dig Vijay dates were round about night 26/27 Feb 1983 to 9 Mar 1983'.

-'On 16 June 1983, A-1 after changing into uniform dropped me at my residence and told me he was going to Brigade HQ (Meerut). He also told me he was not well and that he had been to Brigade HQ on 15 June also'.

-'I did not carry out any joint investigation with A-1 between 19 to 30 June 1983, as after 18 June 1983, I discussed this matter with A-1 on 25 June 1983 only'.

-'It is correct that on 28 June 1983, before the arrival of Colonel Rabbi, A-1 had taken a Muster Parade and there he had announced that anyone having any information of irregularity should go and intimate Colonel Rabbi, the investigating officer'.

-'On 28 June 1983, I left after Colonel Rabbi left, when it was dark. Although I do not remember about any power failure at that time, but petromax and hurricane lamps were being used during investigations'.

*-'On 28 June 1983, while myself, Colonel Rabbi, Major Crass and A-1 were sitting together, Rabbi told A-1: "**Crass has said that if you apologize, the case can be sorted out**".*

-'*While statements of other witnesses were being recorded by Colonel Rabbi and his team, A-1 was not sitting with them all along*'.

-'*On 27 June 1983, I saw A-1 only in the evening when he came for the Bara Khana. He was on leave that day*'.

-'*On 29 June 1983, while delivering the Farewell Address, Scraggly mentioned that he had difference of opinion with A-1 while serving at Army HQ*'. (sic).

(The Defending Officer submitted that the above statement of the witness is only to bring on record the fact of such a statement having been made by Commander during the address, and not to establish the *factum* of what was said.)

-'*Around Apr-May 1984, A-1 had enquired from me about the name of the driver and the members of the working party which had gone for collection of local purchase garnish in question. After this on a number of occasions, I told A-1, I was not able to find out about the names required by him*' (sic).

-'*During Dec 1984-Jan 1985, Subedar Never-loyal told me that the driver of the vehicle was Naik PC,* (who was then) *serving with another HQ Artillery Brigade*'. He was then called and he told me he had gone as driver for collection of garnish to Kashmere Gate. Thereafter I gave his name to A-1, but I could not gather any name of the working party from him or the unit.

-A-1 *had mentioned during one of the Brigade Commander's conferences that he had done local purchase of garnish in large quantities.*

-On 18 June 1983, when I went to the unit with A-1, Battery Commander of 'R' Battery was not there, being on annual leave. I do not also remember seeing Battery Commander of 'P' Battery that day.

-In Sep 1983, once when Brigadier Scraggly came to my office, A-2 was called there; I then left the office for some time. During the dining out of Brigadier Scraggly from my Officers Mess, he told A-2 in my presence he was sorry for he could do nothing for him in the case. I do not remember hearing A-2 telling him: 'It was a conspiracy with his blessings'.

-On 13 Mar 1983 night, while a few unit vehicles were returning on orders of Major Crass, there was an accident in which a Naik was fatally injured.

Verbatim Question and Answer:

-*"Is it correct that during visit of Commander ...Corps Artillery Brigade in April 1983, Major Crass was ticked off by A-1 for his misbehaviour?"*

-*"I do not know this, but the JCOs reported to A-1 in my presence about abusing by Major Crass."*

Cross Examination by Defending Officer of Accused No 1:

-On being shown the Sketch of the unit, he identified his initials and remarks and stated that although the sketch is not to scale, but it does show the relative positions of buildings in the unit area. He then indicated the Main QM Store and the Tentage Store.

Re-examination by the Prosecution Counsel:

-He did not know whether the ledger balances earlier identified by him for 25 Nov 1982 were of local purchase garnish or Ordnance.

-I do not remember as to who in particular used to broach the issue of shortage of garnish during battery commanders' conferences prior to exercise.

-On asking Naik (Driver) PC as to the quantity of garnish, the latter replied 3 different ways: 'not much (*thodi si*'); 12-13 bundles; did not know the quantity.

Re-Cross Examined by Defending Officer of Accused No 1:

-*'I met Naik PC for the first time in Jan 1985'*. Witness did not remember the subsequent occasion when Driver had said he did not know the quantity, as to whether he had called him or he himself had come to the witness.

-"It is incorrect to suggest that in Jan 1985, Naik PC had told me that they had brought one 3 ton full of local purchase garnish or to suggest that on a subsequent occasion I pressurized him to say that it was much less".

Question by the Court:

-Witness produced unit Part II order dated 30 Apr 1983, relating to annual leave of A-1.

PW-10: One More Clerk of Unit QM Branch: (examined on 23-24 July 1986)

Direct Examination by Prosecution Counsel:

-Serving since Feb 1983. In May 1983, he made entries in ledger. On 17 June 1983, he saw A-2 in the unit and Witness 3 hand over certain documents to him.

(Court was adjourned and reassembled the next day, 24 July, when Defending Officer of Accused No 2 stated that despite many earlier requests, PW-3 was being employed in sorting out various important documents given to him in his custody. *Today he was seen talking to Witness No 10 for well over 20 minutes.* He requested proper directions by the court to sort out the matter. Prosecutor, while saying PW-3 has been asking to go back to the unit, refuted all else. *The Court directed that no witness, either already deposed or still to depose is allowed to handle documents relating to this case. Court also directed the Prosecutor that witnesses who have already been deposed* (sic) *should not be seen in the vicinity of the Court, unless required*).

Cross Examination by Defending Officer of Accused No 2:

-Enrolled in Aug 1981; joined the Regt's Rear in Feb 1983, when only A2 and PW-3 were in QM office.

-Witness was examined in detail to explain the exact layout of QM's office and the clerks' office, the telephone recess, layout and distance between various tables/ clerks etc.

-He did the entries ibid in the first week of May 1983; did not remember the exact dates; did them on the basis of the relevant vouchers. He only made the entries and did not know when the officer signed them.

-He had made entries only from Serial 176 onwards in Unit Receipt Control Register based on instructions of PW-3.

-He did not know how and why Serials 203 to 207 appeared twice in the Register. He added that he was new and he did not know; it may have been a mistake.

<u>Verbatim Question and Answer</u>:

-*"I suggest to you that when serial numbers for vouchers in entries 203 to 207 was taken, the existing entries 203 to 219 were not existing."*

-*"I do not know the details of entries in this Register; I did what I was told...*I had only one month's service at that time. The scoring out and fresh entries in the Register were done by me on the orders of PW-3".

-*"I do not know why Serial No 19 was given separately and not in sequence after 207.* Although I know that entries are made in fresh year from 1 Apr 1983 onwards, I do not know why entries pertaining to 1983-84 were put in 1982-83 block."

-"I do not know why the dates for Vouchers given in the earlier page and struck out later are of Dec 1982 because some entries prior to it pertain to Nov 1982".

-'It is correct that the store-holder brings the stock register for ground balance in QM stores and tallies it with ledger balances in QM stores, which is maintained by the Q clerk as per the Distribution Column."

-'I do not know if any ACR size-envelop was received in June 1983'.

-(Thereafter the witness denied a number of suggestions about being ordered to open that envelop, photocopy and re-seal it with gum etc).

-Witness did not remember the date if it was 16 June 1983, but he did get a call from A-2 at Dehradun requesting for a vehicle, which he conveyed to PW-3.

-"I saw A-2 in QM office on 17 June 1983 morning around 1000-1100 hours, once only through the little opening in the wall."

<u>Cross Examination Declined by Defending Officer of Accused No 1.</u>

<u>Re-Examination Declined by Prosecution Counsel.</u>

Two Prosecution Witnesses from Summaries NOT Being Examined!

The Prosecution Counsel then submitted that all witnesses in Summary of Evidence of A-1 have been examined*; and except for Subedar who had handed over to Never-loyal and Quarter Master Branch Subedar Head Clerk, all other witnesses against A-2 have also been examined. Neither the Prosecution wished to examine these two witnesses nor were they available. He then stated the contents of Army Rule 134 and said: Quarter Master Branch Subedar Head Clerk was presently out of India. Several letters along with travelling allowances etc had been sent to civil authorities concerned to procure the presence of the other Subedar. However there was no positive response from the civil authorities on his presence. Although efforts were on, there was no reasonable chance of procuring the presence of these two witnesses. Information has been received from District Soldiers Sailors and Airmen Board (DSSAB), Kangra that (the other) Subedar will not be available till end of August 1986. All practicable efforts have been made in respect of these two witnesses. *Otherwise the case for prosecution is closed.*

A-2 submitted just then that he too has employed Colonel NS Bains (Retired) as his counsel. All efforts have been made for the Counsel to appear the next day, on

(*Wrong statement, as these two had deposed in one Summary of Evidence each, in my case!)

25 July 1986, till when adjournment may be granted; he alone will make a reply to prosecution submission regarding the two witnesses.

Prosecution Counsel had nothing to say.

JA gave his advice. Court decided to permit our submission for 25 July 1986.

On 25 July 1986, my Counsel handed in a written submission to counter the Prosecution Counsel's plea of non-availability of the two prosecution witnesses, citing Army Rule 134; Note 5 to Army Rule 137; and Army Rule 138. Salient points in brief are given below:

-When the accused are tried jointly, the Summaries of Evidence, even though recorded separately against each, are to be treated as one.

-As the charge against both is a common one, whatever is contained in one Summary can be used to support it, which means, the accused can use it to rebut the charge also.

-<u>Regarding Quarter Master Branch Subedar Head Clerk</u>: He had appeared twice: once each in the Summaries of Evidence of both in Feb 1984 (A-2) and May 1984 (A-1). Thereafter he was called as Prosecution Witness for the GCM on 27 Mar 1985 and was present in Brigade at Meerut during Apr and May 1985 also. When the next GCM commenced in July 1985, Prosecutor assured the Court and the Accused that *"best possible efforts were being made to procure his attendance at the earliest."* From this it will appear that Prosecution was aware all the time that he was an essential witness. His evidence is very material for defence inasmuch as he had made the following statements:

-'I also told PW-3 that as per A-2 and Never-loyal, complete stores 75 MM garnish had been received 2 weeks earlier from a firm at Kashmere Gate Delhi.'

-'Never-loyal reported to me that the complete garnish (approx 90,000 M) was received one month earlier, as

tendered for, before preparation of ULPO papers'.

-'As ordered by A-2, I collected 3 to 4 bundles of 75 MM garnish (approx 7,000 to 8,000 M) and handed over to Officer Commanding Workshop, in the first/second week of Dec 1982. At that time, I had seen 35 to 40 bundles of LP garnish (which had no ordnance markings) lying in the veranda of Tentage stores, opposite Unit Mandir'.

-'In mid-Dec 1982, all Battery Commanders had given a certificate each, in writing that they had received all their requirements for exercise and that items and quantities were also recorded in these certificates., including that of LP garnish'.

-'Financial documents are prepared by the Q Head Clerk or concerned Q clerk, only after verification from store holder regarding physical receipt of complete quantity of stores'.

-'...Physical presence of A-1 in the unit till 4 May 1983'.

-'Never-loyal had reported to me in Dec 1982 and replied in answer to my query once again in May 1983 that the complete quantity of LP garnish as tendered for had been brought by him in Dec 1982'.

-Never-loyal never approached me for preparation of NIV (voucher) but had approached PW-3 who was the dealing clerk, as per the procedure'.

-If he is produced as a witness, Never-loyal who is the only PW on the central issue of the charge against the accused persons would stand contradicted by the testimony as above. Prosecution was aware of this and has intentionally made no effort to procure his attendance in July 1985 as well as now. We rely on Paragraph 455 of Defence Services Regulations (Regulations for the Army), 1962 which reads:

> "When an application has been made for a court martial, no military witness will be allowed to leave the station, without the sanction of the authority to whom application for trial has been made. After

trial, witnesses will not disperse without the previous sanction of the convening authority".

-Prosecution Counsel's statement at the Bar cannot be used to prove a fact. It only shows the instruction given to him, but the person who gave him the instruction must appear as a witness to prove the steps taken to produce the presence of this witness in July 1985 as well as now and be subject to cross examination. It is a very material fact and should have been proved by evidence and not by a statement at the Bar. We submit that no efforts were made to procure his presence even in July 1985, as his evidence would have demolished the prosecution's case. Two versions would have come before the Court: one by PW 7, Never-loyal whose demeanour the Court would have noticed , who is also an interested party and who had tampered with the Register containing record of issues; and another by this witness, who is not only senior to him but disinterested also. Defence could have argued and can say with confidence that they would be able to convince the Court that this witness' version is to be believed or at least, there being reasonable doubt, both be disbelieved.

-It is futile to argue that his whereabouts are not known, as every Indian citizen has to intimate to Protector of Immigrants, his address abroad as the Govt has to repatriate him when the need arises. He is also a pensioner and pension paying authority ought to know his address. So evidence is required of action taken to get this witness' presence.

-Regarding Never-loyal's Predecessor Subedar Quarter Master: No evidence has been led here too; summons should have gone to the Magistrate and the latter's endorsement on it need not be proved and DSSAB is not one of the authorities to procure attendance of witnesses...it is only to supplement efforts of judicial authorities and not supplant it. Endorsements, if any, made by DSSAB has to be proved, as it is not a self-proving document. If his availability in Aug is known, so is his address; compulsive measures to procure his attendance could be taken. It will be denial of justice to the accused persons to not so wait till the end of Aug 1986, when he would be available.

-For liberty to natural justice and personal life, 'Time' is of no consideration; we rely on Army HQ Adjutant General's Branch letter No 32908/AG/PS1 dated 18 Apr 1979, which *inter alia* states:

> *"It is requirement of the principles of natural justice that a person being proceeded against is given adequate opportunity to bring out his defence against the averments of misconduct on his part. It may be appreciated, it is not the time, but justice and opportunity to defend the alleged misconduct, which is the soul of justice".*

Honourable Court would also recall that as early as 14 July 1986, Defence had submitted that the presence of Quarter Master Branch Subedar Head Clerk is essential to rebut the testimony of Never-loyal. We would also rely on Note 5 to Army Rule 137 and Army Rule (Read out).

After a reply without much substance by the Prosecution Counsel, Judge Advocate gave his advice; the Court then decided that these were NOT essential Prosecution Witnesses! *The Prosecution case was closed.*

Not examining the two prosecution witnesses who had given evidence more than once earlier was a terrible mistake, I felt, particularly in view of the reasons explained by my Counsel above. We sought a day to prepare our statements. But after a brain-storming session amongst us we agreed that the fight could not be given up so easily! The next day, my Counsel turned the tables; stating that while the 2 witnesses may not be essential to Prosecution, he *requested they be produced as Defence Witnesses,* in the interest of justice and for a fair trial! After arguments from both sides and JA's advice, the Court disallowed this request too of ours. *This I felt was even a bigger blunder by the Prosecution, the JA and the Court;* but they did not seem to realize it!

My counsel withdrew from the scene now and stated that Defence would be carried on by the Defending officers and proceedings would not be held up.

Then we both (A-1 and A-2) were asked if we wished to present any witnesses, and if so whether they were only as to character? Then procedure as per Army Rule 59 was gone through, asking us if we wished to make a statement; we declined. I pointed out that I had given a list of 22 Defence Witnesses on 12 July 1986 to the Prosecution Counsel. After eliminating 7 out of it and adding 3, and after a discussion with my co-accused, I had given the revised list again recently, all of whom may be made available. I requested also adjournment for a day to interview available witnesses; this was granted.

Defence Witnesses were provided to us in ones and twos, whom the Counsel, the Defending Officers, A-2 and I had to interview. We finally produced 14 of them:-

DW-1: BQMH who was stated to have collected a small quantity from Prosecution Witness No 7, for his battery; he denied it was his signature!

DW-2: Driver who went with a vehicle for Prosecution Witness No 7 to collect; he said there were 50 to 100 bundles.

DW-3: JCO who officiated as JCO QM in Exercise location and was stated by PW-7 to have received a small quantity of LP garnish; he denied it.

DW-4: Adjutant, to produce documents to prove NO secrecy and my leave dates etc.

DW-5: JCO QM who took over from PW-7 who knew yet another alleged signatory for his battery, but denied it was that person's!

DW-6: One more NCO, said to have collected only a small quantity from PW-7 for another battery, who too denied it was his signature.

DW-7: Adjutant during my tenure-end, on the events of June 1983.

DW-8: NCO who stayed in the two rooms (alleged by the Prosecution, to be the newly named *junk store*) from where garnish with Ordnance pattern marking was mysteriously recovered on 28 June 1983.

DW-9: The former Deputy Assistant Adjutant and Quartermaster General of Artillery Brigade, to depose for my leave dates.

DW-10: NCO Store Controller from Shakurbasti Depot to vouch for quantities and types of garnish issued to the Regt from Nov 1980 to June 1983. (Prosecution objected to his documents and it was upheld; so DW-12 was produced by us).

DW-11: Regimental Havildar Major who had detailed the working party to go with the vehicle of DW-2 and PW-7; and seen the vehicle loaded with garnish arriving.

DW-12: Store Keeper, a civilian from Shakurbasti Depot, in place of DW-10

DW-13: The Delhi representative of the firm which supplied 58 bundles of garnish from a Transport Company godown to PW-7.

DW-14: Officer from Workshop who had seen a huge amount of LP garnish lying outside Quarter Master Stores and had borrowed some without a voucher.

Just a gist of the evidence by each of them follows.

DW-1: BQMH a 'signatory' to the NIV(examined on 28 July 1986)

Direct Examination by Defending Officer of Accused No 2:

-Was Battery Quarter Master Havildar of 'P' Battery from Nov 1981 to 3 Oct 1983; posted to another unit since Oct 1983. Was on annual leave from 12 Nov 1982 to 11 Jan 1983; reported to unit and was sent to exercise location on 13 Jan 1983; and returned to permanent location on 13 Mar 1983.

-First time heard about local purchase of garnish in the Commanding Officer's *'Durbar'* in Aug 1982, when he had ordered 2 nets per gun and vehicle to be carried for the exercise. Section NCOs asked him for garnish, which was not available. However, when he joined at Exercise location, all guns and vehicles had two good nets each. In his absence, Naik MLD had officiated, but had died in the accident on 13 Mar 1983. At Exercise location, he could not take over fully as all documents were held in Gurgaon.

On being shown the purported NIV (voucher), he stated: *'The signatures indicated to me and appearing under my name are not mine. Neither my name is written in my hand and also my Army Number is not seen written here'.*

-He identified Never-loyal's signature and then said his (Witness') name was also in the handwriting of Never-loyal!

-Whenever he got a voucher, it would have a number, date and would be from the Quarter Master's office. 3 copies would be received, which he would get signed by Battery Commander or Battery 2IC and return one each to QM office and Never-loyal; third being for the Battery.

'-In Feb 1986, when called before Commander Independent Armoured Brigade, (...my CO No 4...) *for "Hearing of Charge", I told him the following:*

> *-'I was on annual leave at that time... have not received this item...It bears no date'* (after he was told it belonged to Dec 1982)*...Separate sizes and colours have not been indicated, as required for garnish'.*

- 'The second time I saw the Voucher was in the Summary of Evidence against our Commanding Officer in a cavalry unit in Ambala, when their CO showed it to me.

-'Before de-induction started on 13 Mar 1983, Commanding Officer addressed a Mandir Parade wherein he ordered that no

vehicle or convoy will move at night and that night halt will be made at Rohtak. However, on 13 Mar 1983 night, on the orders of Major Crass, we started for permanent location in a convoy of administrative vehicles of all batteries. On the way, there was an accident resulting in the death of Naik MLD, who used to officiate for me'.

-Neither Major Crass nor Captain Cassius made any enquiries from me between 14-18 June 1983…No enquiry was ever made from me by any officer till Court of Inquiry…NO document of my Battery stores was inspected by Crass or Cassius'.

-'Commanding Officer's luggage was kept in the unit lines in a room behind the office of Officer-in-Charge Light Repair Workshop, while he was due to go for the Course. (When asked to indicate, he showed the Salvage Store in the Sketch). A log message was seen by me in which two persons were asked from my Battery for shifting the luggage of the CO. Accordingly I had issued Last Ration Certificate for them, 4-5 days before CO's Bara Khana. His luggage was moved, which I had seen while going towards the Ammunition Dump'.

-When I took over charge as Battery Quarter Master Havildar, I went to this room to check for two cots shown on charge, where luggage of Brigadier… had been kept and his two men were also there. I know these men as they had given their Last Ration Certificates to my battery and were dining there. They left the unit after about 1½ months of our return from the Exercise. In the other room also there was luggage, like big boxes and packages, with the name of that Brigadier'.

Cross Examination by Prosecution Counsel:

-'I said Gurgaon, but the actual name is Dundahera; it is generally referred to as Gurgaon for ease'.

-'I do not remember how many vehicles participated in the Exercise, but two guns from my Battery did'.

-'The name of the brigade commander who showed me the voucher (NIV) sounded like '…' I went when persons were called one by one as directed by DAAG, Major…. There were

3, 4 officers including A-1 (my CO) *sitting around; I don't remember anyone else's name. He was writing down whatever I was stating. Not only NIV, he asked about other things also. I did not tell him about luggage of Brigadier... or of my CO, as I was not asked about them.* (He then remembered the correct name of the Commander and gave it out).

-Studied upto class 4. 'Except for my statement as a Defence Witness, before the Lt Col of Cavalry (...in my CO's No 3 ...) *Summary of Evidence, I have not given any evidence, as I was not called'.*

-'It is correct that I did not state anything about the luggage etc before him also as I was not asked about it'.

- 'A-1 never asked me any questions there in front of Lt Col of Cavalry or afterwards'.

-I was only asked about the NIV, No of guns and vehicles for exercise at the Summary of Evidence.

-'After questions by Brigadier in Feb 1986, I have not gone back to ... Medium Regiment or talked to anyone from that unit, and I was posted out in Oct 1983.

-'I am staying with ... Cavalry here since 12 Feb 1986.

-'It is incorrect to suggest that I have deposed as per the bidding of Defending Officer of A-1 or A-1 himself...(then he explains...) *I have deposed as per my own knowledge and have only replied to questions put to me'.*

-'My statement at Summary of Evidence was recorded on 19 Mar 1986'.

Re-Examination Declined by Both Defending Officers.

Questions From the Court:

-'There were two rooms where the luggage of Brigadier and A-1 was kept. Approximately these measured: 15'x15' and 20'x20' respectively. These two men used to stay inside these

rooms, as their beds were placed inside and I also observed some religious photographs also displayed inside'.

DW-2: Naik PC, Driver of 3 Ton for Collection of Garnish (examined on 28 July 1986)

Direct Examination by Defending Officer of Accused No 1:

-A driver by trade, served in the Regiment from 1978 to Jan 1984 in HQ Battery.

-During Oct-Dec 1982 was on Regt QM Stores Standing Duty; went in Dec 1982 to Kashmere Gate for some collection in a Shaktiman 3 ton BA No 81D 4…71 N. Never-loyal who was a Naib Subedar was vehicle in charge and went with him.

-*'There were a few others in the body of the vehicle but I remember only one, as I subsequently spoke to him. This trip was before the 'Durbar' which was held prior to proceeding on exercise. From Dundahera Camp, we went via …(gave the route correctly)*…40-45 KM from Regt… left unit around 1000 hours and returned around 1430 hours. After reaching, all persons left except one who stayed back and we kept sitting and talking. Stores were loaded at that place only.

-*'I did not load anything with my hand nor did I assist Never-loyal in loading. I did not see him loading'.*

-Returned by the same route. No civilian travelled in the vehicle.

-*'I did not take the vehicle to any other place for loading than the place where I had initially parked it'.*

-*'On return, I parked it near Regt Stores, went for my food and returned around 1600 hours. This vehicle is always parked there during duty. Then I took the vehicle to Mechanical Transport Park. I did not do any other collection duty that day. Car Diary was filled by Never-loyal before leaving from the unit. Entry was made at the time of departure and arrival at the Regimental Police (RP) Gate Register. I wrote the mileage while RP sentry wrote the timings. On my return after food, I did not see any distribution being done to the batteries of the stores brought by us. When I returned after food, the stores brought by us were not in the vehicle. I also did not see anyone measuring the stores brought by us. While returning from Kashmere Gate, Never-loyal told me it was garnish which we were carrying'.*

-'During the 'Durbar' held prior to proceeding on exercise, A-1 said that local purchase of garnish has been done and two nets each would be carried; and if anyone faced any problem in this, he should contact him'.

-Went on Exercise on 26 Dec 1982 with the Road Column.

-'Before returning from Exercise on 13 Mar 1983, as per the practice, Commanding Officer(A-1) held a Mandir Parade...ordered that we should move back carefully, have night halt at Rohtak and that no vehicle will move by night'.

-'I was first interviewed about this case by CO Cavalry in Mar-Apr 1986. I have not given any other signed statement. I have never been questioned by Crass, Cassius, Tanjore Doll or Rabbi. No officer has enquired from me about this case'.

-Driver of Duty Vehicle has no responsibility for the stores, as his duty is to drive the vehicle and park as directed. *I have never been responsible for the stores.*

<u>Cross Examined by Prosecution Counsel</u>:

-We reached Kashmere Gate around 1130 hours.

-I do not now remember the name or the Battery of the person with whom I talked. I also did not give his name etc to CO Cavalry or any other officer, as I was not asked about it...I did not remember it also.

<u>Verbatim Question and Answer</u>:

-"Is it that you do not remember it or is it because you just do not know the person's name?"

-"I do not remember. I did not ask the name of the person with whom I was talking" (He added) *"Why should I have asked*

his name?"

-"Therefore either you know his name or did not feel it necessary to ask his name?"

"I did not feel it necessary".

-'I did not see the store being loaded in the vehicle and therefore I cannot say how much store was loaded in the vehicle'.

*-'From my present brigade, I first reported to RHM and Subedar Major only. I did **not** report either to the Adjutant or the Commanding Officer'.*

-He did not remember: when exactly he went for collection in Dec 1982; how many vehicles and guns went in the Exercise; or how many in the road column.

Re-Examined by Defending Officer of Accused No 2 :

-Never-loyal told me to march off at Kashmere Gate and I closed the tail board before marching off.

Questions From the Court:

-When I closed the tail board, I saw the working party persons and some bundles.

DW-3: Officiating Subedar QM in Exercise Area (examined on 28 July 1986)

Direct Examination by Defending Officer of Accused No 2:

-Posted in July 80; P Battery for 2 years; ordered as Subedar QM for the exercise.

-Went as Advance Party In Charge for Exercise on 20 Dec 1982.

-Before Exercise, Commanding Officer had told everyone in a Durbar, that each gun and vehicle will carry two nets; I did for my party vehicles. During Sep 1982 and thereafter also in a Sainik Sammelan, he had said about two nets each.

-During Exercise, did not go anywhere else and continued as the Subedar QM for exercise in that location.

-On receipt of any stores from permanent location, used to report to exercise QM, 2IC or CO before distributing them as per distribution list received from 'Rear', i.e., permanent location.

-'*NO garnish was received at the Exercise location. I did not receive two bundles containing 3,000 M of garnish. No one else other than me was authorized to receive and distribute stores. I kept record of all receipts and distributions. On return to permanent location, I deposited at Q office all the records of receipt and distribution of all stores during the exercise. Never-loyal did not discuss with me anything relating to 3,000 M of garnish. Soon after my return from exercise, I proceeded on 60 days annual leave and returned in first week of June 1983. I started taking over from Never-loyal as Subedar Quarter Master of the unit, as per instruction received*'.

-'*I cannot say whether it was 27 June 1983 or when, but during a Sammelan at that time, Commanding Officer had indeed told all the persons that if anyone knew about the author of a letter received, he should tell him or Major Crass or Tanjore Doll. This was the last Sainik Sammelan addressed by Lt Col... as the Commanding Officer. Bara Khana was held one day prior to the Sammelan; after that Commanding Officer had gathered all the Q staff including myself, Never-loyal, PW 3, Store Hand General Duty ... etc and told that anyone knowing anything relating to a letter received by him, should tell him so. I do not remember now if he said anything about local purchase also. He also said if anyone knew about the name of the driver, he should inform him. He did not ask anything about the working party*'.

-'*During the handing and taking over, I also took on charge a tarpaulin by which some garnish was covered. I did not however take over the garnish on charge, as Never-loyal told me garnish was not on our charge. That tarpaulin and the garnish were lying in the veranda of the Miniature Range. There was no guard on this garnish. Thereafter I had nothing to do with that garnish'.*

-'Sometime...1985, I was ordered by the CO...Colonel Tanjore Doll...to remove(sic) the garnish from the Miniature Range to Tent Store. I counted it carefully and got it moved to Tent Store with a working party, locked the door and after reporting to the Subedar Major gave the key to RHM after sealing the lock. This garnish was about 55,000 M. Some of it was in packing and some of it was loose. Some bundles contained 1,500 M and some 2,000 M. I checked all of them; there were about ***8-10 of them containing 2,000 M'.***

Cross Examined by Prosecution Counsel:

-There were 2 Q Branch vehicles and 2-3 vehicles of each Battery in the advance party of which I was in charge.

-I took over the tarpaulin in July/Aug 1983.

-I am not aware of receipt of any local purchase garnish *during my tenure as Subedar Quarter Master.*

Re-Examined by Defending Officer of Accused No 2 :

-I took over as Subedar Quarter Master in July/Aug 1983.

When asked to examine the next Defence Witness, Defending Officer of Accused No 2 submitted that except for 3-4 witnesses present, whom also he has not been able to interview due to their late arrival, there were no more present. Hence examination cannot continue until they are made available and time is also available for interviewing them.

Prosecution Counsel replied that after his personal conversation with Colonel A at Corps (*who else but*!), 8 were made available from the Regt at 1430 hours on 27 July 1986 to the Defence. (He forgot the speed with which we had examined 3 witnesses in just a day that is, the next day after they were made available!) 2 or 3 have been sent back by the Defence. They were asking for Major Bandicoot and he would be coming on 3 Aug 1986. The name of Rooster was given to him only on 26 July 1986; a summons would go to the Magistrate and also one direct to him. He then started giving the gist of Army Rules 136 and 137 regarding list of and procuring the witnesses for Defence. One Battery Commander of that time requested by Defence is in hospital. Convening Authority has sent out a signal calling for an adjournment, reasons not known to the Prosecution or the Court!

(At that stage, the Court decided to sit beyond 6 p.m. and 6 hours in the interest of justice and discipline.)

Defending Officer of Accused No 2 submitted that out of the 8 made available at 1845 hours (and not 1430 hours) just yesterday (27 July 1986), 3 have been produced in just one day: today and within 24 hours of their being made available; 2 have been sent back being not required; time available after attending the Court and preparing for the next day hardly allowed the Defence to interview the Defence Witnesses. Would like the present Adjutant, before deciding on the ex Battery Commander, who is in hospital. Regarding Rooster, obviously, we could not foresee till an interview of the Driver (Naik PC) was completed; still we had given it a day earlier. Whenever our witnesses are made available with proper documents sought by us, we shall examine them post haste.

JA then gave his advice drawing attention to Army Rules 136 and 82 (3). Court after a consideration in closed court, decided to adjourn till 31 July 1986.

On 31 July 1986 again, JA was late by half an hour; same excuse. Court took a serious view and told the Prosecutor to make foolproof arrangements. Bedi stated that examination will continue to be done by Ramanan and he would only do when necessary.

DW-4: Present Adjutant of the Regiment: (examined on 31 July 1986)

Direct Examination by Defending Officer of Accused No 2:

-Serving since Jan 1978 and as Adjutant since 20 July 1983, produced leave records to show 2 Battery

Commanders were indeed away on leave during June 1983, (while PW 2 had deposed he had enquired from them during mid-June 1983!)

-Also produced the Handing Taking Over Certificate between Subedar Quarter Master who had proceeded on pension (person neither produced by Prosecution as a witness, nor allowed for Defence by the Court) and PW-7 of Nov 1982.

(The Prosecutor informed that two signals...to prove some nasty remarks questioning the very authority of the Commanding Officer by PW-2 and his animosity; (refer to the Chapter on *Dramatis Personae)* ...demanded by us were not traceable; even in A-1's No 3 Summary of Evidence, only Photostat had been attached. Witness was asked to withdraw. Defending Officer of Accused No 2 submitted that all documents now being demanded were attached to the manuscript copy of Summary of Evidence No 1 of A-1. He gave an example of a document produced by the Prosecution through PW-1 from their files! Prosecutor said allegation is not correct, as he had given whatever he had received from the Convening Authority. JA give his advice by reading out Sections 61, 64, 65 (a) and 63 of Indian Evidence Act. After a consideration in closed Court, it permitted the Defence to lead Secondary Evidence.)

Witness was called in and Direct Examination continued:

-He next produced a certified true copy of the Board Proceedings of garnish dispatched and a copy of a letter from A-2 addressed to Major Crass dated 19 June 1983. *(Contents of this letter are not only interesting for its sarcasm, but Major Crass under oath had denied receiving any letter from A-2 along with his letter absolving everyone else but himself regarding the local purchase;* and it reads:

"19 June 1983

My dear (...Crass...) Sir,

Thanks a lot for many things.

This is to request you that I would like the presence of ...Subedar Head Clerk of QM Branch... in the unit and his proceeding on pension may be stopped forthwith.

I have a lot of confidence in you and I hope my request will be honoured.

With warmest regards,

Yours as ever,

...Signature... (SL ....)"

-*RP Gate IN/OUT Register for vehicles is* ***not*** *available* in the Regiment. (*This would have proved the details of date, time, passengers etc of the 3 ton that had gone for collection of LP garnish).*

-QM Branch has said *Bin cards for scrim garnish were* ***NOT*** *being maintained* and so not available. (This proves another statement under oath by PW-7 as false).

-'I ***cannot*** *produce Regt Daily Parade State Register for 1982-83,* as it is now not available. (On a query from Court)... it is presently maintained in the Regt.

-'Regt HQ *Internal Log Book for Dec 1982 (working party details) is* ***NA***; it was sent to Brigade who had further forwarded it to ... Independent Armoured Brigade.'

-'I ***cannot*** *produce* Consignment Opening Board Proceedings (for scrim garnish) for Dec 1982, as according to QM Branch, it is NOT available'.

-'***NO file*** *titled 'Exercise Dig Vijay Feedback' is available* or existing in the unit, so I am unable to produce it'. (Due to security reasons, ALL papers on the Exercise had been destroyed by burning in end Mar 1983!)

(Readers would by now have realized as to how many important documents to prove certain events concerning arrival and distribution of garnish and certificates from Battery Commanders for having received it etc could not be produced before the Court for no fault of ours, as I had left on 1 July 1983, i.e., the day after the Court of Inquiry commenced; and A-2 had not been given the charge back after 2 July 1983).

Cross Examined by Prosecution Counsel:

-Regt Daily Parade State Register for 1982-83 was inadvertently destroyed by the RP Havildar along with a few other documents.

-'*Being the Adjutant from 20 July 1983, I was aware of certain scrim garnish kept sealed in a room. It was initially kept in the Miniature Range and later shifted to a room near Mandir area. I have seen this garnish. However I am not aware as to whether it is ordnance pattern or local purchase pattern. The garnish which was so kept locked and sealed is the same garnish which was subsequently dispatched to ... Independent Armoured Brigade.*

-Driver Naik PC reported to me from ... Artillery Brigade sometime in 1985 in the unit at Dundahera Camp. He was thereafter interviewed by the CO in my presence. He was asked by the CO about the quantity of garnish brought by him from Kashmere Gate, Delhi. He said...remembered having brought 10-15 bundles which were lying on one side of the 3 ton and that he did not remember anything about a working party. He had also said he had gone with Never-loyal'.

Re-Examined by Defending Officer of Accused No 2:

-'I do not remember the date or the month when Driver Naik PC reported to me or when he was interviewed by the CO in my presence. Although there is a register in the unit where interview records are maintained, this interview has ***not been recorded*** *there'.*

(How convenient! **Whatever we needed was destroyed or NA or not recorded!**)

Questions From the Court:

-I am not aware of any amendments being made to the Part 2 order *(regarding my annual leave dates of 1983!)*

At this stage, the Court decided to sit for more than 6 hours, in the interest of justice and discipline.

DW-5: Present Subedar Quarter Master of the Regiment (examined on 31 July-1 Aug 1986)

Direct Examination by Defending Officer of Accused No 2:

-Serving since 1967; Subedar Quarter Master now. During May 1980 to Jan 1983, was Battery Quarter Master Havildar of 'Q' Battery.

-*'First time I came to know about Exercise Dig Vijay was in Aug-Sep 1982; unit went in Dec 1982. We had received instructions that 2 nets for each vehicle and gun have to be carried. 8-10 days prior to move for exercise, nets had been prepared. I received garnish of all colours. I was present in the unit in Dec 1982. Lance Naik JS was my assistant in Battery Stores, when I was the BQMH. It was my responsibility to collect and account for receipt of stores'.*

-Being shown the infamous voucher (NIV), he said, JS *'used to sign in full and this signature is not in full, cannot say if it is his or not'.*

-He then explained the procedure for issue of stores to the battery and the documentation, which has been in vogue since he became BQMH:

-*'I maintain a record of all items received by me for distribution irrespective of their source'.*

Cross Examined by Prosecution Counsel:

-Procedure explained by me is not laid down in any standing order, but was followed by me as Subedar QM; I am not aware of the procedure before me.

Re-Examined by Defending Officer of Accused No 2:

-While I was BQMH, then also I used to get 2 copies of vouchers from the Subedar QM. *When I took over as Subedar QM, I was briefed to follow this procedure by my predecessor.*

At this stage, Ramanan submitted that due to the nature of evidence in the last 4-5 days, it had become essential for Defence to recall Naik PC, the Driver again. Prosecution Counsel submitted that while the Court have very wide powers, recalling a witness should not be permitted without a judicious consideration of all the matters and not for supplementing any negligent performance on the part of either party. Great latitude should be given to the Defence but when Defence is requesting for recall of a witness, they must specify the particular point they wish to bring out in recalling, because the questions have to be put through the Court. Ramanan submitted that since interviews in Jan 1985 and subsequently have been brought on record, by the testimony of PW-9 and cross examination of DW-4 yesterday, we have to per force recall DW-2 to clarify the matter and bring out the truth before the Court. JA gave his advice referring to Army Rule 143 (1) and (4); after a consideration in closed Court, it decided to allow our submission.

DW-4 Naik Driver PC stated when questioned through the JA:

"I left my present unit... Artillery Brigade on 11 Apr 1985 and reported to ... Medium Regiment on 12 Apr 1985". (He thus nailed the lie under oath by two officers!)

DW-6: Another BQMH, Alleged Signatory to the NIV: (examined on 1 Aug 1986)

Direct Examination by Defending Officer of Accused No 2:

-Serving since 1966, except short tenures outside; returned on 11 July 1986 to Regt.

-BQMH of HQ Battery from Oct 1981 to Oct 1982. By mid Nov 1982 having handed over charge to another Havildar, was assisting him; went on annual leave after road column left for Exercise.

-*'On the exhibit Voucher (NIV), although the signature is similar to mine, **it is NOT mine**. My service (Army) **No is also wrong**...'*

-'In the other exhibit (Voucher) dated 21 Nov 1982, I recognize and indicate my signature. I had received the items'.

-'I used to get 2 copies of the Voucher; take items on ledger charge and then one is got signed by Battery Commander or Battery 2IC and returned to QM office and the other is retained in battery office; being shown Pages 58, 59, 61 and 63 from a ledger, along with the (second) Voucher, I recognize them as pages from Unit Equipment Ledger of HQ Battery. I can say stores from the Voucher have ***not*** *been entered in this ledger.*

Cross Examined by Prosecution Counsel:

-As BQMH, I maintain Clothing Ledgers and NOT any others.

-HQ Battery Stores Ledger was being maintained by the clerk in the office; I have seen it there, when I deposit vouchers; but never checked these pages earlier...I have never produced these pages to any one else or at any other enquiry.

... Although items mentioned...*(second voucher)*... were received by me, I cannot say as to what was the pattern of garnish mentioned in it. I cannot say as to who has separated these pages from the Ledger. I do not remember who in particular issued the garnish mentioned in this Voucher or as to whom all were present at the time of the issue.

Re-Examined by Defending Officer of Accused No 2:

-I have never previously given any statement relating to this case anywhere to anyone.

Colonel Ramanan stated that out of the 8 witnesses, we have examined 6 and have sent back the other two; and two more have arrived recently, whom we have not had time to have even a word with them; so request adjournment till tomorrow. NO action appears to have been taken to get Rooster; if a copy of his summons is given, we can make an effort! We have given the particulars of the witness from Ordnance Depot, Shakurbasti and the documents which he has to produce; but Depot says they need permission of authorities for production of documents. Lastly, the location of officer from workshop who collected the garnish is being traced. Prosecutor strongly objected on the pretext that the accused and both the Defending Officers were well versed and should not take more than a couple of hours, *'if they knew their case and their line of defence'*! He kept repeating *ad nauseam* the same tune of 'accused alone responsible to get witnesses not intimated earlier' etc. List of exact documents from Shakurbasti Depot should be given. A Major, who was the Adjutant during 1983 and whom the Defence wanted, was seen in these precincts yesterday itself. He could be examined in an hour. Ramanan submitted again that while we had met that Major yesterday during a break, that won't be sufficient to examine him, as we haven't had the time particularly due to the late sitting of the Court yesterday. JA referred to and read out Army Rule 82 (1), 135 (4) and 136 once again. After considering in closed court, adjournment was accepted till next day and Prosecution was asked to give us a copy of the summons for Rooster.

DW-7: Major..., Adjutant During Mar to July 1983 (examined on 2 Aug 1986)

Direct Examination by Defending Officer of Accused No 2:

-Joined Regt in Oct 1972; after a tenure outside, rejoined on 21 Dec 1982, when appointment within unit was to be decided in and after the Exercise.

-As Officer-in-Charge Rail Column, left on 29 Dec 1982; and on reaching exercise area, was detailed outside the Regt for two weeks and returned on 16 Jan 1983; within 2 days was attached to HQ Armoured Division for manning a Fire Direction Centre, right next to the Regt location.

-Was present in the exercise area...(though with another formation close by)...throughout...During that period, on one occasion, *GOC Armoured Division, after inspecting the camouflage and concealment of the Regt sent a message of appreciation to the Regt and the Commanding Officer.* Thereafter, when all officers were *in the Mess, CO (A-1) mentioned about the local purchase of garnish, as it had not been available for preparation for the exercise.*

-As proper married accommodation was not available, witness' luggage was kept in an isolated hut about 100 yards behind the Light Repair Workshop complex, before he went for the Exercise; and he had visited it, before, and after the Exercise, on a few occasions. One of these rooms was bigger 15 to 16 x 10 feet and the other was small. His luggage was kept divided between both rooms. The smaller room contained his luggage alone and there were no ordnance stores in it. In the bigger room, there was luggage of other officers too, bearing their names. In that bigger room too, ***there were no ordnance stores***, as it was full of baggage. In a corner, however, there was one cot. After return from the exercise, he removed his luggage partially from there to married accommodation allotted.

-Took over as Adjutant after the exercise and continued till 20 July 1983.

-Some of the luggage of CO (A-1), who was proceeding on course and was shifting to a smaller flat, was also kept.

-CO proceeded on leave in early May, sometime around 4 or 5 May 1983. The 60 days annual leave for him was worked out backwards from the date he was to hand over, before going on Course; and this way it was worked out from 29 Apr to 27 June 1983. Witness then produced a letter dated 9 Apr 1983, from Independent Artillery Brigade to the Regt, stating: *"Leave certificate in respect of ... CO... is returned herewith duly sanctioned. Please adjust the date of commencement of leave, subject to GOC... Corps to your unit".*

-Witness was on casual leave for 2 days on 29 and 30 Apr 1983, but in station; rejoined on 2 May 1983. CO (A-1) attended office from 2 to 4 May 1983. *'I was told by him that since GOC ... Corps was not coming now, he had been permitted to proceed on leave forthwith and therefore he would leave on 5 May 1983'.*

-On 4 May 1983, CO handed over a bundle of handwritten essays by officers and told me to hand over the same to 2IC, Major Crass; there was a noting sheet with it addressed to Crass, as to the best and worst essays; he produced the same and identified the date and my signature and remarks.

-Witness then gave a gist of misbehaviour by Crass with JCOs and his subsequent apology (9 and 14 Apr 1983).

-'On 15 June 1983,...wedding of an officer of the Regt locally but CO ... was late by an hour and apologized...he had just returned from Meerut. There he informed me that he had to go to Meerut the next day again and that his fresh ACR form was to be prepared and signed by the Regimental Medical Officer the same night and delivered to him. .... I got it done and sent it to him early next morning(16 June 1983). Before leaving CO called me and confirmed its receipt and also that he was leaving just then. In the evening of the same day, I checked up on telephone from Mrs.... (CO's wife) twice around 1700 and 1800 hours about his return, but he had not come by then. At about 1930 hours I got a call from him while I was still in the office, to inform me about his return'.

-On 17 June 1983, QM...on annual leave...came to the unit around 0930 hours. Then Crass, Cassius, Subedar Major and he came to Adjutant's (witness') office as the telephone in QM office was out of order that day. Crass told me to get CO on line; I did and gave him the handset. Thereafter Crass and QM were on the telephone for an hour... left...returned after about 45 minutes... again started making calls.

-'*Meanwhile on the telephonic instructions of the CO, I told Crass that he should satisfy himself before sending the QM'.* Thereafter, Subedar Major also spoke to the CO in some language, which I did not understand. *Then* ***I heard QM saying on telephone that he had explained and satisfied Major Crass*** *and Cassius and that he (CO) should not worry, for if anyone was to be hanged it was him (QM) and also that he had so many pressing commitments, eg, his mother's 'shradh' in Garhwal. Then* ***Crass also spoke on telephone and said that he had satisfied himself and QM could go back and if anything was left, that could be sorted out later.*** *It was around 1100-1130 hours at that time.* ***Thereafter, myself, <u>Crass</u>, Cassius and the Subedar Major went from the rear door of my office and saw QM off in a waiting vehicle...I did not see QM carrying anything in his hands...****he was in civvies and came empty-handed to my office'.*

-On 18 June 1983, CO came to the office around 0930 hours, with Major Tanjore Doll and called Crass, Cassius and Subedar Major to his office. Around 1230 hours, CO left.

-CO also came to the office for a promotion conference which was held prior to his rejoining duty...on 25 June 1983...I attended the Bara Khana in honour of the CO on 27 June 1983 and he rejoined duty on 28 June 1983.

-On 28 June 1983, CO came to the office around 1030 hours, after certain ceremonial events including a Special Sainik Sammelan, addressed by him. On 29 June, he and Lt Col Tanjore Doll, the CO-designate went to Brigade HQ at Meerut.

-'*On 28 June 1983, Colonel, now Brigadier, Rabbi the Deputy Commander had come to the unit for certain investigation. He remained in the unit till about 2100 hours. I also remained in the office till that time...* ***I was not informed*** *about any incident of recovery of stores to by Cassius'.*

-'*As far as I can remember, apart from the normal guards which are detailed by the Adjutant,* ***I did not detail any other guards on or after 30 June 1983'.***

-CO... staying in Delhi Cantonment... used to come in a separate vehicle. For the rest, 1x1 ton was there to commute...

-'QM left straightway from my office...did not see him going anywhere before he left my office and went away in the jeep'.

-'I heard about the local purchase of garnish the first time, as I had said, when the appreciation had come from GOC Armoured Division. The second time I heard about it was when Crass and QM were talking on telephone from my office'.

-'Although we reached unit on 14 Mar 1983 after the Exercise, CO arrived on 15 Mar 1983 only. On 15 Mar 1983 itself, CO called me and Major Crass, the 2IC, to his office if any report had been sent about the death of Naik MLD. When informed that no report had been sent, he got angry as to why even the first report had not been ... there was a loud discussion between Crass and CO'.

-'Crass rejoined from casual leave on 14 Apr 1983. He was informed by me and the Subedar Major about the collective complaint made by the JCOs. Then on his orders, all JCOs were lined up outside his office. CO called him to his office, when Subedar Major and I were also called. He told Crass that as the complaint had been made to him, the CO, he would sort it out. JCOs were then called in front of CO's office. Some discussion took place between CO and Crass; and Crass finally apologized to the JCOs'.

- 'Sometime later in Apr 1983, ... there was some unpleasantness in the Officers Mess following a remark by Major Crass'.

-'On 7 June 1983...ACR...CO was on leave and was not well... called in...Crass went in first while the rest of us remained in the veranda. ... Crass remained inside for quite some time and I heard a loud discussion or may be some altercation from inside that room. After he came out and during the entire journey back to the unit, Crass remained silent'.

-Witness identified his and others' initials and remarks on the two signals, where Crass had written some nasty remarks.

-'On 20 July 1983, except Major Crass and wife, all officers of the unit and their lady-wives attended the funeral rites of the wife of CO'.

Cross Examined by Prosecution Counsel:

(Before starting, Prosecution Counsel, who had been agitated with this and many other Defence and even Prosecution Witnesses addressing or referring to me as "Commanding Officer" instead of as "Accused No 1" made a sarcastic remark to this witness, asking if he had seen the movie: *"The Man Who Knew Too Much"* and also saying, he was reminded of it, during his Direct Examination. The witness replied: *"If being the Adjutant more than once and having served for so many years with the unit, I did not know what all had happened in my presence and hearing; and did not say it out now, when and where would I say it? There has not been one wrong or false word in my entire statement. Wherever I did not know an event, I had said so"*. This was not recorded in the Proceedings).

-'I had normal relations with A-1, as exist between a CO and an officer'.

... not seen any local purchase garnish in the unit on ground...was never informed by A-1, A-2 or 2IC (Crass) about arrival of any local purchase of garnish.

(The Prosecution Counsel felt elated with this answer and gave a smirk towards me, without realizing, that the witness had *'...rejoined on 21 Dec 1982...left on 29 Dec 1982...detailed outside the Regt for two weeks...attached to HQ Armoured Division...."* etc; obviously, he would know nothing about ARRIVAL of LP garnish ion 13 Dec 1982! He was further stupid later in his 'Final Summing Up', where he specifically mentioned that even the Adjutant was not aware!)

-The rooms where my luggage had been kept were about 300 yards from the Miniature Range, which was in the Main Office building.

...I am aware that a casualty was published about the leave dates of A-1. Dates agreed upon by the Brigade HQ were 29 Apr to 27 June 1983 were published in the casualty. No casualty was published to amend these dates. If any was required, it was the duty of an Adjutant on the instructions of the CO or the officiating CO. I received no instructions from either to amend these dates. Visit of GOC... Corps was cancelled... information I received from the CO only, as explained earlier.

-On 4 May 1983, when CO informed me that GOC would not be visiting, I did not ask him whether I should publish casualty to amend the leave dates. I did not ask Major Crass also. I was also not instructed by anyone else in this regard. After the receipt of Brigade HQ letter with the Leave Certificate, when GOC did not visit, I did not approach the Brigade HQ also for change in leave dates of CO.

-As Adjutant, I did not receive any letter from Brigade HQ about visit by GOC.

-2IC's office does not have a P&T telephone... during the leave of CO, 2IC did not sit in CO's office, but his own. My and CO's office telephones were in parallel on Plan 105. Conversation between Crass at my end and CO at the other was on local purchase of garnish for exercise.

-A-1, Crass, Tanjore Doll, all Battery Commanders or officiating ones, Cassius and Subedar Major attended the promotion conference on 25 June 1983.

-I am aware that some discreet enquiries were being done by Rabbi. I do not know who all were called for investigation; I was not.

-Earlier, when I used the word 'altercation', I did not mean any use of insubordinate language or anyone coming to blows... meant heated discussions.

Re-Examined by Defending Officer of Accused No 2:

-I now refresh my memory from the Regimental Sainik Sammelan Book; from the record written by me of Sainik Sammelan of 22 Apr 1983, I state that CO had mentioned during this Sammelan Major General Artillery and GOC... Corps may visit sometime in May-June 1983. Major *Crass was present* in this Sammelan.

-Casualty return regarding CO's leave was published by the Brigade HQ.

(At this stage, the Court decided to sit for more than six hours in the interest of justice and discipline).

Question from the Court:

-Regarding Casualty, unit is required to forward a draft casualty under signatures of CO or officiating CO to the Brigade HQ.

The Court re-assembled on 4 Aug 1986, when DW-4, the present Adjutant was called and answered questions suggested by us through the Court, as follows:

In Reply to Questions Suggested by the Defence:

-I *cannot produce the Movement Order in respect of Naik Driver PC (DW-2)*, as the same is not available in the Battery or in Regt HQ. He was, however, taken on ration strength on 13 Apr 1985; Part 2 Order also for the same had been published based on the Movement Order. (This was to nail the lie further).

At this stage, Colonel Ramanan wished to bring on record an instruction from 'Lt Col Shifty Eyes' to CO ...Medium Regt dated 1 July 1983, regarding physical holding of all types of garnish in the Regt as on 30 June 1983; so witness was asked to withdraw. Prosecution Counsel submitted...Appendix 'A' would be the Findings of the

Court of Inquiry...would be inadmissible under the law...read out Army Rule 182...in order to help the Defence, witness may be asked as to whether any instructions were received from Shifty Eyes for sealing any particular quantity of garnish. Lt Col Bedi submitted that firstly, it is incorrect to say that this letter is part of the Court of Inquiry proceedings or that it contains the Findings of the Court of Inquiry proceedings. In fact the C of I concluded in Aug 1983 only; secondly the embargo on the proceedings of a Court of Inquiry is on the Prosecution and not on the Defence (Read out "the proceedings of a Court of Inquiry, or any confession, statement or answer to a question made or given at the Court of Inquiry shall not be admissible against an accused")... PW-9 has *inter alia* deposed that he got garnish sealed on 30 June 1983, in consequence of instructions received from Presiding Officer of the Court of Inquiry...this document being the first document that throws light on the fact of the transaction relating to alleged recovery of garnish, being vital may be permitted to be brought on record. JA then gave his advice drawing attention to and reading out Army Rule 182 and Para 94, Chapter 5 of *Manual of Indian Military Law*, Volume 1, 1983; the latter being: *"So also the proceedings of a court of inquiry cannot be called for by courts martial, or witnesses examined as to their contents, nor is any confession or statement made at a court of inquiry admissible* ***against an accused*** *before a court martial (Army Rule 182), the only exception being for giving false evidence before the court of inquiry."* He further stated: The court of inquiry proceedings can however be used by the Defence for cross examining a witness in terms of Section 145 of Indian Evidence Act. After a consideration in closed court, it decided to disallow production of the document in question.

<u>The witness was called and continued</u>:

> -It is correct that instructions were received in the unit in July 1983 to seal some garnish which was recovered. To the best of my knowledge these were brought to the notice of Colonel Tanjore Doll on 4 July 1983.

-He then produced and identified a letter dated 14 July 1983 from the Regt to Brigade, signed by PW-1, Cassius. (This was the letter confirming receipt of the return by brigade of garnish and nets loaned to it in Exercise). *(Readers would remember PW-1's denial of any knowledge of loan or return during his deposition)*.

In Reply to Questions Suggested by the Prosecution Counsel:

At this stage, he wished to produce copy of a Part One Order to show when A-1 proceeded on leave and command was assumed by Crass. My Defending Officer objected saying only original had to be produced. In reply, Prosecution Counsel quoted Army Act Section 142(3). JA drew attention to and read out Army Act Section 133 and Note 2 to it. After a consideration in closed court, it decided to disallow our objection.

-Witness then produced Part 1 Order No 127 dated 30 Apr 1983 regarding assumption of command by Crass.

DW-8: Non Commissioned Officer in Charge of Luggage of Brig ..., Former Commander (examined on 4 Aug 1986)

Direct Examination by Defending Officer of Accused No 2:

-He and another jawan...attached with 'P' Battery...from third week of June 1981 to second week of Dec 1982, to look after the luggage of Brig ....about 2x3 ton loads; important luggage was kept in the veranda of Telephone Exchange and Miniature Range...remainder kept in 2 rooms in the building behind Light Repair Workshop ...both stayed with two pets and had two cots in one, which was 15x12 feet; did not know the dimensions of the other room.

-In the *room where they stayed, there were no tent poles, ordnance stores or garnish kept*. In the other room also which remained locked, he did *not see any ordnance stores being kept or removed*.

-At times, Subedar Major used to visit them to check on welfare and for security of the luggage.

Cross Examined by Prosecution Counsel:

-I do not remember the date but we vacated the room in second week of Dec 1982...Except for this, he had not made any statement anywhere any time.

Re-Examination was declined. Colonel Ramanan submitted that no other witness was available now...we have dropped a few... not been able to contact Rooster. PW-9 Colonel Tanjore Doll may be recalled. We need at least 24 hours after witnesses arrive. Prosecution Counsel said Major Bandicoot and Shakurbasti representative would come by 6 Aug. Additional summons have gone to Rooster, care of Sphere Corporation. PW-9 may be available by 6 Aug. So adjournment may be till 6 Aug 1986. JA then drew attention to the relevant provisions and the court after considering in closed court, decided to adjourn till 7 Aug 1986.

DW-9: Major Bandicoot, former DAA&QMG of Brigade (examined on 7 Aug 1986)

Direct Examination by Defending Officer of Accused No 2:

-He was the A and Q staff officer at Brigade HQ from Apr 1982 to Apr 1984.

-A-1 had applied for leave from 29 Apr to 27 June 1983. His leave was, however, subject to visit of GOC ... Corps and we had written that it would commence after the visit in the first week of May 1983...identified the brigade HQ covering letter of 9 Apr 1983, sanctioning leave, which he had signed. These instructions were issued on the orders of Commander. GOC however did not visit then.

-'On 4 May 1983, A-1 rang me up from Delhi and told me that since GOC was not coming now, could he proceed on leave. Accordingly I enquired from Commander and he gave his clearance. I conveyed the same to A-1 on telephone'.

-During one of the conferences before he proceeded on leave, where I was also present Commander told A-1 that he should be back 4-5 days before proceeding on Course. Leave dates were such that he could proceed on 1 July 1983.

-He then identified the Part II order signed by Commander in respect of leave.

*-'On 15 June 1983 I saw A-1 at brigade HQ around 1100 hours. I saw him also on 16 June 1983 around 1000 hours. He had lunch at Deputy Commander's home on 15th, where I was also present...On 16th also, he told me he was having lunch with some officer at Meerut...*On both the days, he informed me that he was leaving around 1530 hours. He saw the Commander on both the days'.

Cross Examination by the Prosecution Counsel:

*-'On 4 May 1983, when he called me about cancellation of visit of GOC, I was not aware of the same. I am not aware if any casualty was published amending his leave dates. On 15 and 16 June 1983, when he visited the brigade HQ, he was in uniform...*Commander told...(witness)...A-1...could proceed on leave from 5 May 1983 and accordingly witness had called him.

-'I am not aware whether it was Commander who had called A-1 on 15 and 16 June or he had visited on his own. A-1 did not tell me the purpose of his visit...'

Re-Examination Declined.

Questioned by the Court:

-'On 5 May 1983, when I put up the Part 2 Order for Commander's signature, I did not amend the leave dates, as I thought, amendment if any should be sent by the unit'.

At this stage, at the request of Defence, Colonel Tanjore Doll, PW-9 was recalled and cross examined through Court/ JA.

In Reply to Questions Suggested by the Defence:

-'On 30 June 1983, I received verbal instructions as stated earlier for safeguarding the garnish and subsequently I received

these instructions in writing also. From 30 June to 15 Aug, I took measures to safeguard it. Till the time I got it dispatched to this location, I safeguarded it as per my own understanding and initiative; I had not received any instructions in this regard. However, my permission was sought from 30 June to 15 Aug 1983 for opening this by various persons including Cassius. Instructions both verbal on 30 June 1983 and subsequently in writing were the same.

*-'**There is a variation** in the amount of garnish sealed by me on 30 June 1983 and the amount produced by me before the Court. After 30 June 1983, I was verbally informed by Cassius that quantity belonging to sub units had been returned to them. Up to 15 Aug 1983, permission was sought by various persons on various occasions to break the seal since this garnish was to be produced by these persons. Around 15 Aug 1983, the quantity of garnish I saw was less than the quantity I had sealed on 30 June 1983. And I safeguarded this quantity from 15 Aug 1983 onwards...I cannot however say as to what is the exact variation in the quantity, as I have never measured this garnish myself at any stage'.*

At this stage, the Defending Officer suggested the following question: *"What quantity - shade-wise, origin-wise and size-wise, were instructed to be safeguarded by a letter dated 1 July 1983 by Colonel Shifty Eyes, confirming the verbal instructions of 30 June 1983?"* Prosecution Counsel objected to the question and the witness was asked to withdraw. He then said that the question pertains to a document which was not admissible; witness cannot refresh his memory from that document, which is not in his handwriting...Sections 159 and 160 of Indian Evidence Act (which is also only for experts like doctors, ballistic experts etc) refer. Defending Officer of Accused No 2 submitted that the witness has deposed about variations; so in the interest of fair play and justice, he should be allowed to refresh his memory from a document he has seen, initialled and had acted upon; and which had been prepared by orders of brigade commander. Prosecution Counsel said that unless and until the verbal instruction quantity-wise, shade-wise, size-wise etc was clarified from the witness first, he cannot use this document; that too within the wide powers of the Court as Defence claimed it was vital. JA gave advice after referring to and reading Sections 59, 159 and 160 of Indian Evidence Act regarding the nature of evidence; Army Rule 143(1) and (4) regarding recalling of witness and reply; and Section 165 of Indian Evidence Act regarding Judge's Power to put Question or order Production. After a consideration in closed court, it decided to disallow Prosecution's objection.

Witness was called in and the above question suggested by Defence was put to him in inverted commas; he replied:

-"The letter in question was *not confirmation* of verbal directions of 30 June 1983. I received the letter sometime *after 1 July 1983*. I cannot remember the details unless I see it. I now refresh my memory by seeing the letter and I state that the details of garnish required to be sealed by this letter were as under:-

(a) 75 MM MB Green	23,300 metres.
(b) 75 MM Grass Green	21,000 metres; (this included 3,000 M of 'Q' Battery).
(c) 75 MM Brown	9,100 metres.
(d) 75 MM Un-dyed	7,500 metres.
(e) 75 MM Light Green	1,500 metres.
(f) 75 MM Dark Brown	1,500 metres.
Total	63,900 metres.

"As per the letter in question, the above amount of garnish had marking indicating despatch from one Ordnance Depot to another.

"Details of 50 MM garnish are as under:-

(a) Un-dyed	5,000 metres. (All with 'R' Battery).

(b) Light Green 1,300 metres.

(c) Dark Brown 100 metres.

(d): (b) and (c) above were in loose form, with Ordnance cat/part numbers on it.

Bedi submitted, he wished to make a written submission regarding the admission of this particular document as the witness has not stated the correct situation, as reflected in the document. He sought adjournment till next morning. Prosecution had no objection. (At this stage, the Court decided to sit beyond 6 hours in the interest of justice and discipline.) JA drew attention to earlier advice on Page 239 of the Proceedings. After a consideration in closed court, it decided to allow our submission.

The next day, 8 Aug 1986, prosecution submitted that the medical officer normally carrying out medical inspection of accused persons was himself sick; so they were being examined by another and should be arriving soon. So, Defence requested 45 minutes more; Prosecution had no objection. Court was adjourned for 90 minutes.

My Defending Officer read and handed in a written submission; salient points:-

-It is imperative that the letter from Shifty Eyes bearing No 111/C of I/2 dated 1 July 1983 is brought on record to highlight the infirmity in the evidence by PW-9 and Prosecution evidence on record.

-Prima facie, there is nothing to indicate that the letter is inadmissible as per Indian Evidence Act. Court may view it or Prosecution may lead evidence that it attracts provisions of Army Rule 182. The burden of proving a fact lies on the party who substantially asserts the affirmative and not upon the party who denies it; for, a negative is usually incapable of proof.

-Appendix showing details of recovered garnish is already on record by Prosecution Evidence through PW-1 Cassius. (Page 165 of the Proceedings).

-While Army Rule 182 prohibits admission of certain documents, confession etc. in a Court of Inquiry *AGAINST* an accused, it does not bar such transaction in *FAVOUR* of the accused.

-What was produced by PW-1 is, in substance, a copy of the letter in question, dated 1 July 1983, with the *VITAL* variation under column 'Origin', where *"Ordnance marking of COD Kanpur to OD Shakurbasti"* is mentioned in brackets covering Serials 1 to 6, instead of against Serial 2 only. In addition, the words: *"in **used** condition with ordnance cat/part numbers marked"* have been mentioned against a bracket covering Serials 7 to 9 in the Exhibit, instead of the words: *"in **loose** condition with ordnance cat/part numbers marked"*. Also entries against Serials 7 to 9 are shown against 'R' Battery in the Exhibit, whereas in the Letter, it is shown against 'Q' Battery.

-Court too in its observations had said: *"Only ONE package had any markings dealing with OD Shakurbasti"*.

-In addition, the Letter with its Appendix, being in order be permitted to be brought on record, in the interest of justice for the Defence to put Prosecution evidence in correct perspective and to show *'the changing figures of the alleged recovery of garnish and its origin' to suit the hypothesis of guilt being advanced by them.*

-Prosecution Counsel had already stated about the wide powers of the Court in admitting evidence.

Prosecution Counsel replied that Defence had produced the Exhibit through PW-1 and cannot now contradict the same by bringing another document brought on record at their request; on the face of it, the Letter is inadmissible, as it is signed by the Presiding Officer of Court of Inquiry and Para 2 of the same gives out the action taken by it. While the Court's powers are wide, they should be exercised judiciously. If the Court wishes to peruse the document, WITHOUT bringing it on record, I have no objection. Defending Officer then conceded that exhibit was brought on record by us; reliance has been placed by the Defence not only to contradict a witness, but the principle on which it was earlier permitted by the Court; the argument by the Prosecution that the forwarding letter has been signed by Shifty Eyes and so is inadmissible lacks ingenuity. PW-1 had deposed the contents of a different Appendix before all the Summaries of Evidence against A-1 and before the Court another, while claiming it was produced in No 3 Summary of Evidence of A-1; the latter Appendix has not been authenticated by the Officer Recording Summary of Evidence No 3! The letter proposed to be brought on record by the Defence is a document prepared by an independent body and will bring out the truth.

JA gave a very lengthy advice; the Court, after considering it closed court, decided to disallow the submission of the Defence.

PW-9 Examined Again on Questions Suggested by Defending Officer of Accused 2:

-*'Instructions to me were to segregate and seal the garnish...(they) were put in the official dak and were also seen by all staff, including the 2IC. I instructed the Subedar Major to do it and keep in Miniature Range where there was no garnish. I did not get any other instructions from anyone after this. I did not order anyone to distribute garnish belonging to sub units out of this garnish'*.

-Earlier, he had said 3,000 M was of 'R' Battery...based on information given by Cassius (PW-1)... he was personally not aware; nor did he remember when he got this information. As he had not prepared the document, he said he did not want to see it; he was unable to say also if 3,000 M was included in 63,900.

-On 7 Aug 1986, when witness had refreshed his memory by seeing the document and later gave evidence, he gave the details as per combination of his memory and the Document. When more exhibits with different figures were shown, all produced by Prosecution Witnesses, he was unable to say the reasons for differences. He, however, confirmed the initials were of PW-1, dated 2 July 1983.

-After refreshing his memory from a document signed by him, he stated the number of vehicles taken part in Exercise Dig Vijay from the Regt: 12x jeeps/jongas; 21x 1-tons; 21x 3-tons; 1x Recovery vehicle; 9x Kraz's; 1x Dozer; and 6x guns.

-Additional vehicles loaned to other units for the same exercise were: 1 x jeep; 3x 3-tons; and 5x Kraz's.

In Reply to Questions Suggested by the Prosecution Counsel:

-After 15 *May* 1983 (wrongly recorded: it should have been 15 *Aug* 1983), this garnish was taken out on witness' instructions for any inspection and used to be placed back.

Defending officer of Accused No 2 submitted that the next witness was in terms of Section 139 of Indian Evidence Act.

At this stage, the Court decided to sit for longer than six hours in the interest of justice and discipline.

DW-10: Havildar Clerk (Store Control) From Shakurbasti Depot: (8 Aug 1986)

Direct Examination by Defending Officer of Accused No 2:

-He had brought Account cards for Scrim Garnish' 75 MM Grass Green and Un-dyed for 1982-83, which were perused by the Court, who observed that there was no seal or unit stamp to indicate those were from Ordnance Depot, Shakurbasti. The documents did not also bear signatures of any officer. On being questioned by the Court, witness stated that such pages are not stamped; and that one of the initials was of an officer of that Depot but he was unable to say whose.

Witness was asked to withdraw.

Defending Officer of Accused No 2 submitted that the witness had come as the representative of the Commandant of the Depot and the cards would reveal many facts discussed in the Court. He also undertook to prove them in 48 hours, stating they were authentic. Error, if any, in not stamping was not attributable to the witness or Defence. He 'begged' the Court not to penalize the accused.

Prosecution Counsel objected quoting the same observations as the Court. Witness did not even carry an authority letter to prove his appointment. If Defence would be proving it in 48 hours, they could as well produce it at that time. An authorized witness with the entire document of which these pages are part would alone do.

Defending Officer of Accused No 2 submitted that the authority letter addressed to HQ ... Corps was available, for this witness to produce these documents, which have also been mentioned in it.

Prosecution Counsel reiterated his objection that the witness was not competent.

JA then gave his advice quoting Sections 67 (*Proof of signature and Handwriting of the Person Alleged to have Signed or Written the Documents Produced*) and 73 (*Comparison of Signature, Writing, or Seal With Others Admitted or Proved*) of Indian Evidence Act and Section 140 of Army Act (*Presumption as to Signature*).

After consideration in closed Court, it decided to allow the objection of the Prosecution.

Witness was called and informed; he left.

Defending Officer of Accused No 1 submitted that NO other witnesses were available at present; a message had been left at the home of Mr. Rooster on 5 Aug 1986. Copy of summons given to us would reach him today and we expect him to come on Monday, 11 Aug 1986 evening and so, Court may adjourn till 13th.

Prosecution Counsel replied that sufficient time had already been given to the Defence to enable presence of witnesses; Rooster's name was given at the 11th hour; Address of Captain from Workshop given was wrong and it...cannot be certain if he would be available in the next 2, 3 days and *this trial has already been protracted for a very long time*. Any adjournment asked is not warranted and court should proceed. (A question arose in my mind then; but I controlled myself with great difficulty, from asking as to how much of the delay was attributable to the Defence. Luckily for me, Colonel Ramanan would do it in a moment.)

Colonel Ramanan *submitted that it had* ***taken 2 years, 9 months, 23 days, 4 Summaries of Evidence and 40 witnesses by the authorities to bring the case before this Honourable Court****. Court was* ***adjourned more than once for 20 days every time to enable*** *presence of a* ***Prosecution*** *Witness or for getting documents/bundles etc. We accommodated and waited for the relief of JA also. Prosecution should not have referred to Mr. Rooster in statements by Prosecution Witnesses, whereas Rooster is not known to either them or us. Objection regarding 'protracted delay' was not correct. The officer whom he was defending had been denied all his pay and allowances and even Provident Fund subscribed by him! Defence efforts be appreciated and adequate time, even if it runs into months, be given to bring the truth before the Court.*

JA gave his advice referring to Page 230 of the Proceedings and Section 136 of Army Rule.

After a consideration in closed court, it decided to adjourn till 12 Aug 1986.

DW-11: Former Regimental Havildar Major of the Regt (examined on 12 Aug 86)

Direct Examination by Defending Officer of Accused No 2:

-'Served from Aug 1980 to Oct 1983... appointed RHM in Dec 1982.'

-When Basantar Day celebrations were going on in Dec 1982, got a message at 0900 hours, from Q office to detail 6 men for

the Subedar QM to report at 0930 hours as working party for garnish collection…all 6 reported to the JCO in my presence around 0930 hours. Regimental Police Gate was not even 50 yards from where I was present and they left in a Shaktiman 3 ton in front of me after making entry in the Gate Register at around 0930 hours.

-At about 1430 hours, when I was standing in the ground with others, I saw the vehicle returning. I saw the men were sitting in an undisciplined manner and so I tried to stop the vehicle but it stopped only after reaching the Stores. I went and dismounted them and asked as to why they were not sitting properly, as Commanding Officer was particular about discipline. They told me … there was no place for them to sit inside the vehicle. I saw garnish inside. After telling the Subedar QM, I sent away those men for lunch and detailed another party for unloading, which started in front of me. Half the vehicle was loaded. Although I did not count the bundles, they were 50-100. The bundles were 100 in number.

-Two days after this event, when Mandir Parade was held, the bundles were still lying in the veranda of the ('Tentage') *Store near the Mandir, where they were initially kept after unloading.*

-After 2, 3 days, BQMH and RP Havildar brought garnish for HQ Battery and Regt HQ. RP brought the garnish to me, as I was responsible to make a big net for the 'Order Group'. This net was to be so big as to accommodate the entire Order Group. I was responsible to prepare the nets for (…HQ…) *Battery also, which I did.*

-Behind the Light Repair Workshop office, there was a small building which was on charge of Subedar Major and myself; and I had its keys from Mar-Apr 1981 onwards. After sometime, luggage of Brig…came to the unit and it was kept in this building. I saw a pet also with two persons who had brought this luggage. After his luggage was removed, luggage of Captain (…later Adjutant…) *was also kept there. After that was removed, this building remained vacant for sometime. 15 days before Commanding officer was to proceed on Course, his*

luggage came to this building and was on my charge. Till I proceeded to Record Office on Pension on 5 Oct 1983, the luggage remained there.

-In June-July 1983, I saw some garnish lying in the veranda of Miniature Range and it remained there till I left on 5 Oct 1983'.

Cross Examination by the Prosecution Counsel:

-I have never made any statement earlier before anyone.

-Since 4 years have elapsed and working parties used to be detailed frequently, I cannot now remember the names of the 6 persons in the working party.

-The message I had received was from QM; and A-2 was the QM then.

-Working party reported to the then Naib Subedar ... Never–loyal.... I do not remember the name of the driver but it was the standing duty vehicle for the month.

-Before this incident, I had never seen garnish loaded in any vehicle.

-I cannot say as to how many bundles could come in a Shaktiman. I saw all the bundles closed. I do not know how much garnish comes in a bundle. The tail board was closed when the vehicle came back and a jawan was sitting on it. I do not remember how many bundles I had received. Bundle was brought to me after distribution and it was opened by a jawan in front of me.

-I now say that rolls of garnish were only brought to me and not bundles. When I said 50-100 bundles in the vehicle I meant 50-100 rolls.

-Mandir and Miniature Range are about 300 yards apart. Building behind Light Repair Workshop and Miniature Range were about 1 furlong apart.

-I had lifted the tarpaulin and seen large quantity of garnish in rolls.

-One Brigadier sahib had come to the unit; (witness had mistaken Colonel Rabbi as Brigadier)...no lights but hurricane lamps were put.

-Never-loyal was in charge of the vehicle that had gone.

-QM or any other officer did not ever tell me the quantity of garnish brought in the unit.

Re-Examined by Defending Officer of Accused No 2:

-The bundles which I saw in the vehicle were packed in Hessian cloth.

-Two persons were carrying one bundle with great difficulty.

Questioned by The Court:

-By roll I mean a single roll. (*Court observed him giving a circular motion*).

-By Bundle, I mean 8 to 10 or 15 such rolls kept together in Hessian cloth.

-The unloading of vehicle started in my presence and thereafter I kept on moving between the ground and the vehicle to speed up the same, so that the jawans could join the games. (It was *Pagal Gymkhana* for Battle Honour Day!)

DW-12: Shri PL, Store Keeper, Shakurbasti Depot (examined on 12 Aug 1986)

Direct Examination by Defending Officer of Accused No 2:

-Serving since 1973. During 1982-84 was dealing with H-5 Section, which deals with accounting of garnish etc.

-In 1982-83, I had maintained Account Cards for Scrim Garnish Grass Green 75 MM Part No 1080-000012, in my own handwriting. After refreshing my memory from the same, I can say 46,500 M of Scrim Garnish Grass Green 75 MM was issued to ... Medium Regiment *on 7 Jan 1983* on Voucher No 12,699. There was NO issue of this to this Regt in Oct, Nov and Dec 1982. There was also no issue of this to this Regt in Feb, Mar or Apr 1983. (Court peruses the Account Cards and verifies the same).

-On *25 Feb 1982,* 99,000 M of Undyed Garnish 75 MM was issued to ... Medium Regt on Voucher No 29,865. (Court peruses the Account Cards and verifies the same).

Cross Examination by the Prosecution Counsel:

-I have given the statement after refreshing my memory from the documents with me.

-After being shown the Non Availability Voucher of the Depot dated 21 Nov 1982 (an earlier Exhibit), I say that this has been issued by the Depot. I cannot recognize the signature pointed out to me. I cannot also identify the writing above that signature. (He volunteered then to say) This is the No 1 Copy which comes to the unit. Since I do not have the records with me, I cannot say as to what all garnish of all sizes and colours were issued to this Regt prior to Oct 1982 or after Apr 1983.

Re-Examined by Defending Officer of Accused No 2:

-I have here with me records of issue of garnish Grass Green 75 MM from 24 Dec 1981 to 23 Aug 1983 and of Undyed garnish 75 MM from 11 Sep 1981 to 25 June 1984. (Court peruses the Account Cards and verifies the same).

At this stage, Prosecution Counsel wished to re-cross examine the witness as he had stated in categorical terms that he did not have the records with him pertaining to any kind of garnish issued to ... Medium Regt, before Oct 1982 and during re-examination has stated that he has the records of Grass Green garnish from 24 Dec 1981 to 23 Aug 1983. If he had stated so earlier, I would have questioned him on Grass Green from that date onwards.

Witness was asked to withdraw.

Defending Officer of Accused No 1 submitted that after re-examination the right of further re-cross-examination to the adverse party accrues only when new matter is introduced in re-examination. In the present context, no new matter has been introduced but only clarification was sought from the witness on the question asked in cross examination relating to garnish of *all sizes, types, shades and periods*. As no new matter has been introduced there is no right of re-cross-examination.

Prosecution Counsel submitted that since the witness had given categorical answer, his answer, therefore, for all intents and purposes a new matter, as from the reply of the witness I could not have anticipated that the record commenced from Dec 1981.

JA then gave his advice by drawing attention and reading out Sections 138 and 161 of the Indian Evidence Act.

In closed court, it decided to reject the submission of the Prosecution.

Witness was called.

Questioned by The Court:

-7 Jan 1983, as earlier mentioned by me is *the date of posting of entry in my records. There can be a gap between the actual date of issue and the date of posting of entry in records.*

DW-13: Mr. Rooster, Delhi Representative of Sphere Sales Corporation (examined on 12 Aug 1986)

Direct Examination by Defending Officer of Accused No 2:

-Received the summons redirected by Sphere Corporation, Jalandhar to his Delhi office address.

-In 1982-83, was working as Commission Agent of many companies, including Sphere Corporation in Delhi. In Dec 1982, his office was c/o M/s ABC Industries.

-Supplied garnish to ... Medium Regiment in second week of Dec 1982...had gone to the Regt in the first week of Dec 1982 and met the QM Head Clerk but was told QM was not available. Went the next day and met A-2. When he had asked if he could supply any needs for the exercise, QM had asked if he could supply garnish. He had replied that he would check availability from the Delhi market and tell him the next day. It was not available. He then contacted Mr. CS, Manager, Sphere Corporation at Jalandhar, who said it could be supplied.

-He then went back to Major sahib and confirmed he could supply. He asked for rate quotations. (*'By Major sahib, I meant QM and I recognize him'*)...gave as Rs 0.68 P per meter...was authorized to give rate quotation. Total quantity for which rate quotation was given was for 87,000 M in 3 shades: MB Green, Light Green and Dark Brown. Next day again gone to meet and was told by QM that theirs was the lowest and also asked him if they could supply, pending receipt of sanction and supply order. He confirmed.

-He then sent a telephonic message to Sphere Corporation for despatch of garnish in the shades and quantities required. It was received at the Transport Company, Delhi in second week of Dec 1982 and he had received the *'Bilty'* (transport receipt) accordingly.

-He telephoned QM about arrival of garnish, who said to supply immediately. He told the QM, when he expressed urgency that as ... Regt was in Haryana State, it would take 2, 3 more days to get clearance from authorities; so he told him to arrange collection, by sending a vehicle to ABC Industries, from where he could be contacted on telephone. He would then come from the Transport Company and get the good delivered. (Transport Co has two big godowns 15x100 yards in size, with a basement also. It could accommodate 30-35 truckloads of goods. It had a 15 feet long name-board displayed. Vehicles can go right up to the Transport

Co). He reached the godown at 1130 hours on 13 Dec 1982, (the day it was delivered to the Regt); vehicle had reached there already. A Subedar sahib with 5-6 jawans was there. *'Bilty'* was then got released and goods taken out and loaded in the vehicle by the jawans.

-He had *not met this Subedar earlier,* who had a letter of authority from the Regt for collection of garnish. Garnish had arrived as: "Sphere Corporation To SELF".

-'I gave to Subedar 58 bundles of garnish. I had paid Rs 375 for its transportation from Jalandhar to Delhi. One copy of challan had been received which I gave to Subedar sahib and took his signature on the Godown Register. As per the challan, there were: 62,000 M of MB Green; 14,000 M of Light Green and 11,000 M of Dark Brown garnish: all of 75 MM and there were 58 bundles in all'.

- *'I have never supplied jerricans to this Subedar sahib'.*

- 'The entire transport company was burnt down during Nov 84 riots, with all documents etc, as everything was burnt to ashes. Accordingly a case was registered with the Police. *I have with me a Photostat of the FIR which I produce before the court at the request of the Defending Officer'.* (JA observed that it was a Photostat of an FIR addressed to SHO, Lahori Gate, Delhi 110006, bearing signature purportedly of partner of Transport Company).

-Witness stated he cannot identify the handwriting of this document. On the top right there is a very slight impression of the Ashoka Pillar (...not legible).

Prosecution Counsel objected to the production of this document, which was then handed back to the witness and he was asked to withdraw. Counsel then explained the whole procedure then existing on lodging an FIR and that as the witness had not lodged it, he cannot prove it. He had probably brought it from Transport Co. There was no date visible on it. Defending Officer of A-1 stated that this document is indeed admissible in law; Sections 61 to 66 of Indian Evidence Act deal with mode of proof of contents of a document. Under Section 67, the signature of the executor can be proved by the executor himself or by a person acquainted with his handwriting. FIR lodged by the Transport Co bears the signature of its partner and it also bears the address of the location of the incident. Prima facie, it has been lodged at the Police Station under whose jurisdiction its locality falls. Witness may be asked to identify the signature of the partner; if he is able to do so, the document is in order and is admissible. Law does not lay down a format for the FIR. It may be written, verbal or conveyed through a third agency. FIR had been lodged on the same day as the incident, i.e., 31 Oct 1984. Counsel's contention that the witness was not present at the lodging of FIR is misconceived. It is neither requirement of law nor of procedure that this witness had to be so present, in order to make this document admissible. This document is being introduced to support the incident explaining destruction of the register and is of corroborative nature and not the evidence of its contents. Therefore it is admissible, subject to identification of the partner's signature. Prosecution Counsel replied that while an FIR is admissible, it is not in this case, where witness is not the complainant. Primary rule for admissibility of a document is that the adverse party should be able to cross examine the witness on its contents. Date on which it was lodged is most essential; but it does not bear any date. He was at a loss to understand how the Defending Officer of Accused No 1 has concluded that it was lodged on the day of occurrence. Even if he identified the signature of the partner, he is not competent to produce the document. Signature is by partner of ... Delhi Punjab Goods Corporation and not of ... Transport, as he had been saying. It is not admissible; however there is no objection to the Court having a look at the document before deciding.

(At this stage the Court decided to sit for more than six hours and beyond 6 p.m. in the interest of justice and discipline).

JA then gave his advice by reading out and referring to Section 154 of Code of Criminal Procedure (Information in Cognizable Cases); Section 35 of Indian Evidence Act (relevancy of Entry in Public Record Made I Performance of Duty).

After a consideration in closed court, it decided to allow the objection by the Prosecution.

On 13 Aug 1986, the witness was called in.

Direct Examination by Defending Officer of Accused No 2 Continued:

-After the loading, the vehicle marched off around 1230-1245 hours.

-'I was present when the vehicle was loaded. Subedar sahib was standing with me and keeping an account of loading; but I did not see him taking part in loading. He did not open, weigh or measure the bundles. After the loading the vehicle was about ¾ full'.

-Next day, I enquired from Major Sahib on telephone and he confirmed receipt. Then I informed Sphere Corporation accordingly. After this I made a few telephone calls as also visited the unit a couple of times to enquire about receipt of sanction, in Jan-Feb 1983. I was told by Major Sahib that the sanction had not been received till then. I did not meet or talk with anyone in the unit.

-In Mar 1983, when I went, QM Subedar Clerk told me that sanction was about to come and payment would follow soon...at that time, I opened my own firm and ceased working for Sphere Corporation. Around end-Apr or beginning May 1983, Sphere requested me to deliver an envelop to the Regt. I did so; but thereafter I did not contact the Regt in connection with this garnish transaction, but supplied items from my own firm.

-I supply to other units also at Delhi. Subsequent to this, I met Subedar sahib in Mar 1983, when I had opened my firm.

-I have never supplied any plastic jerricans to the Regt in 1982.

-Distance between ABC Industries and ...Transport Co. is about one furlong.

-Full name of ... Transport Co is ...Delhi-Punjab Goods Corporation Registered.

Cross Examination by the Prosecution Counsel:

-On telephonic instructions from Sphere Corporation...had gone to a number of units, including ... Medium Regt, to check for requirements for exercise in the first week of Dec 1982; do not recollect the specific date. It was the first visit to the Regt. Got its location from units at Delhi Cantonment, which I visited. Since 1978, he had been purchasing items from the market and supplying to various firms who further supply it to units in Delhi. In that first visit itself, Major Sahib told him the quantity, 87,000 M and the 3 shades. It was first time he had met him.

-At times supply orders are received before actual supply and at times not so. I gave the quotation in a sealed envelop to Major Sahib the next day at around 1100-1130 hours. While enquiring the rate from Mr. CS of Sphere Corporation, he got the rate of Rs 0.68 P per meter and only then gave it to Regt.

Verbatim Question and Answer:

-*"When you visited the Regt, you went there as Agent of Sphere Corporation, then why did you check for availability of garnish in Delhi market?"*

-*"I looked for it in Delhi also because, had it been available there, it would have costed less as there would have been no transport charges on it."*

-At Delhi he had checked up about the availability of garnish at the whole sale Hessian cloth market at *Khari Bowli* and backside (*sic*) of *Naya Bazaar*. Towards the end of 1st or beginning of 2nd week of Dec 1982, when he spoke to Major, he had said he had applied for sanction and it was awaited. *'I did not send anything in writing to Sphere Corporation about this supply of garnish'*. He added that he did not correspond. *'As I was dealing with 6, 7 firms, I could not correspond with all of them and all transactions were discussed verbally'*.

-*'When I spoke to Mr. CS, I only mentioned the name of Major.... I did not mention anyone else's name'*.

-*'I did not receive anything in writing from Sphere Corporation regarding this transaction...I had received the 'Bilty' and challan one copy'... by ordinary post c/o ABC Industries. I had no personal office of my own, till I opened my firm in Mar 1983. My letters used to be received at ABC Industries, who are wholesale dealers.'*

-*'On Saturday, 11 Dec 1982, when I went to ... Transport Co, the garnish had not come by then, although I had received the 'Bilty' and the challan the same day. On Sunday, 12 Dec 1982, I found garnish had come there. I could not, however, contact Major that day but only on 13 Dec 1982'*.

-*'On 13 Dec 1982, I went to the Transport Co at 1130 hours and after handing over the Bilty to them, got the goods released. I spoke to Major around 0930 hours on 13 Dec 1982'*.

-While talking with him, he said he is sending a vehicle for garnish collection. *'I ...said... that the vehicle should reach ABC Industries around 1130 hours. After that I left a message with ABC Industries that a military vehicle would come at 1130 hours and that they should send an escort with it up to ... Transport Co to show the way'*.

-*'I had no partnership with ABC Industries but I only used to buy goods from them'*.

-The firm which I opened in Mar 1983 is situated in a by-lane behind ABC Industries, about half a furlong away.

-I read the letter of authority for collection of garnish which Subedar sahib had with him; it was signed by Major. I returned the letter back to him, as I did not need it.

Verbatim Question and Answer:

-*"You supplied goods worth more than Rs 60,000 and you handed them over to an unknown person, i.e. the Subedar sahib, why did you not keep that letter with you as a proof of transaction?"*

-*"I had obtained the signature of Subedar sahib on the Register."*

-Since I did not have a register of my own, I obtained his signature on the Transport Co Register. I cannot produce that Register as I have already stated that ... Transport Co had been burnt down.

-*"It is incorrect to suggest that I have deposed falsely here about the burning of ... Transport, because the Register does not have Subedar sahib's signature."*

-"It is incorrect to suggest that I have falsely deposed here that I gave 58 bundles to Subedar sahib, as I had given him only 11-12 bundles".

-The witness explained he indeed gave 58 bundles and the vehicle left around 1230 hours, after the loading on 13 Dec 1982. On 14 Dec 1982, at around 1015 hours he had telephoned Major. *'I told him your representative had come and I had delivered 58 bundles and also asked him whether he had received them alright. He confirmed to me that 58 bundles had been received'*. I did not tell him that I had handed over challan to the Subedar sahib.

-*"It is incorrect to suggest that I did not inform Major about handing over the challan to Subedar sahib, as I had not handed it over to him."*

-'I did not ask Major about payment on 14 Dec 1982...how could I have asked since I knew sanction had not been received'.

-After this and up to Mar 1983, I telephoned Major 2-3 times about payment and supply order etc. He told me the sanction was about to come. I cannot remember the date or month of these telephone calls made by me, but all of them were made before noon.

-The closed envelop which I received from Sphere Corporation in end-Apr/beginning May 1983 was addressed to the Regt and not to QM or any other person. Next day I went to the Regt and handed it over to QM Subedar Clerk. I did not obtain any receipt as it was not necessary.

-Name of the Subedar sahib who came to collect the garnish was "... (Never-loyal)..." as it was written on his name plate and also written on the authority letter brought by him.

-I did not meet that Subedar "... (Never-loyal)..." after Mar 1983, as my grown up sons have been visiting units for business. I did not meet Subedar "... (Never-loyal)..." ever after 13 Dec 1982 when he had collected garnish.

-I had informed Sphere Corporation that supply had to be made pending receipt of supply order and sanction. Manager told me that it was all right as they had been dealing with the Army and had been supplying in this manner. Mr. CS never asked me to progress payment... I was commission agent only and it was their own matter.

Verbatim Question and Answer:

-"When Major... told you that sanction had been applied for and was awaited, did you not in the meantime ask for supply order?"

-"How can one ask for supply order in the absence of sanction? Hence I did not ask for supply order."

-'It is incorrect to say that during Dec 1982 to May 1983, I

was reminded several times by Mr. CS regarding payment for goods supplied by them." The witness explains he, however had, on his own, telephoned the Regt 2-3 times during this period to enquire about receipt of sanction.

-*'I did not ask about payment from Major between Dec 1982 and Mar 1983. During this period I visited the Regt 2-3 times, and also made the earlier-mentioned 2-3 telephone calls to Major. During these 2-3 visits I enquired from Major only about receipt of sanction and not about payment'.*

Re-examination Declined.

Questioned by the Judge Advocate:

-Once the delivery was made to party concerned by me, I used to inform Sphere Corporation on telephone that the delivery has been effected properly but did not use to send any written confirmatory report or any other document in this regard.

-Before visiting ... Regt in first week of Dec 1982, I had never earlier visited any Army unit personally to strike any deal. However, I have been commission agent since 1978.

In Reply to Question Suggested by the Defending Officer of Accused No 1:

-In the trade of commission agents, they generally confirm the delivery of goods by them to parties, verbally and not in writing, to their principals.

In Reply to Question Suggested by the Prosecution Counsel:

-I cannot say about other commission agents, as no one reveals their trade secrets.

DW-14: Captain Who Had Served Earlier With Workshop: (examined on 13 Aug 1986)

Direct Examination by Defending Officer of Accused No 2:

-Was...attached with ... Medium Regiment as their Officer in Charge Advance Workshop Detachment (AWD).

-On 14 Dec 1982, learnt ...Medium Regiment had plenty of garnish...So I requested QM ... told me that he could give me 5 bundles only. Around 1330 hours, I collected those 5 bundles from Subedar Clerk QM Branch...Garnish was ... plenty in the verandah of the Tentage Stores, when I collected...loaded in my vehicle by the 4 persons from the AWD whom I had called. One bundle was carried by two persons. Physically I did not measure the length of garnish. Each bundle was triangular in shape and as per my estimation, each contained about 1,500 M. Since I was visiting the Regt daily and being practically a part of it, I knew that it was Tentage Stores.

Cross Examination by the Prosecution Counsel:

-When I first saw the garnish while going to QM office, I saw it wrapped in Hessian cloth. It was not covered with any tarpaulin etc.

Re-Examination Declined.

Questioned by the Court:

-I went to QM to request for garnish at around 1000 hours on 14 Dec 1982. After that I went to Central Ordnance Depot, Delhi Cantonment for some official work...

-These five bundles were given to me without any voucher or receipt...since AWD was almost part of the Regt and used to get items as required, there was no such requirement. These were carried in a 3 ton upto my Workshop Company at Meerut.

No Questions Suggested by the Defending Officers

In Reply to Questions Suggested by the Prosecution Counsel:

-Whenever any item was taken by AWD from the Regt, no NIV, loan voucher etc was prepared or signed...The requirements of AWD as such were negligible. Once I asked for 3 litres of paint which also I had got and also when the garnish was required, it was given.

ANNEXURE 7: GIST OF CLOSING ADDRESSES (THIRD GCM)

BY DEFENCE ON 18 AUG 1986

1. In order to refresh memory, the Charge Sheet was read out first. The fundamental principle of our criminal law is that an accused person is presumed to be innocent until proved otherwise. It is NOT for the accused to prove his innocence but for the prosecution to bring home the guilt, NOT by mere inference or conjecture, but by reliable and dependable evidence adduced in the course of trial. Besides legal presumption of innocence, law of evidence lays down that 'burden of proof' is on the party who alleges a fact. Only after the prosecution proves the charge beyond a shadow of doubt, the onus of disproving shifts to the accused, but not to the same extent. It will be sufficient onus even if the accused created a reasonable doubt about the prosecution version. Court has to be satisfied beyond a reasonable doubt that it is the accused who has committed the offence.

2. Prosecution examined 10 witnesses and has mainly relied upon Subedar Never-loyal, PW-7; so we shall discuss it in the perspective of overall evidence on record; (*all Page Nos cited are from the GCM Proceedings*):

   (a) PW-9 deposed that 80 vehicles took part in Exercise, with 2 nets each.

   (b) PW-3 and 9 as also DW-12 deposed that 75 MM garnish available with the batteries on 25 Nov 1982, was as follows: MB Green NIL; Light Green 10,900 M; Dark Brown 2,500 M; Undyed 99,000 M and Grass Green 10,000 M (i.e., 56,500-46,500), thus totalling to 1,22,400 M; NO stock in Regt stores at STB on 25 Nov 1982.

   (c) PW-3 had given out the requirement of garnish for various types of nets; and also that the last receipt in the Regt of MB Green 75 MM was on 30 Dec 1981 and of Dark Brown on 10 Nov 1981: both 75 MM.

(d) Thus the total requirement of garnish for 235 equivalent nets of size 10.7x6 M @ 856 M each worked out to 2,01,160 M. Deducting the holding in ledgers (although not discounting the non-utility mostly of Undyed), it comes to 2,01,160 LESS 1,22,400= 78,760 M.

(e) It was in this background that Local Purchase (LP) was resorted to against the Non Availability Voucher given by Shakurbasti Depot on 21 Nov 1982. This simple, straightforward innocent deal has been given colour by the Prosecution, who gave a further twist by producing *'allegedly recovered garnish'* six months after going for the exercise and 3½ after return from it.

(f) Prosecution has not explained the reasons behind the mysterious and often-varying figures of this alleged recovery; mentioned in detail).

(g) It was observed by the Court itself that the markings as deposed by PWs 1, 2, 7 and 9 did NOT exist on the Material Evidence. This so-called recovered garnish was nothing but Undyed (unused balance of 99,000 M) plus 15,000 M returned by Brigade HQ after the exercise; Defence Stores Holding; Signal Section Holding and 50 MM balance held in the Regt.

(h) The actual transaction was given out by PW-8, who explained how DW-13 had liaised with the unit, gave the rate quotation and delivered 58 bundles totalling 87,000 M of 75MM garnish in 3 shades as contracted. He also deposed that rate per meter being 68 paise, the total was Rs 61,526/20 P, including 4% sales tax. He also gave the despatch details through ...Transport.

(i) DW-13 deposed unambiguously the arrival of PW-7, vehicle, driver and working party; the loading; PW-7 signing on Transport Co godown, in the absence of an office for him; handing over of challan etc.

(j) As per evidence on record, PW-7 Never-loyal had taken over duties as Subedar QM on 16 Nov 1982 after everything was found correct; (*he produced the certificates also as exhibits*!). He also deposed that during first or second week of Dec 1982, A-2 told him that he was to go to one ABC Industries at Kashmere Gate, Delhi and collect (*'some'*) garnish from one person *Rooster & Co*, which was attached with *ABC Industries*. When witness checked with A-2, on quantity of garnish; need for working party; vehicles required and authority for collection, he had told him: no need of working party; to take the already attached vehicle to the witness; and *"to collect whatever quantity of garnish ...given"*. He also told him that a Sikh person from Rooster & Co would meet him at ABC Industries and deliver the item. Accordingly, he left at about 0900/0930 the same day in a Shaktiman 3 ton, driven by *Naik PC* and reached ABC Industries at 1045/1100 hours. He met the owner of ABC Industries and told him the purpose, who told him to wait for the representative of Roster and Co. The person (Sikh) came, (whom the witness *had seen* earlier in the Regt, supplying local purchase items) and led him to a transport Co *"1/2 to 1 ½ KM away"*. He asked for the unit and was told ... Medium Regt & the name of A-2. *'He then showed me a few bundles and asked me to take them. I asked him as to how many bundles are there. He told me to count myself. ...I counted 13 ...and 1500 M in each, totalling 19,500 M. Bundles were packed in thin Hessian cloth and could be seen through that it was UNDYED (khaki) ... no marking... driver and I loaded in vehicle. ... Each bundle weighed approx 15-20 kg.'* After loading when asked where to sign, voucher, challan etc, he was told the person had spoken to A-2 and no need of anything. He reached back at 1245-1300 hours. Reported to A-2 he had brought 13 bundles totalling 19,500 M of garnish. A-2 ordered him to issue it straightway. '*When I asked him any NIV to be prepared, he told me to issue the garnish first. He also asked me to issue equal quantity to each battery, a little to HQ battery and keep rest with me*'. He '*then collected a voucher form from Clothing Stores and after putting battery-wise distribution on it, and having obtained the signature of battery representatives, I issued the material the same day*'.

(k) The witness had then produced a voucher (Nominal Issue Voucher or NIV, in short) bearing digits 601 made in his own hand and purporting to be serial number of NIV (Issue?) Register maintained by him. When confronted with Serial 601 in the "*Issue Register 1983*" and pointed out its anachronistic entry vis-à-vis other entries tried to wriggle out saying it was '*meant for his personal record*'! Strangely he wishes the court to believe that: "*As the proper NIV is prepared in the office, this document was prepared for my own record and I had written NIV on it*". Indeed this document has not only been conceived, prepared and authored by PW-7, as the sub unit representatives whose signatures it purports to contain have not only denied the receipt of the garnish mentioned in it but also the alleged signatures. DW-6 and DW-1, two of the alleged signatories have denied it was their signature(s); ***the third and the fourth have not been proved by the Prosecution till date***.

(l) This NIV was seen for the first time only on 18 June 1983. NO separate sizes or shades alleged to have been issued are mentioned! Nor corresponding entries exist in battery ledgers, which is why Prosecution has not led any evidence to get them on record. On Page 189 of the Proceedings, PW-7 has also stated that he had distributed 46,500 M of LP garnish vide another exhibit and that was the corresponding voucher for 'this NIV'!

(m) Wanting to take this matter to an end, he deposed that he had sent the balance 3,000 M to the exercise location whence a demand had come but was unable to produce any document, although claiming that he had a record of all items sent to exercise location. The Subedar who had functioned as Subedar QM in the exercise area deposed that he kept a record of receipts and showed them to CO/2IC but did not receive any garnish bundles. He had also deposited that record with QM office; oddly Prosecution has not produced that record!

(n) In order to re-establish his credibility, PW- 7 deposed that on **06** Nov 1982, he *'issued 4,600 or 46,000M of garnish'*, when there was NO stock of 75 MM garnish in the unit as per the exhibits and deposition of PWs 2, 3 and 9! During cross examination, he could not tell the exact quantity and in re-examination, he could give neither the shade nor produce any document in support. It is on record from his own deposition that he had taken over only on **16** Nov 1982!

(o) Evidence of PW-7, the prima donna of Prosecution is contradicted in every material point. He has made false statements even on insignificant points:

- not carrying a *'Dandaman'* (the person to be carried compulsorily in every heavy military vehicle to warn the driver by beating a baton on the driver's side panel of vehicles wanting to overtake) or a working party, while taking a vehicle during the rush hour, through the busy roads of Delhi Cantonment and old Delhi (Kashmere Gate area!);
- he, along with the driver loading the vehicle (contradicted by DWs 2, 11 and 13)
- his attempt to give a totally false image of ...Transport Co, as being a small tin shed with no walls and a telephone on a table under the tin shed, with garnish bundles lying behind the table

etc, whereas the correct picture was given by Rooster, DW-13, as ...Transport Co's godown having the capacity to hold 30-35 civil truckloads;

- his statement that he had approached the former QM Subedar head Clerk, when not satisfied 'with this method of distribution' (as given by QM, A-2);
- he having seen/met Rooster both in the unit and in the latter's office and having collected plastic jerricans from Rooster, which was denied by the latter, saying he had never supplied that item to the Regt and that he had never met PW-7 earlier before this garnish-trip!
- the manner in which he attempted to make the court believe that he had made 13 trips from the godown to the vehicle to load the '13 bundles' (each being at least 25 to 30 kg), all done in less than 30 minutes, over ½ to 1½ KM!

(p) The evidence of PW-7 is to be judged with reference to his conduct vis-à-vis PW-8 and DWs 2, 3, 11, 13 and 14 and the presumption of probability legitimately arising in this case and applying the test whether the evidence of PW-7 is consistent with the common experience of mankind, in the usual course of nature and human conduct with well-known principles of human action. In view of the mere concoction of NIV in support of his oral testimony, NO reliance should be placed on his evidence, when weighed against untarnished and unchallenged testimony of PW-8 and DWs 2, 3, 11, 13 and 14. It is on record in Page 194 of the Proceedings: "***The court observes that the witness has to be pointed out now and then to answer specifically to questions put to him and not to reply in a vague manner***".

(q) It is submitted that *'from the way in which a witness gives evidence, one can often discover whether... is a liar, partisan, or has a bias, or whether he is a truthful witness struggling to tell an honest tale. If he is over forward and over zealous in ...favour of one side, but reluctant to make any additions ...against that side; if his memory is clear and precise on all points that tell in favour of one side, but hazy and obscure when truth would benefit the other party, then it may safely be concluded that he is a liar, or a partisan as such unreliable'*. (Powell, 9th edition, pages 506-7).

(r) The learned counsel may try to buttress the claim of PW-7 of having brought only 19,500 M only, by arguing that he had NO animosity with A-1 and A-2 to depose falsely against them. But his entire testimony is on defending himself, as *he has NO proper documentation with him even today* to account for the LP garnish and as such he succumbed to the pressure exerted on him by PW-2, who was bent upon embarrassing the image of A-1, proceeding on HC course, to settle scores with him for various admonitions and perceived slights (who had ill feeling against A-2 also, due to the report about his misuse of transport):

- after the accident on 13 Mar 1983;
- on 9/14 Apr 1983 after his abuse of JCOs;
- at the Mess on 22 Apr 1983;
- his own ACR on 7 June 1983.

The degree of ill feeling could be gauged from the fact that PW-2 did not even attend the funeral of the wife of A-1, who had died under tragic circumstances on 20 July 83.

(s) Had PW-7 not brought the whole quantity of 87,000 M, he would have had no hesitation in taking PW-1, 2 and 9 to ABC Industries or Rooster or ...Transport Co.

(t) In order to avoid contradiction of his claim, he had even hidden the name of the driver till Apr 1985!

3. Other PWs: With the exception of PW-4 (ex DDOS at Corps HQ, who had sanctioned the LP); PW-6 (Clerk from Corps Ordnance); PW-8 (Shri CS) and PW-9, Colonel Tanjore Doll, the evidence of the remaining PWs except for their personal data, everything else is full of self-contradictions in deposition or contradicted by other evidence on record. See examples below.

4. PW-1 Captain Cassius. Having reported to Regt on 4 Mar 1983, has very little personal knowledge; is a narrator of events as told to him by Never-loyal or QM clerk and as directed by PW-2, Crass. Glaring contradictions in his deposition:

   (a) Page 75: 'checked files only on 16 June 1983 vs. Page 82: on 14 June 1983.

   (b) Alleged telephone conversation by PW-2, Crass in his presence, with A-1 at Delhi on 16 June whereas A-1 returned from Meerut only late in the evening.

   (c) Alleged entries got done by A-2 in ledger on 17 June 1983 (Page 163) contradicted by PW-10 at Page 230 that he (PW-10) had done the entries in May 1983.

   (d) On Page 163 he states that he produced 'all the documents' from the QM office before Colonel Rabbi on 28 June 1983, whereas besides quotations, nothing (supplier's bills, forms D (except in one case) and CTC of voucher) is available in the office even today and not produced on record either.

   (e) He was not aware of any instruction from Court of Inquiry regarding safe custody of 'allegedly recovered garnish' (Page 165); but PW-9, the new CO (Page 335) deposed that PW-1 had initialled the letter on 2 July 1983!

   (f) He was also warned by the Court on variations in figures (Page 166).

5. PW-2, Major Crass. The less said about him, the better it is. Court had watched his demeanour and warned

him more than once. His animosity and rancour have been brought out (as in Para 2(s) above). Major discrepancies in his deposition are:

1. On Pages 105 and 111, he deposed neither A-1 nor anyone else told him anything about LP during a conference, Durbar or on exercise. PW-9, successor CO (at Pages 211 and 225) deposed that during conferences A-1 had mentioned about LP. DW-2, Driver deposed (Pages 262 and 263) that in a durbar before the exercise, A-1 had told all ranks that LP has been done and two nets will be carried and if anyone faced any problem, he should contact him (A-1). Many other witnesses deposed about *'Durbar'*; Adjt showed from *'Durbar'* Book, PW-2 had been present and had signed it!

2. He deposed at Pages 99 and 109 that he had spoken on telephone to A-1 who was at Delhi at 1200 hours on 16 June 1983, whereas A-1 was away to Meerut that day from about 0800 to 1930 hours, as deposed by PW-9, DW-7 and DW-9.

3. On Page 104, he deposed that he had done 'joint investigation along with A-1', when in fact A-1 had visited the unit during June 1983, only on 18 and 25 June for a discussion and Promotion Conference respectively, before a Bara Khana on 27th and rejoining on 28th, as per PW-9 (Pages 231 and 226) and DW-7 (Page 296). PW-9 has also deposed that *"...on 18 June 1983, there was a 'discussion' in the presence of A-1, in which, I', Cassius and Crass all participated"* (and NOT a JOINT investigation, as he alleged!)

4. On Page 105, he deposed that he was not aware of Corps Commander's expected visit in May 1983 but contradicted himself on Page 109, that "there was a letter from Brigade HQ telling A-1 to adjust his leave depending on the visit of the Corps Commander

to the unit". He was also present and had signed the Sainik Sammelan Register, where the fact of the expected Corps Commander's visit was mentioned.

5. On Page 107, he deposed that he had checked with Battery Commanders of P and R Batteries regarding LP transaction during his preliminary investigations, whereas PW-9 and DW-4 have both deposed from Records that these two were on leave for the whole of June 1983!

6. When questioned on collateral matters, he does not remember anything or has not taken appropriate action as the officiating CO. *Pages 102 to 104 are full of "I do not remember" from him.* Pages 109 to 112 are full of his failures to take action as the officiating CO, eg, stock position of garnish in the Depot; ground balance of garnish (used and unused); quantity of ordnance pattern garnish that ought to have existed; documentation by batteries; holdings by BQMH's; supplying agency's documents; bin cards; brigade SOP on local purchase etc.

7. The Court would have noticed the discrepancies in deposition by many other PWs, as also the quality of evidence.

8. Once again, it is for Prosecution alone to prove the charge: eg, 6 contingent bills with various dates having been submitted. PW-6 Ordnance Clerk from Corps Ordnance Branch (who performed so till end June 1983) has deposed that *'after being returned in May 1983, those contingent bills were not received back anytime'*. Ex DDOS, PW-4 has also deposed on Page 156 that "*the above*" contingent bills were not received back from...Medium Regiment during his tenure. ***Although it is not the Defence case that no contingent bills were prepared or submitted, our submission is that we did not submit the bills as averred in the charge sheet.***

9. Our case is that Local Purchase of garnish was resorted to after obtaining the verbal sanction of DDOS, Corps, as spoken by Brig Scraggly, against Non Availability Certificate issued by Shakurbasti Depot. In pursuance of the nod from Scraggly, 87,000 M of 75 MM scrim garnish was purchased from M/s Sphere Sales Corporation, Jalandhar, through their Delhi rep, Rooster; and physically collected by Subedar Never-loyal, PW-7 in Dec 1982, in a vehicle driven by Naik PC and brought to the unit, which was unloaded under the supervision of the then RHM, (DW-11) and kept in the verandah of a stores barrack. Documents were prepared, signed and sent to DDOS Corps, soon after, for sanctions. These were received in Apr-May 1983 and *contingent bills were accordingly submitted with dates as 2, 5, 17, 22 and 27 Apr 1983 and 2 May 1983, as produced by us through PW-4*. Soon after A-1 and A-2 had proceeded on leave. These contingent bills appear to have been received back with observations, when A-1 and A-2 were away. These were duly corrected by PW-3 and PW-5, *on their own,* as is apparent from the deposition of PW-1, who has *inter alia* deposed that on the forenoon of 16 June 1983, he did not hand over the mail to A-2, when the latter came to the unit on a personal visit, but asked him about the details of the LP transaction. *PW-1 then produced before the Hon'ble Court six sets of exhibits as having been the six shown to him by A-2 on 16 June 1983. He has also pointed out the dates on Contingent Bills as 9, 12, 23 and 28 Apr 1983 and 4 and 10 May 1983.*

10. *It is an established fact that A-2 explained LP transaction to PW-1 and PW-2 on 17 June 1983 only and NOT on 16 June 1983*. It is also submitted *that PW-1 while producing the six sets of exhibits before the court did NOT state the dates on the contingent bills were different from the ones which are existing on them now*. It is apparent that PW-1 was shown the contingent bills by A-2,

with dates as now appearing on the prosecution-exhibits. His subsequent effort to indicate the amended dates as deposed on Page 90 is an endeavour to mislead the court. PW-1 has also not accounted for his whereabouts on 17 June 1983. The forwarding letters for these corrected documents appear to have been got signed by A-2, when he had come on a private visit to the unit to thank the officers for the help rendered for his son's wedding on 23 May 1983. Having explained the details of the transaction, he had proceeded back to his leave station (*'empty handed'* as deposed by DW-7) around 1130 hours, with the approval of PW-2, the officiating CO, *who saw him off*! After his visit, the vested interests ganged up to distort the facts and in order to embarrass A-2 and (through him) A-1, made the documents disappear, as 87,000 M of garnish received had not been paid for yet. As prudent officers, would the court believe that after 1½ hours of discussion on this very topic of LP and having seen the documents, PW-1 and PW-2 would have allowed A-2 (who had come to the unit on a private visit) to carry away those very official documents?

11. For argument's sake, if the documents were really carried away by A-2, what was the necessity for A-2 to hold them back or destroy them and not forward for payment, having got the necessary sanctions, especially when the Defence case is that contracted quantity of garnish had been brought and used; and A-2 was to be on annual leave till 14 July 1983 and office copies were in unit files, including the covering letters and A-2 had not taken them away?

12. By inventions and blatant lies, an open transaction that has been done with the involvement of former QM Subedar Clerk and PWs 3, 5 and 10 (all clerks) and PW-7 the store holder Subedar Never-loyal;

fully discussed in unit and brigade conferences; and announced in Sammelan more than once was converted into a hush-hush affair by the Prosecution. In order to confuse further, the learned counsel has further tried to marshal evidence to show that documents were backdated or signed while on leave etc, to show *'mens rea'* (Guilty mind). Assuming though not admitting that were the case, even then it would not show *mens rea,* as Justice Subba Rao had observed in the case of Dr. Vimla vs. Delhi Administration (AIR 1968, SC 1572): *"Where there has been no intention to cause harm or undue gain to anyone, the accused cannot be held to have acted with the intent to defraud (...) in spite of the fact that the accused might have acted falsely or adopted some deceptive methods".*

13. I may also submit before the Hon'ble Court the confirmed and accepted legal view about the appreciation of oral evidence, as pronounced from time to time by various high courts: *"Where a witness is shown to have made deliberately a false statement, he is prima facie utterly unreliable and there is no question of truth of any statement made by such a witness".* (AIR 1953 MP 250)

    "Primary duty of court is, when it finds the prosecution case false and manufactured in material and vital particulars and supported by prejudiced evidence, is to throw the whole case without delay; and the practice of the court to search laboriously and anxiously with a microscope for some truth which may be buried in the evidence, is wrong; a waste of valuable time and a danger to public, which frequently results in innocent persons being convicted". (AIR 1933 ALL 896).

14. In the absence of positive and irrefutable evidence to establish that only 19,500 M and not the contracted quantity had arrived, the accused CANNOT be held GUILTY of the charge. In a criminal case, no inference

or presumption can be drawn on points of fact; the onus lies on the prosecution to prove the case and NOT on the Defence to disprove it.

18 Aug 1986 (Signed) NS Bains, Colonel (Retired)

BY THE PROSECUTION COUNSEL ON 19 AUG 1986

1. Charge: The accused persons have been arraigned before you on a charge under Army Act Section 52 (f) for committing an act, with intent to defraud. (Charge read out).

2. Relevant Provisions of the Law: The terms 'Fraud' and 'Intent to Defraud' have NOT been defined; but Section 25 of IPC defines 'fraudulently', as *'A person is said to do a thing fraudulently, if he does that thing with the intent to defraud and not otherwise'*. He then went on to define a few other terms: Injury, Person, Govt, Intention (or knowledge) not being capable of proof etc. He then went on to 'Facts to be Proved' and dissected every word of the charge sheet and defined terms like 'Proved', Disproved' and 'Not Proved'.

3. First Fact: A-1 was CO and A-2 was QM at Dundahera Camp during Apr to June 1983. Then the controversy over the leave dates of CO was explained one-sidedly, though in writing he had mentioned the evidence of my presence in office on and up to 4 May 1983. *'Technically he is divested of his duties but he nevertheless retains his appointment as CO of the Regt during leave'*. Then, while explaining my presence/absence, he missed out some para/lines both verbally and in writing.

4. 'Together Submitted'

   - He then explained the sequence of preparation of documents for seeking LP and then submitting Contingent Bills etc, which had been signed by both. Without explaining how and what manner, he stated: *'Thereafter the accused persons obtained the sanction of*

DDOS... Corps for LP of scrim garnish'. He then gave out the description, number, date and signature of every enclosure of the documents; (these were office copies!).

- The next statement that '...*The above documents were a part of the whole set of documents which were prepared and kept by the accused'* does not convey anything: what formed the *Set*? Kept where and by whom?

- He committed another major mistake where he talked next of a Demi Official letter from a Lt Col at Corps Ordnance (part of the infamous *'envelope'*, which is said to have created the initial doubts in the minds of PW-1, Cassius and PW-2, Crass during 4-16 June 1983!) and said *'the draft was given by DDOS Corps to Lt Col...'*, whereas PW-4 was never asked about this Lt Col and this letter; but the one who had signed a letter dated 7 Mar 1983! PW-6 on Page 176 has clearly stated that Major... (who later as Lt Col wrote the letter) gave the draft of DO letter in the name of A-2.

- His next major lie and NOT proved anywhere is when he stated: *"Thereafter the documents remained in the surreptitious possession of the accused persons, until during the cross examination of PW-4 (DDOS), Defending Officer of A-1 produced the forwarding letter in original from his custody"*: firstly, it was Defending Officer of Accused No 2 and NOT mine, as Bedi had asked just one question about his (DDOS') presence in office throughout in May 1983, to which the witness had answered "Yes"; secondly, these documents were from DDOS' office, which is why they were ORIGINALS, with DDOS' initials in all of them dated 23 May 1983, including this one and thirdly, these were brought by the clerk from Corps Ordnance, who was to be PW-6 and was with the knowledge and permission of the Prosecution. How and why else would anyone 'help' the accused? The dates on all the documents being what I (and QM, A-2) had signed during our physical presence and functioning in the office upto 4 May 1983 were the ones available at DDOS' office; so all dates mentioned in the 'amended documents' are incorrect as none of the amendments has been initialled by me!

- He again committed the same *blunder* when he stated next: *"In this connection, I invite the pointed attention ...that vide (exhibit) these documents were forwarded by name to A-2, whereas at the trial, all the covering letters (such as the above) were produced by Defending Officer of Accused No 1. This proves irrefutably the commonness of intention on the part of both accused persons who together submitted contingent bills as averred in the charge"*. Once again, it was Defending Officer of Accused No 2 and NOT mine, as mine (Bedi) had asked just one question as above!

  (UNFORTUNATELY, IN THE LEGAL SYSTEM AND PROCEDURES, THE DEFENCE DOES NOT GET AN OPPORTUNITY TO REBUT SUCH NON-SENSE AND LIES IN ADDRESSES BY THE PROSECUTION AND THE JA; THE JA TOO DOES NOT POINT THEM OUT, AS HAPPENED BOTH IN AUG 1986 AND AGAIN DURING ADDITIONAL SUMMING UP BY JA IN NOV 1986! You will read later.)

5. Whether or Not Accused Submitted Bills for 87,000 M well knowing only 19,500 M was Received.

- He relied mainly on the evidence of PW-7.

- In addition, he tried to find holes in the evidence of DW-2 the Driver (who had said that when he closed the tail board, *'he saw some bundles inside'*) and DW-11, the ex-RHM, who stated 'he saw 50 to 100 bundles' and had answered in Cross Examination: *'by bundles I meant rolls'*. He had never served in Q jobs; *any person with a modicum of unit life would have known the difference between Havildar Majors (who deal with personnel, discipline etc) and Quarter Master Havildars (who deal with barracks, material and stores etc).* This had been immediately rescued during Re-examination when he answered categorically, that the 'rolls were covered in Hessian cloth' and that *'Two persons were carrying one bundle with great difficulty'*; again the learned Prosecutor omitted this, as it was inconvenient! *How could we have reminded the Court, when the JA whose duty it was, did not do it?*

- There is NO record or anything in writing with M/s CS or Rooster to show supplies were made by Sphere Sales Corporation and if so how much. They never insisted on early payment for supplies for over Rs 60,000/-. *(Being from Punjab and the trader's caste, the Prosecution Counsel pretended not to have any knowledge of 'business-worldly' affairs! He did not draw attention to the fire in the godown of ...Transport Co. If for 87,000 M, there is NO record, where and how did "only 19,500 M" spring from?)*
- He then made an unsubstantiated statement that PWs 1, 2, 3, 7 and 9 *"have stated they are not aware of any receipt of LP garnish"*. Into this denial, he ropes in also DW-7, (whose deposition clearly states that he had arrived in the unit, only in third week of Dec 1982, AFTER the nets had been knitted and had gone in the Rail Column and stayed away attached till end of Exercise elsewhere!) If LP garnish had not been bought, with the availability of only 1,22,400 M, how could two nets each needing 2,01,160 M have been knitted; loaned 68 to Brigade and the Regt could have got an appreciation also?
- He then questioned the signing of Urgency Certificates etc as a CO. (Obviously when the need was emergent and move to Exercise was nearing, the deal was over and done with in Dec 1982 ; these were only covering sanctions sought in May 1983).

6. Intent to Defraud. Once the court concludes that the accused had submitted bills for 87,000 M well knowing that only 19,500 M had been received in the unit, it is deception and possible loss to the Government. Without indicating how, he next says: *'There is definite proof of secrecy. ... Once when the DO letter from Lt Col at Corps HQ arrived, the cat was out of the bag. ... The amendment to the LP documents is though a conduct subsequent to the occurrence. ...Right from Dec 1982, the whole transaction smacks of nothing but fraud....When stores had been received, supply orders are falsified documents.... once the court comes to the conclusion about intent to defraud, a special finding regarding variation in dates of documents as per Army Rule 62 (4) and (5) will be required'.*

7. He concluded by saying: *"If you have that amount of certainty upon which you would act in the affairs of your own life, then it is your duty to convict".*

BY THE JUDGE-ADVOCATE: 21 AUG 1986

1. If I express any opinion by mistake, please disregard it. ... You are the sole judges. ... The cardinal and most important principle of criminal law is that the accused is presumed to be innocent and the Prosecution has to prove the case. ...Burden of proof, howsoever complicated, remains on Prosecution. ... Onus on *'special issues'* shifts to the accused where the standard of proof required is the same. ... If Prosecution is not able to prove beyond reasonable doubt, the accused is entitled to be acquitted. ... While I shall define *'Reasonable Doubt'* later, I shall first do so about: *'Proved, Disproved' and 'Not proved'* from Section 3 of Indian Evidence Act. ... Proof cannot be mathematical. ... *Evidence* can be classified in to *Direct* (whether Oral or Documentary) and *Circumstantial* (Facts relevant or otherwise admitted); the latter is in no way inferior and may in some cases be superior to Direct Evidence.

2. Charge and Law Relating to It. ...Army Act Sections 52 (f) and 3 (xxv)... *'Intent to defraud'* NOT defined, so

we lean on Section 25 of IPC, where it is explained but not defined. ...Two essential elements: *Deception* (and NOT mere secrecy) and *Injury*. ...Design, foreknowledge and action before or subsequent to it. ...Motive is not be confused with Intent.

3. Prosecution and Defence Cases. (Generally he repeated the addresses by Defence and Prosecution Counsels as above).

4. Issues. Prosecution MUST prove three issues:

   - *A-1 and A-2 while being CO and QM of ... at....*
   - *'well knowing that only 19,500 metres were supplied'*
   - *'together with intent to defraud signed during May 1983, contingent bills for Rs ...'*

5. Evidence Discussed on the above 3 Issues.

   - *Status of A-1 and A2 as CO and QM*: there does not appear to be any doubt. Only point of dispute appears to be whether A-1 ceased to be CO or not, when signing. *Location of Regt at Dundahera Camp*, well proved.
   - *'Well knowing that only 19,500 ...'* can be seen in two parts: first, the amount of garnish received and then, 'well knowing':
   - Evidence explained threadbare of PW-7 as against DW-13. Also, consider testimony of Direct Evidence of PW-7 and DW-13 vs. Circumstantial Evidence of PWs 1, 3 and 8 and 9; and DWs 2, 11, 12 and 14. (All relevant portions extracted and read out). ***Defence has disproved NIV (exhibit) to be false***. If Defence contention of 46,500 M issued on another voucher when there was no stock held in the Regt other than LP garnish, you may see if the total quantity as contracted is accounted for. You should also consider since PW-7 has NO documents, whether it is he who is responsible to account for 87,000 M OR total quantity has been expended for during the exercise

OR only 19,500 M was received. *If you conclude full 87,000 M was received, then you should acquit the accused; on the other hand, if you conclude only 19,500 M was received, then you may consider the next part of 'well knowing'.*

- Only if you conclude that 19,500 M was received, the question of *'well knowing'* has to be considered. The following evidence on record has to be seen:
  - First set of applications for LP in Dec 1982; see which pages have the signatures of A-1 and A-2. Although the dates are in dispute, the signatures are well proved.
  - PW-9 has deposed A-1 had mentioned *'large quantity of garnish contracted'*.
  - DW-1 has deposed A-1 had stated in Sammelan prior to the exercise, two nets to be carried and LP being resorted to.
  - PW-7 reported to A-2, he had brought only 19,500 M.
- You may see LP applications (exhibits) and by using your general military knowledge of men and everyday affairs, conclude as to under what circumstances were they signed and whether these are routine documents only. Direct evidence from state of mind, speech or act would tell you whether the accused knew of the quantity received, before signing and submitting the contingent bills.

<u>Third Issue</u>: Consists of 3 parts; *'together'*, *'with intent to defraud'* and *'submitted to DDOS, Corps...'*.

- Taking the last part, *<u>'submitted to DDOS, Corps...'</u>* first: Evidence is on record regarding preparation of documents by PW-3, 5 and 10 (all clerks) quoting A-2 or former QM Subedar Head Clerk; then by PW-4, ex DDOS on identification of documents produced by Defence with his initials, while he was unable to say whether those produced earlier (by PW-1&3) and these were the same, as his initials did not appear in the latter. PW-3 stated A-2 had read out the DO letter loudly on 16 June 1983. PW-5 identified the amendments done by him as ordered by PW-3 who had written the pencil dates. Then you may decide if these were the contingent bills submitted to DDOS with dates as mentioned in the Charge. If you are convinced they were not, then you may decide in favour of the accused. If not, proceed to the next step.

- '*Together*': JA drew the attention of the Court to Section 34 of IPC and explained terms such as *pre-arranged; pre-meditated; common intention; inference by conduct or circumstances of the case* where direct intention cannot be seen, etc. He then explained the evidence on record and placed before the Court to see, if any *'prior meeting of minds'* and *'commonality of criminal action'* existed. If you conclude that there was prior intention, was it by both or some part by both or either. ...There are two types of offences: *'conjointly'*, such as mutiny, dacoity etc; and *'jointly'*/ *'singly'* such as murder etc. ...In peculiar circumstances, separation of liability is possible. ... . If only 19,500 M of LP garnish had been received, what was the commonality of intent in sending documents to DDOS?

- '*Intent to Defraud*'. Defence case is full 87,000 M had been received and used; so documents had to be sent to DDOS. If you conclude that only 19,500 M came, then you may see the two components: Deceit and Injury. NO handing over points on LP of garnish were given by A-2 to PW-1 nor by A-1 to PW-2; PW-3 has deposed the whole sequence of preparation of documents from Dec 1982 onwards as directed by A-2. Now, returning to 87,000 M vs. 19,500 M again: DW-13 stated he was unable to produce any documents. Leave dates of A-1 had not been amended. Touchstone is: on duty or leave. If you conclude A-1 was on leave, then he is liable. Then you may see if there is evidence of Secrecy or not. Next comes *Injury*: If documents had gone to CDA, Government would have been at a loss; that is injury.

In summary, JA stated he had not read out the entire evidence. So the Court can and should refer to the records...may see whether Prosecution has proved the case beyond reasonable doubt; if you conclude it has failed, acquit the accused. If you conclude that it has proved all the ingredients of the charge beyond reasonable doubt, then you must convict.

-Some Other Points:

-Sketch of Unit Area (exhibit): Evidence should have been duplicated. *Evidence (based on the Sketch) of a witness who had not prepared it, has to be affirmed by the person who had prepared it. So disregard this testimony.* (Wrong advice as PW-9 had identified his initials on it: see first question in Cross Examination!) Oral account given by any witness may be considered vis-à-vis overall evidence.

-Refreshing Memory: Witness may only refresh and not read out; Sections 159 and 160 of Indian Evidence Act refer. Even then, it cannot form the basis of the correctness of its content. You may see evidence of PW-9 at Page 326 of the Proceedings regarding the amount of garnish to be sealed, in this light and you may only take it into account if it meets this criterion.

-Credibility of Witness. Depends on a variety of factors and truthfulness has to be seen while weighing character, integrity, courage, sense of duty, concern to facts, and the evidence of other witnesses. Section 134 of Indian Evidence Act refers. Quality and quantity is of evidence is what matters. Evidence is to be weighed and not counted. Just as for conviction, the evidence of a single quality-witness would suffice, the same is true for acquittal too. Weighing of evidence is to be done based on Bearing and demeanour; Integrity; Position in life; Interestedness; Motive; Consistency of Testimony; Conforming to previous written testimony; and Discrepancy in material facts etc.

-Discrepancies: Do not demolish testimony. Trifling ones are ignored.

-Reasonable Doubt: *'A doubt which is reasonable and crops up in a reasonable person's mind'*. Absolute certainty in criminal cases is rarely ever possible.

-Addresses of Counsels: Are not evidence, but only arguments and suggestions.

6. In the end, JA drew the attention of the Court to Army Rule 143 (4).

ANNEXURE 8: GIST OF MY PRE-CONFIRMATION PETITION

1. My Pre Confirmation Petition dated 29 Nov 1986, under Section 164 of Army Act and Para 474 of Defence Services Regulations (Regulations for the Army) (DSR:RA) against the Revised Finding and Sentence was addressed to the Chief of Army Stafr, through Army Commander, Western Command. (*This is ONLY a gist and does not cover names and identities of anyone.*)

2. Introduction and Brief History. After an Introduction, I had given the Brief History of the case and how ham-handedly it had been dealt over 4 years, change of 3 stations, 4 (including my co-accused, QM's) Summaries of Evidence, 3 General Courts Martial and a Revision, just to satisfy the ego of the A and JA staff officers (named) at Corps and Command HQ, who would again

be rendering advice on not only this Petition but on the Revision Proceedings too!

3. My Prayer. It was: "*I request you NOT to confirm the Proceedings and to acquit me honourably*". (That happened after another 15½ months!)

4. Layout. The Petition was laid out in 6 headings (as under) and 92 Paras.

DENIAL OF JUSTICE IN PREPARATION OF MY DEFENCE

5. Right from the start, authorities at HQ...Corps had made up their minds to deny me natural justice by placing all possible hindrances in preparation of my defence. Briefly, these were as under (with authority and *Page No of GCM Proceedings quoted against each*):-

   (a) Action on a Pseudonymous Letter Against the Provisions of Army Order 69/73. (Covered in the narrative; so not being repeated).

   (b) Character and Military Reputation. Para 518 of DSR: RA clearly lays down that when the character and military reputation of an officer is likely to be a material issue, the Presiding Officer of the Court of Inquiry, wherever possible, will be senior in rank and other members at least equivalent in rank to the officer; also amplified by Army HQ letter No 46440/AG/DV-1 dated 11 Aug 1983. When the court of inquiry had been convened to inquire into the local purchase of garnish in ...Medium Regt, obviously it would be doing so into my (and QM's) actions. Even if not done initially, when during its proceedings, some witnesses had made indirect assault on my character, NO action was taken by ... Corps.

   (c) Non Provision of a Defending Officer for GCM on 27 Mar 1985. I had given on 25 July 1984 itself the name of Major HS Bedi, available locally.

(d) Incomplete Staff Work by A and JA Staff of Corps. They had failed to ensure compliance of Army Rules 22 and 25, despite my written demand, thus causing me avoidable harassment and delay.

(e) Continued Attachment Under Direct Influence of HQ...Corps. (Self- explanatory).

(f) Non Response to My Pleas and Appeals to Ensure Justice. (Covered in Narrative).

(g) Victimization, Harassment and Humiliation due to Vindictive Attitude of Corps HQ A Staff. Instances are a legion; just a few of them:-

- Ordering my presence at Court of Inquiry when I was on furlough and was arranging for my wife's cremation the same day on 20 July 1983.
- Denial of married accommodation at any of the places I requested on extreme compassionate grounds (already covered in the narrative, not being repeated).
- Even a first time car loan was denied without mentioning reasons.
- Sought an interview with Army Commander on 25 Feb 1985; when asked to state the reasons, gave it on 13 Mar 1985; reminded on 24 Apr 1985. NO reply till this petition!
- Even a day's casual leave was not sanctioned for performing obsequies; (as covered in the narrative).
- Requests for annual leave (30 days from 11 Dec 1984; 13 days from 1 May 1986) to spend time with my motherless minor girls in the absence of a married accommodation that was denied to me, *have not even been replied to till date of this petition*!
- The number of repeated disciplinary proceedings in the name of fairness causing me misery.

- The humiliation of close arrest throughout 3rd GCM, when I was no threat whatsoever, all because of the vindictive attitude of Colonel A at HQ...Corps.
- Non provision of Many Documents in preparation of my defence; list given.
- Stress and Strain led to my admission to ICU at MH with 'breathlessness' and my medical downgradation for the first time.
- Harassment Even at ICU and Refusal of Leave to go to Delhi to Engage a Counsel (as covered in the narrative).

ILLEGALITY AND FLAWS IN GCMs TILL REVISION

6. While GCMs No 1 (27 Mar 1985) & 2 (20 July 1985) were dissolved due to technical flaws...the cause being the A and JA staff indolence and carelessness..., the authorities as well as GCM No 3 just bulldozed their way from 21 Apr 1986, till we were arraigned on 25 Apr 1986; (most points having been covered in detail in the narrative, are only enumerated):-

   (a) Contrary to Army Rule 34 (3), names of members were only given 36 hours in advance (not 96), and AT NIGHT, when I was at MH!

   (b) Despite Para 459 (b) of DSR: RA, all members less Presiding Officer were junior to me and two were Officers Commanding minor units.

   (c) All detailed from local units and directly under HQ ... Corps.

   (d) Challenge of Members as per Army Rule 44 was denied to me, when I insisted on the presence of my Counsel still to be engaged, due to leave not being sanctioned.

   (e) Objection to an 'interested' JA by Accused No 2 was

rejected, who gave partisan advice for my objections also on Army Rules 44 and 51 (Pages 33/34 of Proceedings and exhibits); change of a 3rd to 4th CO and 'dictation' by Corps HQ on it; incorrect advice on Army Rule 24 (1) (b) regarding provision of witnesses.

(f) Non provision of Essential Witnesses (Army Rules 134, 137 & 138 and Pages 334-336 of Manual of Military Law and Pages 237-8; 181-3; 189; 238; 240-44; 248-251; 230-1 & 293-4 of the Proceedings; Army HQ letter No 32968/AG (PS)-1 dated 18 Apr 1979; and exhibits).

THE REVISION ORDER AND MY SUBMISSION

7. Deputy JAG at HQ...Corps who had written the Report on Application for Trial in my case and was designated to move to Command HQ was allegedly influencing the activities of JA Branch and officers and got Report on Trial written to ensure that a difficult person (read, '*me*') who continuously proved the inefficiency of JA Branch at ... Corps under him, was sorted out by a Revision Order. By then he had moved 'up' also! Thereafter I had mentioned a summary of the flaws in the Revision Order, as covered seriatim by my Counsel in his address.

WEAKNESSES IN ADDRESS BY COUNSEL OF CO-ACCUSED, AN EX JAG

8. This learned counsel though not directly associated with the case for the past 3½ years, may have done so at JAG Branch at Army HQ! So was he right in accepting the brief of A-2? Why is there no bar to such blatant misuse? Some weaknesses in his address:

(a) Not having served in an army unit as such, he lacked an understanding of daily unit life. The relation between any Adjt/QM and a CO are just that; as a staff officer and commander. The only commonality of interest was that the Regt which has had a fine name and laurels under my predecessors, should not get a bad name by not having the 2 nets as ordered for the biggest ever exercise of the Indian Army (under me!); that and the non-availability were what compelled us to go in for LP. Accused No 2 himself had said so in his voluntary statement at his S of E (when I was 1000 KM away on a course and which I got to see for the first time in Mar 1985): "I apprised the CO of my efforts and my inability to procure the same ...(garnish)...*from local market, who again directed me to procure the same IN ORDER NOT TO LET DOWN THE FAIR NAME OF THE UNIT AND HIMSELF*".

(b) It is on evidence at Pages 392, 137 and 278 that there were Monthly Consignment Opening Boards under my command and one was there in Dec 1982 also. If the Regt was unable to produce it today, fault was not mine.

(c) About my being '*fully in picture about surplus and deficiency of garnish*', evidence is on record again in Pages 258 (DW-1); 293 (DW-7); 312-3 (DW-8) & 345 (DW-11). PW-9, Tanjore Doll had also said at Page 225: "...*there were a number of conferences of subunit commanders during Sep-Dec 1982 onward in which shortage of garnish was discussed*". A-2 himself had voluntarily stated in his S of E: "...*subunit commanders raised the point of garnish...I was directed by the CO to meet their requirements by personal liaison with OD, Shakurbasti....On receiving the NA, I apprised the CO of the same and the garnish situation in the depot. He then directed me to resort to LP*".

(d) He then talked about '*the matter of DO letter from*...an officer of Corps Ordnance Branch to A-2...being blown out of proportion by' me. When Paras 11 and 13 of Revision Order pointed an accusing finger at me for this DO, I had to give out the truth that this letter had NOT been shown to me till date!

(e) His next barb: "*The way A-1 has tried to shift blame on A-2 is most unbecoming of a CO*". It is unfortunate that for whatever reasons the wise men of the Court after long deliberations had found me NOT GUILTY on 21 Aug 1986, while finding A-2 Guilty. I have maintained the same stand from 30 June 1983 when I gave a statement before the Court of Inquiry and till date: '*I have only done what any ordinary and prudent Commanding Officer would have done under similar circumstances, i.e., had total faith in his QM and as per his verbal report and Certified Receipt Vouchers etc, I had signed the contingent bills*'. In fact, to state the truth, it is due to oft-changing and most misguided statements of QM at the Court of Inquiry that any doubt at all was created in the minds of authorities to proceed to the next step: attachment, S of E etc. Even though the Hon'ble members of the Court were not expected to give credence to counsel's address, when the JA too (... who was just a Major under this Counsel when he was JAG and his Superior Reporting Officer for ACR for 2 years) included it in his address, probably their minds got influenced?

(f) In view of the peculiar procedures wherein I could not defend myself AFTER the address by this counsel (and the JA), I am suffering today.

ANALYSIS OF ADDITONAL SUMMING UP BY JA

9. The Revision Order states clearly: "*...if it becomes necessary to clarify any point/points raised by the accused, the JA may give a further summing up*". But the JA in this case, exceeded his brief in order to victimize me and to keep two of his superiors (one past, the ex-JAG and counsel for A-2; and the other his current one, the DJAG command who had just moved there from this Corps). Despite clear mandate in Army Rule 105 (8) that he '*is expected to be entirely impartial*', his conduct did not appear so. It is an irony of such outmoded legal system

such as our Army, whereby the accused will never get a chance to rebut false, mischievous and misleading statements in JA's summing up. Some major points are:

(a) Former Subedar Head Clerk of QM Branch as a witness. He said that the *'admission of the prosecution*...(regarding this witness)...*has come into the proceedings under special circumstances'*, as if the JA who had written the RT/Revision Order was ignorant, but does not state as to what those special circumstances were:

- Is he an essential witness?
- Is he a material witness to the defence?
- Is the requirement for his production by the defence genuine?
- Have reasonable and sufficient steps been taken to procure his presence since July 1985?
- Is the delay in his arrival acceptable vis-a-vis denial of justice to the accused?
- Any presumption as per Illustration 'g' to Section 114 of Indian Evidence Act necessary?
- Does not his presence become mandatory as per the direction in the Revision Order?
- Was the apprehension by the defence about his non-production justified?
- Are the circumstances quoted by the defence needing his presence at Pages 181-3; 237 to 244 and 384 to 391 justified?
- Was there a need or not for him (JA) to cover Notes 4 and 5 to Army Rule 137; an advice for adverse inference against the prosecution as directed by the Revision Order and prayed by defence?
- Was there any need for him to bring fresh points such as Motive for the witness to be an accomplice,

which far exceeded his brief as per regulations and the Revision Order itself?

- JA repeated ad nauseam that PW-7 stated that *"...immediately after collection... he told... (the witness)... that he had brought 19,500 M". (Where is the other party to this conversation, when the JA at GCM No 3 in his Summing up/Address had stated that the Defence has disproved that infamous voucher (NIV) of PW-7?)* PW-7 had stated in the S of E of A-2 that he had reported to PW-3 on arrival after collection; this changes from July 1985, once it was clear (as briefed by the prosecutor) that the former Subedar Head Clerk of QM Branch would not be produced, as seen from the half-hearted efforts by the prosecution (to have not even approached Controller of Immigrants or Pension Paying authority for the present address!).

(b) Addresses by Counsel. JA states: '*These are not evidence but arguments of facts and the Court should exclude them from consideration*'. But, he himself starts quoting verbatim from the address of Counsel for A-2 (his former superior) only portions where he had thrown barbs at me!

(c) Signing While on Leave by A-1. This matter was settled once for all during the Address by JA at No 3 GCM, when he had gone step by step and had said '*on leave or not is the touchstone*'; and it was NOT part of the Revision Order also; still this JA exceeded his brief in raking it up and gave his own conclusion that I had been on leave when I had signed the Contingent Bills, dates in all of which had been amended and some extended to my leave dates, whereas in the office copy produced by PW-4, the DDOS, the last bill had been identified as signed by me on 2 May 1983, when I was in the office. In two of my S of E, PW-3 had stated that he had handed over all documents ready for despatch to QM (A-2) on 6 May 1983. *Any person would know that if despatch was involved, obviously signatures would have been done prior to that date and also the clerk would have taken a day or two to check all documents* for correctness; thus it was proved indirectly that I ought to have signed them latest by 4 May 1983, the last day at work before my leave.

(d) *Handing Over Notes to PW-2.* This again is NOT a part of the Revision Order; nor mentioned by either counsel. JA at Revision had NO business to bring this up; not only that during the reading of his summing up, JA had done another unethical act at this point; he had said: Why did A-1 not do so? '*Only to draw an iron curtain over his deed?*', which was NOT part of his written address.

(e) Secrecy. The fact that there was NO secrecy and that all ranks not only in my Regt but some in the Brigade too were aware of my announcements in unit/brigade conferences about LP and Sainik Sammelans; more than 3 clerks were involved in preparation of the papers; it was done with Scraggly's concurrence; stores seen and requested by other units etc, I would draw attention to PW-9 Page 225; DW-1 Page 256; DW-5 page 280; DW-11 Page 344-5; PW-9 Page 212; DW-7 Page 293; PW-9 Pages 219 and 228; PW-4 Pages 156-7; PW-7 Page 178; DW-13 Page 353; PW-3 ages 117-121; PW-5 Page 168 and PW-10 Page 131.

(f) Despatch of Documents by DDOS to CDA for Payment. This was the MOST misleading and damaging statement and an unwanted one (as per the guidelines of the Revision Order) by this JA. PW-6 had stated clearly that when forwarding so, a copy would be endorsed to the unit. When I was on leave, how could this copy be hidden, if it had come? If the JA had even a modicum of a unit functioning, he would not have made such a stupid statement, but where is the time for the Court to weigh up each of his tendentious statements? CDA would NOT have accepted the documents after the alleged amendments; but returned them as per Rule No's 39 (vi) and 46 (i) and (ii) of DSR (Financial Regulations). How could this transaction have ever been hidden?

(g) DO Letter from Corps Ordnance. My lack of knowledge of it has been brought out by PW-3 (Page 141-2); PW-5 (Page 169-170) and PW-1 (Page 90). A-2 had allegedly got amendments done in documents based on this DO; if he had wanted to hide it, he need not have read out the letter in PW-3's presence and could have got amendments done elsewhere and dispatched them? I had not seen or heard about its contents as evidenced by the above PW but became aware of it, only after I read a copy of the Court of Inquiry demanded by me under Army Rule 184 in Mar 1984.

(h) Handing Over Notes to PW-9. This is one more mischief by the JA and not covered in the Revision Order. If I had any dishonest intention, even on 28 June 1983 when so-called alleged recovery of garnish took place and I came to know on 30th, I could have convinced all concerned as technically, I was still the CO and had 2 more days to hand over. Why should I have hurried and handed over in less than a day, *included the point in the Notes myself* and gone to Scraggly the next day? I could have 'sorted out matters' and then gone. Even when Scraggly had suggested why should I have included it in the Certificate, if I had any evil intentions? I could have insisted we would come back on 1 July, or I could have foregone my course and stayed back as CO (till MS Branch issued another posting) and "sorted out" matters and thus avoided all this humiliation and harassment.

(i) Relevant Points Conveniently Omitted by This JA.

- The disproved NIV of PW-7.
- PW-7 should have been recalled and asked proof of distribution of at least 19,500 M and to prove the signatures for the "*4,600 or 46,000 M*" which he claimed to have issued on 6 Nov 1982 through another NIV which he called a formal one in place of this fake NIV.
- Again with zero experience in men and matters in a unit, this JA declared without anything having been proved that garnish was collected and issued from OD, Shakurbasti on another exhibit: all on the same day, *22 Nov 1982*. Where did he get this from? No signature except that of A-2 has been proved by anyone! The only signature of A-2 is for RECEIPT by and NOT issue in the Regt. *It is actually the Non Availability Voucher dated 21 Nov, which is the basis for LP*!
- Reasons for not floating a voucher could have been brought out by the prosecution, which were: The date when PW-7 had brought the garnish was 13 Dec 1982, correctly stated by DW-13, Rooster who had issued it: the date is significant as the first Basantar Day (pagal gymkhana) was going on the first day of the celebrations; the unit was in a celebratory mood till 15th and then got busy knitting the nets. Obviously floating vouchers etc became secondary when the emergent item had been received and the unit was getting ready to depart on the scheduled date 20 Dec (postponed later to 25 Dec)! In the absence of sanction, this could not have been taken on charge.

(j) JA Giving Directions to the Court. While talking about the NA Voucher which he had mistaken to be an Issue Voucher in the unit, he said and I quote: *"Thus you should decide (...not 'may'...* like all other

JA's) *that when the garnish was issued by OD Shakurbasti on 22 Nov 1982 and received by the unit the same day and further issued...how could it be part of the garnish which was sealed on 30 June 1983...?"*

(k) Loan to Others and Physically Holding More Garnish Than Required for Exercise. As for the loan, it was NOT 15,000 M given to brigade HQ as stated by the JA, but 68 knitted nets had been given and they chose to return plain nets separately and 15,000 M garnish in July 1983. Only a dimwit could have made such a statement after explanations in the proceedings many times of total requirements and holdings. (A simple calculation of the MINIMUM garnish needed for the smallest size net being 490 M, these 68 nets [assuming they were the *smallest* size], unit should have got back *33,320 M; where had this amount of garnish originally come from when given to Brigade HQ on 25 Feb 1983 in the exercise area?*)

(l) Facts on Record Missed Out by the JA.

- The point about knitted nets having been loaned and NOT 15,000 M is covered above.
- 2,01,160 M of scrim garnish would have been required for a total of 235 nets authorized, @ 856 M per medium net. Details were given out by PW-3 on Page 146 and PW-9 Page 225 and 335.
- On the day, A-2 was ordered by me to go in for LP sometime in the end of Nov/early Dec 1982, (after the Non Availability Certificate was received), unit could not have held garnish more than its authorization, as per the Stock Taking Board of 25 Nov 1982 which included the ledger and ground balances; as per PW-3 at Page 130-1. Unfortunately for me that sincere and conscientious Major, ('P' Battery Commander) having died in Oct 1984 cannot come and testify that he had not only checked every place in the Regt but had taken certificates as

per SOP from all store-holders that 100% stores had been laid out and none was held anywhere else in their custody/charge. If this JA is to be believed, the unit was holding garnish FAR IN EXCESS of its authorization, viz, Used in exercise 2,01,160 M + Loan to workshop 7,500 M + alleged recovery 73,300= 2,81,890 M LESS holding as per ledger 1,22,400 and allegedly distributed by PW-7 on fake NIV 16,500= 1,43,060 M!

– There was NO *junk store* in the unit but only a Salvage Store (as earlier explained and written on the Sketch by PW-9!) and it had been occupied by the luggage of many officers successively right from July 1981 onwards as brought out by DW-1, Page 258; DW-7, Page 293; DW-8, Pages 312-3 and PW-11, Page 145; as also PW-7, Page 189 (who changed it to 'Junk Stores' during Re-examination)! *The only person who had allegedly SEEN garnish INSIDE the 'salvage/junk store' and 'recovered' it, is the store holder himself (PW-7) on 28 June 1983*, in a remote corner of the unfenced unit at about 7 p.m., when there was a power failure in Gurgaon area (and even Rabbi was carrying out investigation with petromax and hurricane lanterns); but the only other person *who saw it (PW-2) after a report from PW-7 at about 7.30, saw it OUTSIDE 'the LUGGAGE ROOM'* and says it had not been brought out under his orders but it was seen by PW-2 but the latter denies it! (PW-7 Pages 188 to 190; PW-1,Pages 91 to 95 and PW-2, Page 102). Later, PW-1, when asked in further cross examination (Pages 166-7) if he had replied in the Court of Inquiry (when asked whether he *had checked the state of garnish in the unit between 14 May and 16 June 1983)*, about ordering Never-loyal to check the state of garnish *on 6 June 1983* and the latter having reported to the Witness: "Garnish was lying in Salvage Store in sealed bundles. On being asked to check, he reported, 55,000 Metres approximately of garnish being held". The witness denied it and was then confronted with the recorded statement. He then volunteered and stated that he *'had clarified it as 6 July and not 6 June in the Summary of Evidence'*. So when did he actually see it?

(m) <u>Alleged Lack of Knowledge of LP by PWs 1, 2 and 9 Cited by Prosecution Counsel and JA.</u>

- PW-1 arrived in the Rear on 14 Mar 1983 and went on leave; was recalled on 24 Mar to relieve A-2. How would he know what happened in Dec 1982 or even till 14 Mar 1983, the date of return of the unit from exercise? (PW-1 Pages 74 and 92).

- PW-2 is a chronic liar and the Court had warned him for demeanour. The fact of his presence in ALL the sub unit commanders' conferences in my office and the Sammelan(s) as has been brought out by PW-9, Page 211 and DW-2 Pages 262-3. It is amazing that as the 2IC and Security Officer of the unit, he did not know that in Dec 1982, a huge amount of garnish was lying outside the stores, which even an attached workshop officer had seen and borrowed from! (DW-14, Page 367).

- PW-9 has NOWHERE stated that he 'did not know about the local purchase of garnish'; he has himself stated at more than one place that shortage was discussed and that I had mentioned about LP of garnish not only in the unit conferences but in a brigade conference also. He has stated that his '***battery had received garnish for completing the second net in Dec 1982 but ... not aware if it was LP or Ordnance origin***'. Where else could he have got it from, unless we believe this 'magician' JA who can produce garnish more than DOUBLE the authorization!

INDEX